CULTURAL FEELINGS

Cultural Feelings: Mood, Mediation and Cultural Politics sets out to examine the role of feelings and mood in the production of social and cultural experience. By returning to the work of Raymond Williams, and informed by recent 'affect theory', it treats feeling as a foundational term for cultural studies.

Ben Highmore argues that feelings are political and cultural forms that orchestrate our encounters with the world. He utilises a range of case studies from twentieth-century British culture, focusing in particular on Home Front morale during the Blitz, the experiences of Caribbean migration in the post-war decades, the music of post-punk bands in the late 1970s and early 1980s, and more recent 'state of the nation' film and television, including *Our Friends in the North* and *This is England*. He finds evidence in oral history, in films, photographs, television, novels, music, policy documents and journalism. Through these sources, this book tells a vivid and compelling story of our most recent history and argues that the urgent task for a progressive cultural politics will require the changing of moods as well as minds.

Cultural Feelings is essential reading for students and researchers with an interest in affect theory, emotion and culture.

Ben Highmore is Professor of Cultural Studies at the University of Sussex. His most recent books are *The Great Indoors* (2014) and *Culture* (2016). His book *The Art of Brutalism: Rescuing Hope from Catastrophe in 1950s Britain* is due to be published in 2017.

CULTURAL FEELINGS

Mood, Mediation and Cultural Politics

Ben Highmore

Routledge
Taylor & Francis Group

LONDON AND NEW YORK

First published 2017
by Routledge
2 Park Square, Milton Park, Abingdon, Oxon OX14 4RN

and by Routledge
711 Third Avenue, New York, NY 10017

Routledge is an imprint of the Taylor & Francis Group, an informa business

© 2017 Ben Highmore

The right of Ben Highmore to be identified as author of this work has been asserted by him in accordance with sections 77 and 78 of the Copyright, Designs and Patents Act 1988.

All rights reserved. No part of this book may be reprinted or reproduced or utilised in any form or by any electronic, mechanical, or other means, now known or hereafter invented, including photocopying and recording, or in any information storage or retrieval system, without permission in writing from the publishers.

Trademark notice: Product or corporate names may be trademarks or registered trademarks, and are used only for identification and explanation without intent to infringe.

British Library Cataloguing-in-Publication Data
A catalogue record for this book is available from the British Library

Library of Congress Cataloguing-in-Publication Data
A catalog record for this book has been requested

ISBN: 978-0-415-60411-6 (hbk)
ISBN: 978-0-415-60412-3 (pbk)
ISBN: 978-0-203-13044-5 (ebk)

Typeset in Bembo
by Out of House Publishing

Printed and bound in Great Britain by
TJ International Ltd, Padstow, Cornwall

CONTENTS

List of Figures   *vi*
Preface and Acknowledgements   *ix*

1   Feeling our way and getting in the mood (An introduction)   1

2   Cultural feelings (Some theoretical coordinates)   20

3   Morale work (Experience feeling itself)   54

4   Bombsites and playgrounds (A wrecked, indifferent calm)   75

5   City of strangers (Qualities of disappointment)   93

6   Deep doubts and exorbitant hopes (Something is happening)   119

7   Mood, generation, nation (Feelings and cultural politics)   137

8   Post-referendum blues (Postscript)   158

Bibliography   *164*
Index   *176*

FIGURES

3.1	Humphrey Jennings, *Fires Were Started*, 1943.	56
3.2	Propaganda image from the Ministry of Information.	61
3.3	A land army at work, from *Listen to Britain*, dir. Humphrey Jennings and Stewart McAllister, 1942.	69
3.4	Ritual play in *Listen to Britain*, dir. Humphrey Jennings and Stewart McAllister, 1942.	70
4.1	Slum clearances, Gorbals, Glasgow, 1960s.	77
4.2	Children play on the site of demolished houses in Byker, Newcastle.	78
4.3	Boy destroying piano, Wales.	87
4.4	What is left of 'Saturday morning pictures' from *Whatever Happened to the Likely Lads?*, Series 1, Episode 4 'Moving On'.	91
5.1	Jamaicans on board the *Empire Windrush*, unattributed photograph in *The Sphere*, 3 July 1948.	102
5.2	A man on the doorstop of a terraced house, Notting Hill, 1961.	107
5.3	Still from *The Nine Muses*, dir. John Akomfrah, New Wave Films, 2010.	111
5.4	Still from *The Nine Muses*, dir. John Akomfrah, New Wave Films, 2010.	113
7.1	Slum housing, *Our Friends in the North*.	145
7.2	Edwards' System Building, *Our Friends in the North*.	146
7.3	Promotional film for Edwards' Systems Building, *Our Friends in the North*.	147
7.4	'New' slum housing, *Our Friends in the North*.	147
7.5	National Front supporters and Union Jack flags in *This is England*.	150
7.6	A royal wedding (Prince Charles and Lady Diana Spencer) in *This is England*.	150
7.7	*This is England '88*.	151
7.8	*This is England '90*, Park Hill Flats, a suitable case for photographic treatment.	153

Any kind of political project must have the 'making and using' of mood as part and parcel of the project; for, no matter how clever or correct the critique or achievable the project, collective action is impossible if people are not, so to speak, *in the mood*.

(Flatley 2008: 23)

Moods are modes of feeling where the sense of subjectivity becomes diffuse and sensation merges into something close to atmosphere, something that seems to pervade an entire scene or situation.

(Altieri 2003: 2)

PREFACE AND ACKNOWLEDGEMENTS

Cultural Feelings picks up where a previous book of mine (*Ordinary Lives*) left off (although this book, like the other, stands on its own). It is a continuation of the same project: namely the investigation of social aesthetics. If Raymond Williams insists that culture is ordinary, I insist that aesthetics is ordinary, or to say it slightly differently, that aesthetics is unavoidable. It is not just there in the beautiful and the sublime but, to echo the philosopher Austin, it's there in the 'dumpy and dainty' too. And, of course, aesthetics is not limited to the domain of art. Social aesthetics points to a host of qualities, atmospheres and experiences. To push aesthetics into the study of cultural feeling and mood isn't to push it out of joint (to try to make it do so much work that it ends up doing nothing); it is to see aesthetics realised in its most everyday guise. Feelings and moods are aesthetic forms at their most social, their most insistent, and at their most ubiquitous.

The examples I use in *Cultural Feelings* are nearly all located in Britain (though mainly England) as a provincial outpost of a global context; an outpost that is affected by national history, migrations, international trade, regional particularity, as well as the various different national cultures that make up Britain. My book uses British case studies partly because the question of nationalism is central to my project, and because Britain is my immediate context: it is where I live, where I teach, where I vote and, crucially, where I conduct research. I have access to research resources that are primarily national in reach (for instance, I have access to a range of newspaper archives that are national [British] in orientation). I would hope, however, that the book as a whole suggests a range of themes, orientations and methods that could be developed in other national and transnational contexts.

During the writing of this book, I tried out some of its arguments in a variety of critical and convivial settings and I want to thank various hosts, respondents and friends for their encouragement and their questions: Epp Annus, Tony Bennett, Tim Bewes, Paul Bowman, Svetlana Boym, Charlotte Brunsdon, Neil Campbell,

Ella Chmielewska, Ann Cvetkovich, Gail Day, Catherine Driscoll, Jonathan Flatley, Michael Gardiner, Mellissa Gregg, James Hay, Doug Haynes, Michelle Henning, Richard Hornsey, Michael Lawrence, Alphonso Lingis, Meagan Morris, Greg Noble, Mary O'Connor, Elspeth Probyn, Ramaswami Harindrinath, Bryony Randall, Greg Seigworth, Michael Sheringham, Rob Shields, Richard Stamp, Carol Tulloch, Megan Watkins and Yoke-Sum Wong.

The journal *New Formations* feels to me like my intellectual home, and the editorial board has been a sustaining influence on this work. I would like to thank Sara Ahmed, Jeremy Gilbert, Scott McCracken and Jenny Bourne Taylor in particular for their help and contributions to the *Mood Work* issue that Jenny and I edited. At the University of Sussex, I would like to thank all my colleagues and my graduate students. Particular thanks are directed to Caroline Bassett, Catherine Grant, Kate Lacey, Sally Munt, Sue Thornham and Nick Till. For general inspiration in this venture, I want to thank Epp Annus and Katie Stewart. Meaghan Morris and Rita Felski provided supportive words at just the right moment.

This book contains material that has been reworked and adapted from previously published work:

'Habits of Mood: Cultural Pedagogy and Home Front Morale', in Catherine Driscoll, Greg Noble and Megan Watkins, eds., *Cultural Pedagogies and Human Conduct (Culture, Economy and the Social)*, Abingdon: Routledge, 2015, pp. 173–185, © Taylor & Francis.

'Feeling Our Way: Mood and Cultural Studies' in *Communication and Critical/Cultural Studies*, vol. 10, no. 4, 2013, pp. 427–438, © Taylor & Francis.

'Formations of Feelings, Constellations of Things', *Cultural Studies Review*, vol. 22, no. 1, 2016, pp. 144–167, Creative Commons Licence.

'Playgrounds and Bombsites: Post-War Britain's Ruined Landscapes', *Cultural Politics*, vol. 9, no. 3, 2013, pp. 323–336, © Duke University Press.

1
FEELING OUR WAY AND GETTING IN THE MOOD

(An introduction)

This book is about feelings and moods. But it isn't about moods and feelings as internal states, experienced by individualised sovereign subjects. Or it isn't primarily about that. We live across mood-worlds. We live through a plethora of feelings. Some moods and feelings are dramatic and intense; their presence is emphatic, insistent. Other feelings are relatively inconspicuous because they occur too often to be noticeable, or because they saturate a particular situation. Some are just a low hum. We don't notice the mood of the place where we work until it is somehow 'off'. But the day-to-day mood of our workplace isn't the absence of mood. We know this because it is significantly different from the atmosphere in our homes, even though we might not notice that mood either. All of the feelings we experience are relational — my boredom, for instance, is directed towards something even though it feels so internal and empty to me — and to a greater or lesser extent those relations are deeply entwined with the social worlds that we inhabit.

This book is concerned with moods and feelings as social and historical qualities. As a modest claim, I want to suggest that moods and feelings are an important aspect of the world, and that we need to take account of them. More immodestly, I want to claim that unless we attend to moods and feelings we are not engaging in the sociality of social and cultural enquiry. How the world feels to us, and how it has felt to us, is the phenomenal form of the social: this quality is the sense of promise and defeat, of opportunities found and lost, of ease and disquiet, of vibrancy and dourness.

In the chapters that follow, I work both theoretically and historically to chart some of the ways that mood, feeling and atmosphere help us to describe various periods and moments of British post-war social and cultural history. In the next chapter I will explain more precisely why I'm using a word like 'feeling' rather than the more theoretically elaborated term 'affect', and why I'm conjoining feeling with the equally vague term 'mood'. For now, I just want to say that I *don't* subscribe to the definition of 'feeling' in a statement such as: 'feelings are *personal* and *biographical*, emotions are *social*, and affects are *prepersonal*' (Shouse 2005, emphasis in original). My interest in the term 'feeling' (and my claim for its usefulness) is precisely because it isn't locked into the personal and biographical. Indeed, in ordinary speech we use the verb 'to feel' in a whole range of ways that include forms of learning and habit ('she was getting a feel for the job'), intuition and insight ('they had a feeling that it wasn't going too well'), tactility and practice ('they felt their way in the dark'), and these uses often relate to collective and social experience. I want to use the terms 'feeling' and 'mood' precisely because they can range across the habitual and the emotional aspects of experience, because they can incorporate both the mundane practicalities of everyday life and the intense eruptions of more sensational moments.

In the case studies that I pursue in this book, I'm particularly concerned with tracking patterns of feeling at a national level, and this has meant that my focus is often on cultural texts such as films, novels and music. I have been less concerned with the feelings that are attached to material culture.[1] In this introduction, however, I'm going to write, often anecdotally, about mood and feeling as a way of showing how they matter and function at the level of everyday life, in both the ordinary things that surround us and the elaborated forms that supply us with imaginative articulations of moods and feelings. My anecdotes congregate around a number of themes that can be written as a set of axioms. These axioms don't itemise distinct aspects of feeling and moods; rather they point to active forces that are always in play *simultaneously* in the arena of cultural feelings. If cultural feelings and social atmospherics constitute something like the 'chemical' solution of the social, then these axioms name the active processes that are always at work in such a solution.

The first axiom is that *moods and feelings are material*. I want to pursue an approach to mood that refuses to treat mood or feeling as some sort of ethereal spectre that is manifest by sympathetic magic, whereby we all start feeling what others feel as a mimetic chain reaction. Instead I want to insist that moods are embedded in cultural forms (in narrative and musical genres, for instance, or in institutional protocols and conventions) and that these forms often have technological delegates that perform mood work (dimmer switches, corporate furniture, customer feedback forms, and so on). This is simply to say that I want to privilege the conveyors and mediators of mood and feelings, whether these exist in vernacular figures of speech or in complex narrative forms, or whether they are active in a style of clothing or in the architecture of a workplace. The second axiom is that *moods and feelings are a form of labour*. Moods and feelings don't just happen; they are produced, and most of the time their production is the result of specific work. Mood work, for instance, is undertaken by the 'caring professions' (populated predominantly by women), but also by journalists, media producers and by the hordes of 'spin doctors', publicists and advertisers working for governments, charities and large corporations. We are all, in some way, involved in mood work through our roles as citizens, daughters, prisoners, teachers, students, sons, lovers, customers, criminals, patients, consumers, parents, carers, workers, voters, *et al.* Such social roles (which of course overlap) implicate us in networks of work relations with their concomitant hierarchies and power relations. Today's social media has greatly increased the way we can be seen to participate in mood work, even if we don't all use emoticons ☺.

The third axiom, and probably the one that is most central to this book, is that *moods and feelings are historical*. To put this simply we could say that what makes *this* moment different from another is often the orchestrations of mood, atmosphere and feeling. Of course, all sorts of things change over time but we could claim that a moment's *this*-ness (its presence, for want of a better word, or its deictic character, to use more technical vocabulary) is to be found at the level of mood and feeling. We know this when we think about our own past and the specific atmospheres and moods that give a time and a place a particular flavour that is different from the flavour of another time and place. How we remember the past, and how the past is remembered for us (in films, novels and on TV) is often accomplished through the registration of mood, of generating the right atmosphere, which is often secured by incorporating material items that resonate with the social feelings of a time (the furniture that doesn't just signify a period but embodies a series of cultural practices and social attitudes, for instance).

The last axiom is most fundamental and encompasses all the previous ones: *moods and feelings are social*. By this I simply mean that the shape and texture of social experience is often best grasped as a pattern of feeling and mood. There may well be moods and feelings that aren't directly social (for instance, forms of psychosis) but they are not the subject of this book (hence the qualifier 'cultural' in my title). But what exactly does it mean to claim that something is social? It doesn't mean, I don't think, that something is simply shared by a population (in the way that the national electrical grid is, for instance). After all, one of the defining characteristics of contemporary capitalist society is that it is riven with social hierarchies: class and gender differences that are aggravated and extended by systemic and widespread racist proclivities and discriminations aimed at sexual minorities, those with disabilities, and so on. To say something is social, then, is to claim it is simultaneously collective and existing within a diverse and divisive arena. It is the quality of being both generally felt and specifically articulated that is mood's domain.

To fill out these axioms and to make them palpable, I am going to tell some anecdotes: some of them are mine, some are not. I will start out with a fairly lengthy description of a job I used to have working as a projectionist in a regional arts cinema. It was the second half of the 1980s, a time when new digital forms of video production were just beginning to be incorporated into film, but where the future of digital projection wasn't yet fully imagined. It is a particular cultural form that was experienced by many as a form of leisure. As a form of labour it wasn't, I don't think, particularly unique. The interlacing of labour, material circumstance and the specifics of cultural feelings are constellations that can be found in any number of situations. The following then is just one situation in particular.

Moods and feelings are material

The trick was synchronicity. The trick was fading out the background music just as you're bringing down the house lights and opening up the curtains and starting the projector running, so that at the key moment when the house lights are nearly out and when the curtains are over halfway open and when the silence is just beginning, you can flip the switch that allows that intense beam of light to be thrown from the projector onto the screen and connects the speaker system to the soundtrack of the film. It took a bit of practice. To start with I'd panic and forget to dim the lights or not flick the switch that opened the light source on the projector. Or worse; I'd not quite get the bottom reel to take up the film and it would jerk, causing the film to snap, followed by the manic spooling of film onto the projection-booth floor (which meant I had to stop the film before I drowned in celluloid). But as I started getting it right, I'd take pride in choosing some pre-film music that I liked, cueing it up so that the song itself was just fading out as I doused the lights, opened the curtains and started the film. If I liked the film, I'd try to find some music that shared some of the same resonance. But often I felt that Nina Simone singing the title song of her 1978 album *Baltimore* did the job.

The song 'Baltimore' was written by Randy Newman, and Nina Simone's vocals seemed to imbue each phrase of the song with a world of hurt and a lifetime of picking yourself up off the floor and carrying on. Simone seemed to have a way of taking the songs of melancholic men (I'm thinking of her versions of songs by Bob Dylan and Leonard Cohen) and amplifying the misery while also dialling up the feeling of buoyant resilience. Her voice and her approach seemed to act as a sort of tough-love resonator. 'Baltimore', the song at least, is filled with pitiful exclamations: 'Hard times in the city, in a hard town by the sea … Oh Baltimore, ain't it hard just to live.' No doubting that it's a hard life: no questioning that Nina Simone is going to live it, and live through it. But it's that voice, singing those words, set in that sonic landscape of surging strings punctuated by reggae guitar chops that struck a chord with me. It seemed like a good prelude to a film.

It was 1987 when I started: the film titles that I screened easily spring to mind – *Something Wild*; *Roxanne*; *Withnail and I*; *Angel Heart*; *Raising Arizona*; *Jean de Florette*; *Manon des Sources*; *The Lair of the White Worm*; *The Moderns*; *Torch Song Trilogy*; *Distant Voices, Still Lives*; *Patty Hearst*; *High Hopes*; *Red Sorghum*; *Rita, Sue and Bob Too*; *Prick Up Your Ears*; *House of Games*; *Bagdad Cafe*; *Babette's Feast*; *I've Heard the Mermaids Singing*; and so on and so on. I can remember some of the films exceptionally well, but mostly as fragments or as sensual particulars. I can remember the colour of *Bagdad Cafe* but not the story; I can easily call to mind a couple of scenes in *Distant Voices, Still Lives* – the part where everyone is smoking in the cinema and then someone falls in slow motion through a glass ceiling; I think I could still impersonate the manner of enunciating in *House of Games*. I think I would remember something of any of them if I chanced upon them unwittingly now. Searching them out wittingly, however, was often disappointing. When I watched bits of the film during twice-nightly screenings for two weeks as a projectionist I just loved

Wim Wenders' *Wings of Desire* (especially the long travelling shot through people's apartments that starts the film), but when I sat and watched it in the auditorium it seemed to be mainly about a middle-aged man falling for a younger woman with strikingly tousled hair (like the films of Tarkovsky: the existential dilemma of fancying someone). The cinema where I worked was, and still is, an 'art house' cinema, which showed the usual diet of quirky, indie fare, as well as more experimental avant-garde programmes compiled by the British Film Institute (always in the small second cinema). I remember meeting the wonderful Margaret Tait who ate her sandwiches in the projection booth while her windswept filmic poems were showing in the smaller auditorium. She seemed slightly shy about showing her films, maybe because they slowed down time.

I can remember most of the films I showed in the two years of being a projectionist, not because I was diligently checking to make sure that they were in focus (although I was) or because I loved movies (I did then, much less so now) but because I was scared. I was scared most of the time, anxious about messing up. I just never got the hang of it. Not in two years. My boss tried to teach me something about electronics. I even read books about it. But when things went wrong – and they did – I was always flummoxed; my default position was panic. I was totally unprepared. For some reason I thought that it would just be easy work and that I could work my way up from the bottom: start as a projectionist and end up as a film programmer, perhaps a curator of film festivals. What I wasn't prepared for was the fact that being a projectionist at this pre-digital time was a fairly heavy, dirty, technical and industrial job. I didn't mind the dirty, heavy work, it was the technical aspect that panicked me. What they needed was someone with a bit of technical know-how – someone who might be able to tell a resistor from a carburettor at least! Not someone with a fine art degree who liked arty movies.

I thought of myself as a filmmaker-in-waiting doing my rotation in the 'back room'. Really I was being cured of acute cinephilia. The projection booth was like an overdose of Brechtian alienation effects by way of an ultra-materialist concentration on the filmic apparatus. It blocked a good deal of the mood and tone of the film that was supplied by the soundtrack (the grain of an actor's voice, the soundscape of place and so on). I can remember getting ready for change-overs (when you have to start the parallel projector to take over the film as the reel on the other projector came to an end). In my anxiety, I'd often get ready too soon, so I'd end up crouched, looking through the glass, staring and staring at the top right-hand corner of the screen waiting for the little scratched circle to appear. Sometimes I felt that I was ogling this corner for hours, but it was often at least a few minutes. The industrial whir, clank and clang of two Gaumont Kalee 21 projectors supplied the insistent soundtrack. However mellow and languorous it was down there in the auditorium, up in the booth it was always the frenetic snatching (24 snatches a second) driving that large mass of celluloid through the machine that provided the overarching soundtrack and tempo.

Sometimes if I was particularly keen on a film, I would watch it on my days off in the auditorium. This was usually a mistake: I'd be too concerned with the quality of the focus; too jumpy when the change-over marks appeared; overly concerned with aspect ratios and volume. I'd managed to turn every 'classic-realist text', with all that character identification that it was meant to promote, into a structuralist-materialist experience of 'film-as-film'. Sitting there I would try to get the measure of the experience of those around me – a sense of the theatricality of the presentation. Listening to my much-loved Nina Simone from down there was awful: it just sounded like wine-bar good-taste. But it was amazingly ignorable. What wasn't ignorable and worked like some sort of hallucinatory charm was the dimming of the lighting. Dimming the lighting was like turning the volume down on the audience. You could see them adjust themselves in their seats; reorient themselves in relation to their companions, their seating and the screen. The dimming, recalibrated space, made neighbours recede and intensified the pull of the screen. People hunkered down; we were in for the long haul.

And as the curtains opened and the film began you could feel people feeling their way into the film (I was one of them of course), picking up cues and clues. Scrutinising the pre-title sequence; listening to the soundtrack; anything that might indicate what sort of pleasures and pains were waiting to greet us. Would we need an armrest to grab? Should we sit forward slightly in apprehension of someone being apprehended? Or will we arch back so as to laugh out loud? Films were genre cues, mood enhancers and mood introducers: little signs to prepare yourself, to sensitise yourself towards a future that may turn out well or badly or hilariously or indifferently.

So far this section could be thought of as a 'mood memoir', but if so it is one of a particular hue. It does not particularly dwell on the emotionality of mood, nor does it spend much time thinking about my own emotional mood beyond mentioning a certain amount of work-anxiety and disappointment in relation to film experience. I could have described a different set of experiences (visiting a hospital, the first days at school) and made them similarly moodful. This sort of mood description pursues the presence and absence of expertise (someone who can work a projector, for instance, or someone who can diagnose diseases), some form of institutional setting (although it could be very informal like a cinema), and a set of material techniques and associated sensual and sensorial material supports. In the previous section I have chosen to concentrate on settings where concentration and attention, as moodful orientations, are foregrounded. And in this the sensorial 'supports' seem to be hugely important: indeed, the light dimmers and curtain motors might well be doing the bulk of the mood work, or at least in this setting they might be doing more preparatory mood work than the sentiments conveyed by the Nina Simone song (where the surging strings and choppy guitar, rather than the lyrics, might be carrying the bulk of the atmospherics). Also important was the fact that all signs of film labour were hidden: the heaving of heavy metal film boxes, the industrial clang and whir of the projectors, the assemblage of the reels, the hunkered waiting for change-overs were all absent. The work of mood very often requires the obscuring of work.

The mood cues of social genre are important as a way of dealing with the unknown, of preparing for it and anticipating its demands (re-attuning your attention, silencing yourself, as the lights go down in a cinema, for instance). Mood is future-directed even when it is overcome with reminiscences. Mood is the activity of gauging the atmospherics of the hospital ward, for instance, so that you are sensitised (and sanitised) to certain ways of being and less likely to make a fool of yourself: the endless antiseptic hand-lotion dispensers are now an important prop in this performance. It would be interesting to write mood descriptions of the first few weeks of an army recruit. But new environments (the hospital visit, the first day at school or in the army) are just moments when mood is most vivid: for mood and feeling to be a central aspect of cultural investigation we need to attend to the moods that have become second nature and when we are least aware of the moodfulness of life.

The science laboratories of today's secondary schools (or high schools) look roughly similar to the ones I remember from my school days. There are some crucial differences: the gnarled wooden worktops and stools have been swapped for what looks like Formica, aluminium, plastic and steel; blackboards have been junked and replaced by shiny whiteboards and smart-screens. But much is the same: the Bunsen burners are the same; the large posters of the Periodic Table are still there, of course; the height of the work benches is the same, as is the convention of having stools rather than chairs for sitting on. Similar too is the distribution of activities.

To enter a science lab for a chemistry or a physics lesson (or some combination of the two) is to anticipate conducting an experiment (or to watch one being conducted). Such expectations are embedded in the furnishings, in the gas taps, in the large, deep sinks, in the vast cabinets of test tubes, beakers, tongs, pipettes and more complex instruments, as well as the locked store of chemical ingredients. The expectation is different from going to the cinema, of course, where we expect the equivalent of a sodium flare from the get-go. In a science lesson we know that there are going to be flat periods of copying down equations, or listening to the uninspired voice of the science teacher explaining some chemical process or other, before anything approaching special effects (which could turn out to be a damp squib) will take place. A science lab, like any other classroom, is specifically a machine for orchestrating attention. The lab orchestrates attention in its layout, in its posters, in its screens and in its workbenches. But undergirding all this is a 'literary' or at least a textual genre.

The mood of the science lab is most successfully guaranteed via a highly conventionalised form of writing: the write-up of the experiment. I remember being in a science class and there must have been a new kid there because the teacher made an example of him when he didn't know the conventions for the science write-up because he handed in what the teacher took to be a stab at disrespectful humour: 'It was a bright September morning when I got to the science block…' He wasn't trying to be funny; he just drew on the only resources he had for writing an account of something he had experienced. He didn't know about writing out a hypothesis or aim, predicting a result, showing a method (that was the bit I loved as it meant I could draw a diagram of the apparatus – my favourite item was the water-cooled condenser), detailing the results and observations, and rounding it off with a conclusion. With your grubby lab coat on and the knowledge that you would have to do a write-up for that week's science homework, science experiments were a performance of a certain mood, a set of deliberative actions with a goal in mind (getting the homework done). But it wasn't a mood that you would describe in terms of emotions and seemed generally affect-less. Some of us were, of course, disruptive and sought to alter the mood by mucking about: yet the mood of the experiment was set and it seemed impossible to aim the mood towards something as foreign as wonder – even in the face of the explosive purple flares that potassium makes when it hits water.

The genre of the written experiment is a material element that organises in advance how we orient ourselves to the situation we are experiencing. Just as we know to 'hush' as the lights go down in the cinema, so we are sensitised to certain forms of noticing, certain forms of alertness as the experiment commences. These are all material elements, but they also suggest that mood is hardly the result of happenstance. The form of the science write-up has been shaped over time, as has the convention of furnishing school laboratories in particular ways. This shaping is a form of labour, as is the replicating of these practices over and again. So too is the business of being a projectionist. But mood labour takes other forms as well.

Moods and feelings are work

The second mood axiom insists that a crucial feature of our contemporary world consists of moods and feelings as forms of labour, aspects of our working worlds. We have already seen this by drawing attention to the mood work undertaken by cinemas, hospitals and schools. Such institutions are an assemblage of human and non-human agents working to promote and sustain certain feelings and not others, specific atmospheres and not others. In the world of interior design, whether for hospitals and libraries or nightclubs and airport lounges, energy and money is spent on achieving the right mood. When an expensive 'luxury' hotel claims that during your stay you will luxuriate in a mood of tranquillity and serenity, for instance, you expect to see such atmospheres being generated not just by the care and attention of the hotel staff, but also by the décor, the branding and the facilities on offer (a 'therapeutic' spa, for instance). In one hotel I stayed in (one of the perks of attending academic conferences), the little bars of soap came packaged in a little box that told you that this soap was a form of 'Mood Therapy' and that this particular mood was called 'alive'.

The hospitality industry is, in many ways, selling you feelings and moods. Moods and feelings, then, aren't just the result of happenstance and contingency (the miserable weather, the delayed train, the burst of sunshine, the unanticipated good fortune) but are often the result of purposeful actions.[2] One feature of recent studies in the political sociology of labour, particularly as it has been witnessed in Western countries where a production-centred economy has been transformed into a service-centred economy, is the increased focus on the sort of work where the 'products' are, to some extent, feelings and moods. What social scientists and political commentators call immaterial and affective labour is mood work.[3] In the pioneering work of the sociologist Arlie Russell Hochschild, the management of feelings and mood is central to the emotional management and emotional labour that is her topic (and what Hochschild terms 'emotional' is an aspect of the world of cultural feelings). Based on ethnographic work conducted in 1980, Hochschild's book *The Managed Heart: Commercialization of Human Feeling* takes us into the moodful world of flight attendants. Hochschild's book is both about the physical and psychological cost of such labour and about how unevenly emotional labour is distributed (for instance, within patriarchal family structures where women often perform the vast majority of care). She also points to the growing ubiquity of emotional labour:

> But most of us have jobs that require some handling of other people's feelings and our own, and in this sense we are all partly flight attendants. The secretary who creates a cheerful office that announces her company as 'friendly and dependable' and her boss as 'up-and-coming', the waitress or waiter who creates an 'atmosphere of pleasant dining', the tour guide or hotel receptionist who makes us feel welcome, the social worker whose look of solicitous concern makes the client feel cared for, the salesman who creates the sense of a 'hot commodity', the bill collector who inspires fear, the funeral parlor director who makes the bereaved feel understood, the minister who creates a sense of protective outreach but even-handed warmth – all of them must confront in some way or another the requirements of *emotional labor*.
> (Hochschild 1983: 11)

Emotional labour in Hochschild's example has specific emotional consequences (flight attendants can often feel emotionally drained after having to deal with difficult, angry passengers)[4] but the industry is set up to make flying as 'flat' an experience as possible. Emotional work, then, is an element within a much larger world of cultural feelings where the management of atmospheres, feelings and moods is often aimed at lessening and often obliterating emotional responses.

If we stick with Hochschild's example of the experience of flight attendants, airline companies and flying, then we might initially suggest that mood incorporates the entire situation as well as the 'players' within it. While Hochschild brilliantly describes the work of airlines where 'spontaneous warmth' is sold as a commodity, and supplied by a steward who can't show that such spontaneous warmth is studied or laboured or drains the spirit and the body, she is less interested in all the other work that takes place to fashion the mood of the contemporary transatlantic flight. Of course, she was doing her ethnography as someone committed to studying the hidden injuries of jobs undertaken mainly by women. And, of course, she was writing before 9/11 made security the dominant issue for commercial airlines and airports.

Today, if we started to enumerate the kinds of material forms and forces that shape the mood of a flight, we might include alongside the 'spontaneous warmth' of the flight attendants at least the following: the queues through security and hand-luggage scanning; the reasons for the journey (for fun, for work, for keeping contacts among diasporic families, for necessity); the status of your passport (will you be welcomed with suspicion at the other end? Pulled into interrogation and body searched?); the classing of seating (first, business, economy, and that dispiriting walk past the business booths before you find your place squashed into an economy seat in what is also known as 'cargo class'); the colour of the security code (is it orange or red?); the in-flight entertainment; the noise of the flight; the weather conditions; and so on. We could say initially that mood is made up of individual and collective feelings, organic and inorganic elements, as well as contingent, historical and slow-changing conditions. A sudden jolt of turbulence can produce general muted gasps among all but the most seasoned traveller and crew; hours of flying in noisy, cramped conditions can produce a sense of not being fully present, a not-quite-aware mood.

We could then suggest that mood is an orchestration of many factors. For instance, the emotional labour that the flight attendants perform is often aimed at decreasing the emotional and affective intensities of passengers. A 'normal' flight, then, might have as a base mood a low-level anxiety coupled with that familiar sense of flatness that immobile waiting provides. We could say that the flight (and all the agents that this points to) attempts to instil a 'good-enough' mood of low intensity and it does this through the training of the flight crew and through the various rituals of flying: the safety announcement telling you how to disembark if you land at sea; the regular 'gifts' of drink and food; the intermittent announcements; the restful voices of cabin crew; the endless cacophony of jet engines; and the hugely important stream of in-flight entertainment.

The labour of many people is often aimed at maintaining cultural feelings; we are always entangled in a world of feeling. But just as people labour to produce moods and atmospheres, so too do animate and inanimate objects. Indeed, it is usually the synchronising of humans and machines, bodies and tools, people and techniques that produce achievable and sustainable mood-worlds. But as we have already seen by marking the distance between Hochschild's research in the early 1980s to our situation more than 35 years later, cultural feelings are far from static. History shapes cultural feelings and is shaped by cultural feelings in all sorts of ways: clearly the events of 9/11 have fundamentally altered the mood of aviation, but it hasn't just done this as a cultural memory that preys on people's minds when they fly. The aftereffects of 9/11 have been felt in all sorts of protocols and mechanisms, they have been embedded in scanning equipment, in traveller profiling, in the routines of airport security. To say that moods and feelings are historical is to look to the changing habits and routines of everyday life and the large structuring effects of political and social events.

Moods and feelings are historical

My little memoir of being a cinema projectionist could be extended enormously to pay some proper attention to the mood-worlds of the films that I screened and to ask some historical questions about the relationship between the atmospherics of this set of films (starting with the UK productions) and the historical moment that included seeing Margaret Thatcher voted in for a third term as prime minister of the United Kingdom. While there might not be a 'national mood' in any hard and fast way, there are clearly levels of optimism and hope, of fear and anxiety, of joyousness and pessimism, that are more or less available at particular times for particular constituents of the population. What sorts of moods were circulating at a moment that saw the birth of the YBA phenomena (the careers of Young British Artists such as Tracey Emin and Damien Hirst took off at this time); that made it hard to imagine forming an alternative to Tory rule (a moment that didn't yet know the compromises that would be performed to make that deal); a moment that had triumphantly rousted most institutional bases of actually existing progressive social action; but a moment that had also set up schemes for young people to act as cultural entrepreneurs and allowed sorts of 'businesses' that allowed bands like Portishead to emerge; and a moment where 'political correctness' was seen as becoming a new bogeyman, and where the actions against so-called political correctness were a palpable and effective ideological force?

Our own pasts might be remembered via a host of cultural items (songs, TV programmes, meals, houses, friends and so on) that seem strongly flavoured: our memories have an atmosphere, a mood and a series of feelings. And just as our own past is enfolded by feelings, so too is our collective past constantly *mooded*. But this isn't the result of professional, academic scholars. It is the work of politicians, journalists, advertisers, filmmakers and television programmers who want to vividly paint the recent past with a moodful palate: the 1960s is painted as all exuberance and irresponsibility, all permissiveness and misadventure; the 1970s as flared trousers and tank tops and endless picket lines. It is not hard to see that such moodful representations are often grotesque oversimplifications. It isn't hard to see that such felt histories often work as dire warnings for the present, disparaging forms of collective politics and collective social relations, discouraging experiments in more democratic forms of teaching, less patriarchal forms of living, and less competitive forms of working. By this I mean that we get a sense of a particular period by trying to grasp its moods, and that such moods are probably the most difficult things to grasp with any confidence. Moods and feelings are not innocent and unmotivated: registering moods of fear and trepidation, of elation and expectation, nearly always takes us into the realm of the political.

Take, for example, what might be one of the most 'over-moodful' moments of recent British history: the 'Winter of Discontent'. For many citizens of a certain age, the very phrase brings to mind a barrage of images culled from newspaper front pages of rubbish-strewn, rat-infested streets. In the particularly cold winter of 1978–1979, pay disputes caused strikes among local authority refuse collectors. The resultant build-up of rubbish was widely photographed by the press and accompanied by editorials denouncing the power of trade unions.

Whatever else we can say of that historical moment, we can say that the 'mood work' that was performed by leading politicians of the right and their newspaper supporters was frighteningly successful. It still is. A set of relatively small disputes have supplied the sensorial and sensual mood-markers that other much larger (and more economically significant) strikes simply couldn't offer. The fact that late 1978 and early 1979 have been tied to a mood of 'discontent', which is realised by trash in the street and the odd sighting of vermin, is the moodful alibi that is used time and again to explain the 'inevitability' of Margaret Thatcher (who became prime minister in May 1979). Today the dread of that moment ('whatever else happens, we don't want to go back to that') is a mood consensus enacted in popular journalism, in the lazy historicising of TV programmes, by Labour politicians (of the 'New Labour' variety) as often as Conservatives. It is enacted almost on a daily basis, endlessly naturalising Thatcherite conservatism and the break-up of the post-war social settlement.[5] A cultural approach to mood might see the re-mooding of such historical periods as a particularly useful but hugely difficult task. This book is an attempt to participate in this re-mooding, to look at cultural feelings with a degree of political sensitivity that recognises that particular forces are at work in determining what moods and atmospheres dominate and saturate a particular period, a particular set of activities.

The historicity of feelings and moods, as I have mentioned before, doesn't just relate to the realm of eventful social and political history: it also exists in what can look like a more banal, everyday setting. Take, for example, the university seminar. The seminar, for many of those working in the arts and humanities and the social sciences, is the central platform for pedagogic labour – it is where curricula are delivered, challenged and discussed. If a lecture offers a playing-through of ideas, then seminars are where ideas become inhabited. Orchestrating the mood of the seminar becomes a skill that any university teacher interested in trying to promote an ethos of openness and experimentation needs to develop. Skills are developed over time, through trial and error, through witnessing the practice of others. You recognise productive moods when they appear: the right levels of energy – not too hyper, not too placid; the right rhythms of time – people listening to each other, not talking over each other, but still eager to contribute; the right permissiveness – people willing to try out ideas but also to take responsibility for their positions. Such moods might include little that could be called emotion, or affect: the mood is about attentiveness, about conviviality, about a willingness to share the time with each other. It is a mood that you hope takes a collective form of mutual support, where you hope that the shy and under-confident will feel able to contribute and where you hope that the easily confident will take a lead but not dominate.

But anyone who has taught for even a miniscule amount of time will know that, however gifted they are at teaching and orchestrating seminars, and however much they try to practice the same 'best practice' for each seminar group, in the end the collectivity of the seminar often means that the gift of mood is not always the teacher's to give. Two seminar groups discussing the same texts in the same room, taught by the same tutor at the same time on consecutive days, can have quite distinct moods. One seminar is great – lively, discursive, funny, joyous – the other seminar isn't particularly problematic, it's just a bit flat, it hasn't taken shape, and it is hard work. And when you try to work out why this is so, it is almost impossible to point to anything or anyone as the causal agent – there isn't a snarling bundle of disdain sitting in the corner casting a pall of negativity over the proceedings. Contingencies, it would seem, are important in mood work: perhaps one seminar collectively 'simply' got out of the 'wrong side of the bed'. It is no wonder then that one of the metaphors shared by many of those interested in moods is weather. Moods are like weather, they have their own pressure systems, there is never a possibility of having 'no weather', and they exist as an atmosphere. Perhaps the non-metaphoric weather was responsible for the initial condition of flatness that the one seminar group could never quite shrug off.

But there are other determinants involved in the shaping of mood and the most important of these are social and historical. To recast a well-worn sentence, we could say that 'people make their own moods but they don't make them just as they please; they do not make them under circumstances chosen by themselves, but under circumstances directly encountered, given and transmitted from the past'.[6] We live the mood-worlds we've inherited. But our mood-worlds are also determined by the force fields currently at work in society. To go back to the seminar for a moment, we could ask what has changed over the past 20 or 30 years that could affect the seminar? Seminar groups have got bigger, rooms have become more and more anonymous, the length of time for the seminar has become shorter, seminar groups are now bombarded with online demands for their assessment of courses, very few students now get grants and most will have to pay £27,000 for their three years of undergraduate learning. It would be odd if this didn't have a determining effect on the feelings circulating in the seminar.

But how has this determined the mood of the seminar? One seasoned veteran of the seminar said that 30 years ago, when a student complained about something 'not being relevant' they meant it wasn't relevant to understanding and changing the contemporary world; today when they said something wasn't relevant it meant they weren't going to be assessed on it. We can overcook these stories of creeping instrumentalism, and downplay the actuality of the situation that students find themselves in and the ways in which they respond. We could say, however, that the anxieties of the seminar, which have probably always been there, have taken on new hues and tones and part of this is the worry of 'wasting money' by not getting the requisite marks to show your worth. We could also say that in a performance culture, it is likely that we as teachers have altered too, knowing that how our students rate the seminar will be available for scrutiny by line managers and human resources (HR) departments. Are seminars slightly more brittle now, but also more focused? Do ears prick up more quickly when marking criteria is being discussed? Is discussion less wandering, less open to random surprise? Mood shows us how the determinants of history can be felt 'in the air', so to say.

Moods and feelings are social

To claim that moods and feelings are social is simply to say that at some point they are collective. At times this seems to go against how we experience certain feelings, especially those that seem to bubble up from within, casting us into isolation and social withdrawal. Yet even those intensely isolating feelings like grief and lost love hurl us into a world already marked collectively by shared moods, by common experience and by cultural conventions. Sometimes collectivity itself appears to be a mood or at least a modifier of moods. To be in a place with thousands and thousands of others can intensify celebratory moods or solidify forces of dissent. Protests, for instance, are a world of atmosphere and mood that are defined by their sense of collectivity: solidarity means some sort of mass unification of mood and feeling. Similarly, the exuberance of a festival requires hundreds or thousands of bodies exuberating together. In this way, certain moods and feelings can be a shared disposition that would be very hard to experience outside of mass collective experience.

But mood and feeling are also social in ways that don't seem to require the sharing of physical space. During the global financial crash of the winter of 2007 and into 2008, we witnessed a massive mood-diagnosis of what was happening. TV pundits routinely described the unconfident mood of the market, the sense of a mood of disbelief: as if the booming of the market had to stop because people were no longer in the mood for it. Of course this might be nothing new: we might have been economically moody for some time. The cultural critic Jani Scandura writes:

> In the nineteenth-century United States, the term 'depression' was generally used with a modifier, such as 'economic'; 'melancholia' was the term of choice for 'blue devil' moods. After the 1929 stock market crash, however, 'depression' came to refer simultaneously (and without antecedent) to psychological ill health and financial collapse in American clinical and popular discourse. The so-called Great Depression was marked both by economic and mass psychological depression.
>
> *(Scandura 2008: 4)*

It is part of ordinary economic understanding that markets are prone to fluctuate according to contingent feelings, as though spikes and plateaus in the market are some sort of indicator of how a population feels, whether it is happy and thriving or anxious and tentative. But in another sense, to connect the economy to moods and feelings is just another way of saying that the economy is ultimately unpredictable (like a mythic moody teenager) and that it is, in its present state, unplannable and indeterminate.

It isn't just the economy that is discussed in relation to mood: at a very general level, we could say that there are endless relays between a vocabulary of feeling and mood and all sorts of social and cultural endeavour. This book is based on the belief that these relays and connections are worth exploring as an investigation of cultural forms. As the rest of the book is aimed at showing the extent and importance of these interconnecting relays between feelings and various social phenomena, I won't say anything more about the sociality of feelings and moods here, apart from to say that it is often part of very ordinary speech to ask about the morale of a workforce, the atmosphere of an event or the spirit of a nation. Such a discourse is often the bread and butter of daily and weekly journalism (in print, as broadcast and online). It is always part of the elaborate dramas that fill TV schedules and movie theatres (and their digital online surrogates). Cultural feelings are intricately entangled in a world of mediation: rather than think of feelings as our internal life, cultural feelings name an elaborate exterior world experienced through our acculturated nervous systems and through our worlded skin.

Most of the examples I've used so far in this introduction are part of a micro-analysis of moods and feelings. In what follows I am primarily interested in larger units of feelings, such as those that can be seen to organise and orchestrate national experiences and spaces, periods and moments. The questions that drive this book (even though it knows in advance that no ultimate answers will be forthcoming) are designed to explore the scope and scale of cultural feelings. They are unanswerable questions because there is no general size or shape to cultural feelings: they can animate a room and saturate an epoch. Nonetheless they are worth asking precisely because they sensitise us into qualifying each time the range and reach of a cultural feeling as it circulates. My questions then are relatively simple and relate to time (what is the duration of a mood or feeling? How do we periodise patterns of feeling? What is the temporal unit that we use to apprehend cultural feelings?), to space (where do we locate moods and feelings? Where are their borders? Are moods and feelings connected to institutions, to national phenomena, to global forces or are they articulated much more locally in relation to a milieu?) and to people (who do we name when we say that cultural feelings are collective: a national population; a class; a particular set of experiences relating to gender, sexuality, age, ability?). At the base of these questions lies a more methodological question aimed at the practice of cultural investigation when it is attuned to moods, atmospheres and feelings: how do we render an account of cultural feelings that can offer a sense of the general orchestration of feelings and moods at the level of national and global culture, while also being sensitive to and articulating the ways in which these orchestrations affect different groups in different ways. What follows is simply an attempt to render a set of orchestrations of cultural feelings, ones that can pick up the major melodies as well as the harmonies and descants.

The structure of this book

This book is about feelings and moods, but it is also about the way that these qualities are made manifest, the way that they are conveyed and sustained, and the social effects and affects that they have. As my title claims, this book is about the cultural politics and the forms of mediation that mood and feeling take and have taken. The cultural politics of this book is twofold: on the one hand, it seeks to describe situations in which the cultural and political aspects of mood and feeling become vivid; on the other hand, it seeks to pursue its own political path in the choice of what phenomena to look at and in the accounts I provide of such material. Writing counter-moods for our recent history is a form of cultural politics. But re-mooding the recent past isn't a question of swapping one mood palate for another; painting the 1970s as prosperous and lively rather than full of discontent, for instance. Instead it means generating more realist, more complex mood-worlds that more accurately articulate the various patterns of experiences that attach themselves to an epoch or a moment, and being able to negotiate and orchestrate conflictual and contradictory feelings. If the period of the Blitz, for instance, has tended to be painted as a period of unerring valour, as the very exemplar of what courage means, it is not in anyone's interest simply to reverse this image. But it is in all our interests, I would have thought, to offer more complex orchestrations of the mood-worlds that greeted aerial bombing in 1940–1941 or the patterns of feeling that ushered in the Margaret Thatcher government at the end of the 1970s.

While my emphasis throughout is on forms of cultural and historical description, in the next chapter I undertake a fairly long account of the main theoretical coordinates for what follows. In this, I lay out a foundation for approaching moods and feelings as objects for cultural analysis. The chapter is split into three uneven parts. In the first part (the longest), I return to Raymond Williams' project of mapping 'structures of feeling' as a central aim of cultural studies and ask what, precisely, that suggestive phrase meant for Williams and what it could mean for cultural investigation today. My sense is that while Williams' phrase is routinely used, we don't always investigate the nature of Williams' deployment of this term and what he included under the heading 'feelings'. In the middle part, I look at the work of Martin Heidegger as offering suggestive philosophical coordinates for thinking about mood or what he terms *Stimmung*, meaning both mood and atmosphere. In the last part, my concern shifts to the current interest in affect theory and new materialism to ask how foregrounding mood and feeling both continue and refashion some of affect theory's primary concerns.

Chapter 3 argues that the study of mood and habit provides a useful platform for examining the pedagogic work of aspects of culture. Using the example of British wartime film propaganda, this chapter suggests that a pedagogic understanding of propaganda aimed at increasing Home Front Morale needs to mobilise a formalism that is attentive to the phenomenal form of cultural objects. In this way, we can recognise that often the pedagogical job of culture is not to *tell* us what to think and feel but rather to *show* ways of attuning ourselves in relation to current circumstances. One of the important aspects of this chapter is to recognise that a good deal of mood work is aimed at de-dramatising social circumstances and atmospheres, to undo forms of anxiety and stress, and so on. Importantly, then, much of the mood work performed by institutional set-ups promotes low-intensity moods that are often hard to spot as mood-forms. This chapter concentrates on a set of cultural feelings that were tied very specifically to a set of historical circumstances, namely that vast industrial-military assemblage called World War II and the particular address made to what was called the British 'Home Front' at this time.

If Chapter 3 is concerned with a specific historical period, Chapter 4 is concerned with a particular kind of space. The chapter argues that bombsites in Britain were a vivid component of a social imaginary that informed the post-war social settlement. Post-war reconstruction, which often involved additional demolition, also produced ruined landscapes that were complexly associated with war damage. The bombsite-demolition site as an accidental or purposeful playground for children added to the vacillating meanings of these ruined landscapes, as they signalled both the destructive power of modern industrial violence and the resilient and resourceful power of children and play to reconstitute and repair such landscapes. The image of children playing among ruins joined these two meanings together making the bombsite into a habitat for 'feral' youth or the 'juvenile delinquent' as the imagined threat that haunts the Welfare State. By attending to the material and symbolic landscapes of post-war ruins we can see a cultural politics struggling with internal anxieties and ruinous identifications.

Chapter 5 focuses on the experiences of particular groups of people over a relatively long period of time. It looks at the experience of migration within Britain as generating particular cultural forms that convey a pattern of feeling whose tone might be described as mixing elements of regret, resilience and exuberance. Its overarching mood is one of disappointment. Yet that mood of disappointment that is everywhere recounted in the testimony of migrants to Britain in the post-war years isn't simply a response to a situation that didn't live up to expectations. It is a feeling that is exacerbated through the production of cultural work (in newspapers, on radio, on television) that constantly registers the migrant as social problem, rather than, say, heroic voyager. This is mood work that forms of mediation perform. As an antidote to that mood work I look at a film by John Akomfrah as one particularly powerful practice of producing counter-moods around the representation of black British settlement. Re-mooding the world is a practice of cultural politics. At times it is also a utopian practice.

Chapter 6 is primarily concerned with music as the conveyor of feeling and mood. In the late 1970s and early 1980s, 'post-punk' (or DIY aesthetics) emerged out of the anger and disdain of punk and the new regime of Thatcherism. Itchy and fractured guitars, lolloping and looping bass lines, mottled and abrasive drumming and singing that stretched to almost hit the right note characterised the sound of bands such as the Raincoats, the Slits, Gang of Four and the Au Pairs. Promoted by record companies like Rough Trade and mongrelising a range of musical genres (most particularly reggae, funk and punk), such music orchestrated a rough alliance between feminist, anti-imperialist and anti-capitalist politics; a grassroots amalgam of squatters, students and hedonists; and promoted purposeful musical eclecticism. Startlingly optimistic soundscapes were hewn out of the rock of purposefully deskilled musical accomplishments. As a way of engaging with the evanescence of this musical firmament, I have written this chapter not as a sustained investigation and argument but as series of short descriptive and analytic fragments.

As a final case study, I look at two long-form television and filmic projects that chart a set of feelings and moods as they change across important (and overlapping) periods of time. Generation is, I argue, a useful way of refracting cultural feelings as it suggests that there are feelings and moods associated with the time of the life-course as age is intertwined with historical events and processes. The TV drama *Our Friends in the North* follows four friends from the north-east of England across the years 1964 to 1995 and looks at their changing fortunes. The drama is set against a political landscape of a left-wing local council and its housing policies in the 1960s, of police corruption and the criminal underworld in the 1970s and of the miners' strike and the rise of Thatcherism in the 1980s. The drama details how the four characters' lives are both entangled with these events and with each other. Shane Meadows' *This is England* project (which started as a film set in 1983 and then followed with three TV series set in 1986, 1988 and 1990) is smaller in historical scale but is concerned with a larger cast of characters. It is set in an unnamed seaside town and is concerned with a large group of young people (in their teens and twenties) who, in 1983, are skinheads. Their relationship to political events (the Falklands War and the rise of Thatcherism) provides an overarching feeling although it doesn't direct the narrative. It is the relationship between the way in which a period is presented as a set of cultural moods, and the feelings displayed by the characters as they live this period that this concluding chapter is concerned with. The question of how large-scale social and cultural forces are lived out is, I argue, the practice of a cultural politics that sees its arenas as the rendering and shaping of moods, atmospheres and feelings.

Finally, I end with a short postscript that reflects on cultural feelings today and the possibilities for a cultural politics that engages with moods, atmospheres and feelings.

Notes

1 I am pursuing this aspect of cultural feelings in a book I am currently preparing on the shop Habitat. This book will be published, in due course, as *The Making of Taste: Habitat, Lifestyle, and Class in Postwar Britain* by Manchester University Press.
2 Within the world of retail and marketing research, a great deal of attention has been paid to the way atmospheres can be used to increase sales; see Heide and Grønhaug (2009) for representative work on the Norwegian hotel industry. Heide and Grønhaug cite a study of the restaurant industry that 'indicates that atmosphere is often perceived by both guests and staff as the single most important characteristic of the establishment – rated even more important than the food itself' (2009: 29).
3 Classic accounts of affective and immaterial labour are provided by Maurizio Lazzarato in his essay 'Immaterial Labor' (1996) and by Michael Hardt in his essay 'Affective Labor' (1999).

4 When I used to work as a waiter it was always the unexpected responses that undid me. One very busy Sunday lunch service, the two chefs that were on duty had a fist-fight and were sent home and the manager stepped in to cook the food. My job that day consisted primarily of apologising to the customers who were waiting an inordinately long time for their food. Mostly the reactions were understandably grumpy or angry. I set about parrying such aggressions with offers of free drinks and effusive apologies. After several hours of this, one couple stopped me to tell me that I had been doing a wonderful job. I couldn't take this and had to leave the restaurant floor in tears, and wait ten minutes until I had recovered enough to rejoin the fray.
5 See Thomas (2007) for an excellent account of this.
6 Adjusted from Marx (1852: 96). Marx is talking about the conditions under which history is made.

2
CULTURAL FEELINGS
(Some theoretical coordinates)

In this chapter I am going to build on some of the descriptive elements that appeared in the first chapter by setting out the main theoretical coordinates that can be seen to undergird them. This task requires some ground-clearing and clarification of the main terms and concepts deployed throughout this book. The central core of the chapter will involve an extensive discussion of one of the architects of cultural studies, Raymond Williams, and his phrase 'structures of feeling'. In some sense, the entire book is aimed at drawing out the critical potential, as well as squaring up to the problems, that 'structures of feeling' (as a form of enquiry) generates for the investigation of culture. For Williams, 'feeling' always pointed towards a politics of culture that could somehow correct the overemphasis on economics and ideology within cultural politics and more particularly within left-leaning and socialist approaches to the humanities.

Feelings, Williams insists, are not necessarily practised in a sentimental register, nor are they simply coterminous with emotions or affect. In an essay that was first published in 1975 ('You're a Marxist, Aren't You?') he makes clear that a progressive politics will need to mobilise feelings and other less-rationalist phenomena:

> The task of a successful socialist movement will be one of feeling and imagination quite as much as one of fact and organisation. Not imagination or feeling in their weak senses – 'imagining the future' (which is a waste of time) or 'the emotional side of things'. On the contrary, we have to learn and to teach each other the connections between a political and economic formation, a cultural and educational formation, and, perhaps hardest of all, the formations of feeling and relationship which are our immediate resources in any struggle.
>
> *(Williams 1989b: 76)*

I think that today we are so used to associating feelings with emotional responses (particularly in the regions of an individual's sense of themselves as sad, happy, hurt, angry, etc.) that we find it hard to imagine something like 'socialism' as a feeling. What would constitute the feel of democracy, for instance? What sort of feelings would encourage or discourage a sense of community within a neighbourhood, a city, a country? What precisely Williams means by 'feeling' and how formations, patterns and structures of feelings arise and get disseminated will be one of the crucial questions that I hope to clarify in this and further chapters.

This chapter will start by considering Raymond Williams' work on cultural feelings and establishing its genesis and place both within Williams' oeuvre and as part of his cultural moment, as the term emerged within a dialogue between anthropology and literary studies. While I think Williams' mobilisation of the word 'feeling' is endlessly productive, I want to supplement my discussion of Williams with an account of the philosopher Martin Heidegger's use of the word *Stimmung* (an untranslatable word meaning mood, atmosphere and attunement). Heidegger's philosophical ambition is enormous but also banal (and I think that this was central to his project) and he makes *Stimmung* an invaluable foundational term within his existential phenomenology. I finish this chapter with a discussion of recent affect theory, focusing specifically on the work of Lauren Berlant, who, while not being representative of work taking place under the title 'affect', offers perhaps the most exciting and challenging deployment of the term.

Patterns of feeling

The phrase 'structures of feeling' names the approach that Raymond Williams developed throughout his career as a literary analyst. The phrase names an attention to social change that occurs at the level of cultural feelings and where the evidence for such change can best be found in the emergence of new literary and dramatic conventions, in alterations in the connotations of certain words (his 'key' words), and in the changing figural aspects of culture. This, I think, would be one way of describing the phrase 'structures of feeling' as it was mobilised by Williams in his professional work as a historian of drama and literature:

> The point of the deliberately contradictory phrase, with which I have never been happy, is that it was a structure in the sense that you could perceive it operating in one work after another which weren't otherwise connected – people weren't learning it from each other; yet it was one of feeling much more than of thought – a pattern of impulses, restraints, tones, of which the best evidence was often the actual conventions of literary or dramatic writing.
>
> *(Williams 1981: 159)*

In this quotation from Williams' book of dialogues with the editors of *New Left Review*, we get the sense that we should approach the phrase with some trepidation (it is clearly an approximation rather than an analytically precise technical term), but also that it names a form of attention (a sensitivity towards 'tones, impulses, restraints') as well as an object of study ('literary or dramatic writing').

We shouldn't be surprised that Williams singles out literary and dramatic writing rather than, say, the changing practices of financial exchange, the transformations in pop music, or changes in mealtime habits – he was after all a professional historian of drama and literature. Yet literature is a vehicle rather than an endpoint in Williams' analyses, and his wider ambition is to find a way of attending to a much more general realm of life: 'For what we are defining is a particular quality of social experience and relationship, historically distinct from other particular qualities, which gives the sense of a generation or of a period' (Williams 1977: 131). It is this ambition to pursue the investigation of culture with the aim of trying to register particular qualities that would characterise a particular historical period or a particular group experience that I see as essential to his project. It might turn out that drama and literature are two of our most productive ways of accessing these qualities, yet it would be foolhardy to imagine that these would be the only ways of accessing them, or always the most productive route.

During the 30-odd years that Raymond Williams deployed the term 'structures of feeling', it could point to an entity as vast as the dominant feelings of an age (of the Elizabethan age, for instance) or as historically specific as an emergent (or even pre-emergent) set of concerns coming into focus for specific groups (for instance, in the new social movements of the 1980s and beyond). 'Feeling' could at times be covered by the word 'experience' and would include a massive terrain of attitudes, manners, actions, behaviours and so on. 'Structure' seems to be a word that is primarily used to suggest a commonality, a series of relations and repetitions, a way of insisting that 'feelings' aren't the private property of an individual but are part of a common *social* culture. And I think that 'structure' is also a word that attempts to toughen up the phrase (or masculinise it), to stop it sounding too emotional. In many ways I think that the phrase could be adjusted to 'patterns of feeling' (which is a phrase that Williams also uses) without losing any essential features.[1] But whether it is 'structures of feeling' or 'patterns of feeling', the phrase is vague; the question is, is it *necessarily* vague? Does the vagueness of the phrase allow it to do the sort of work that a more precise set of terms would inhibit?

The features of the phrase that require more clarification here are not, I don't think, the temporal or spatial units that can be described by a structure of feeling (local, identity-specific, national or international; the *longue durée* of an epoch or the relatively short time-span of economic booms and busts, for instance). In this, 'structures of feeling' is an abstraction, just like 'culture'; it is fundamentally tensile in quality and will always require clarification as it tries to apprehend the empirical. As Paul Filmer suggests: 'as with any concept formulated to assist in the analysis of the emergent flux of social process, it is likely to require clarification whenever it is introduced into critical discourse and whenever it is applied to the critical analysis of concrete, empirical social and cultural practices' (2003: 201). Indeed, one way of thinking about the critical lexicon that Williams produced during his career is that it was principally aimed at providing just such tools for clarification. So the finely wrought distinctions between 'oppositional', 'alternative' and 'incorporated', and the dynamic temporal situation that the terms 'emergent', 'residual' and 'dominant' point to, are all ways of clarifying and qualifying formations of feelings.[2] The question of the scale and scope, the range and the reach of a structure of feeling can only be addressed through actual case studies, and this is something that motivates the chapters that follow this one.

In this chapter I want to concentrate on the term 'feeling', and to provide a context for Williams' use of that word. The detailing of the direct and indirect influence of anthropology on Williams' concept of 'structures of feeling' allows, I think, for a much fuller discussion of what Williams meant by 'feeling' and the sorts of qualities and phenomena that could be included within the term. It is also worth remembering the specific context of what was called 'Cambridge English' for understanding Williams' position both as a continuation and as an intervention in that formation. It is also necessary to look beyond his emphasis on dramatic and literary forms as evidence for structures of feeling. Throughout his writing, particularly at moments of autobiographical performance, there are clear indications that he saw structures of feeling as being conveyed and sustained by much less representational forms; conveyed and sustained by forms that have a ubiquitous presence within the everyday; for instance, clothing, buildings and, for many, religion.

The phrase 'structures of feeling' was first used by Williams in 1954 in his jointly authored book (with the documentary filmmaker Michael Orrom) *Preface to Film*.[3] In this book he coins the phrase as a way of holding together an argument that insists that dramatic forms are recognised as part of a social totality, and as providing the most vivid evidence of what that totality is like as a living form (its qualities or attitudes, for instance). While cultural historians and literary critics might seek to grasp the world as divided up into separate entities (religion, leisure, family, politics and so on), this is not how the world is experienced: 'while we may, in the study of a past period, separate out particular aspects of life, and treat them as if they were self-contained, it is obvious that this is only how they may be studied, not how they were experienced' (Williams and Orrom 1954: 21). This is an issue that the historian faces. It is an argument against the atomising effects of disciplinary specialisation (the specialisations that produce separate realms of economic history, social history, political history and cultural history, for instance). He goes on to use an analogy that he will return to each time he discusses 'structures of feeling': 'We examine each element as a precipitate, but in the living experience of the time every element was in solution, an inseparable part of a complex whole' (Williams and Orrom 1954: 21; the same formulation is reiterated 23 years later in Williams 1977: 133–134). Initially the phrase is used to encourage a particular form of attention towards dramatic works. Its aim is to transform finished artworks, that might be available for specialised and atomised interpretation, into unfinished, socially responsive works, that are 'still' emerging within the melange of a dynamic culture, and that rather than requiring specialist interpretation, require understanding, contextualising and connecting. The phrase is intended to direct our attention towards the work's historicity; its role as documentary evidence of 'the native's point of view' (so to say), for a particular community, at a particular time.

'Structures of feeling' are, for Williams, what get remaindered when atomised disciplines get their hands on culture and divide it up into distinct realms of 'psychology', 'society', 'economy', 'history', 'art' and so on. 'When one has measured the work against the separable parts,' writes Williams, 'there yet remains some element for which there is no external counterpart. This element, I believe, is what I have named the *structure of feeling* of a period, and it is only realizable through experience of the work of art itself, as a whole' (Williams and Orrom 1954: 21–22, emphasis in original).[4] We should be wary of thinking, however, that this means we can *only* recover structures of feelings from artworks: the emphasis of the 'only' might not refer to 'art' so much as to the idea of experiencing it as a 'whole' (as a whole way of life, as a world). Such emphasis seems to be clarified when he writes, 'all changes in the methods of an art like drama are related, essentially, to changes in man's radical structure of feeling' (Williams and Orrom 1954: 23). Thus while art (film, plays and novels, primarily) might be the privileged documentary route to recovering a structure of feeling, it is human, 'lived experience' – as an entirety – where structures of feeling exist.[5] As such, structures of feeling are not an aspect of life (or art) that can be siphoned off and analysed; they saturate the lifeworld in complex ways, as mood, attitude, manners, emotions, and so on. Anyone even slightly familiar with Williams' work will recognise that 'structures of feeling' echoes with his emphasis on treating culture as a 'whole way of life'.[6] 'A whole way of life' is Williams' way of signalling that culture needs to be seen through the transdisciplinary optic of anthropology, or an anthropologically attuned sensibility.

Cambridge and experience

To get a fuller understanding of what Williams meant by structures of feeling, it is worth situating the phrase, initially at least, within Williams' own life and experience during the late 1930s and throughout the 1940s. The phrase 'structures of feeling' becomes at once more vivid and more tangible when it is recognised, not as a vague formation of manners and attitudes that hangs in the ether, so to say, but as a living triangulation between an individual's biography (his or her stock of life experiences, which would include their upbringing, education and so on), their contemporary social position (which might include their sense of political agency or lack of it), and the larger national and geopolitical forces at work (including international tensions, national political narratives and so on). 'Structures of feeling' is a phrase that points at one and the same time to an overarching orchestration of energies, attitudes and emotions, and to the fact that 'we' may experience this orchestration differently depending on our background and current situation. In other words, groups of people can feel a structure of feeling quite differently (depending on, for instance, whether they feel part of a specific generation) and yet the overarching aspect of a structure of feeling is what articulates this difference. In this sense, 'structures of feeling' operates like Jacques Rancière's phrase 'the distribution of the sensible': it names a differentiated social terrain that is unevenly experienced precisely *because* of its overarching orchestration, not *in spite of it*.[7] In other words, within societies structured around an uneven distribution of resources, forms of prejudice, bias and unequal opportunity will constantly fashion the structures of feeling in constitutive ways.

Raymond Williams was brought up within a Welsh village (Pandy) among proud working-class men and women, but received a scholarship to attend a grammar school in Abergavenny (also in Wales) and from there went to study at the University of Cambridge at the outbreak of war, where he was active in left-wing politics (he joined the student branch of the Communist Party). Between 1941 and 1945 he fought in the war as part of the Guards Armoured Division and was demobbed as a captain. In the academic year 1945–1946 he completed his MA degree at Cambridge and then took the position of extra-mural staff tutor within Oxford University, where he taught as part of the Workers' Education Association and where he remained until returning to Cambridge in 1961 as a lecturer in English.[8] Even in these few sentences there is a sense of life being lived across substantially different spaces and times, and that these crossings registered dramatic social and historical upheavals at both the biographical and the geopolitical levels. To move from Pandy to Cambridge wasn't simply to move from a working-class milieu to one where the ruling class were in the majority: it was to be made aware of what Ernst Bloch called 'non-synchronous simultaneity' (Bloch 1935). For instance, in 1958, looking back at his first years at Cambridge, he remembers 'learning' that the word 'neighbour' no longer meant what it did in Shakespeare's day, yet also knowing that in Pandy, where he grew up, 'neighbour' still meant precisely what it did for Shakespeare:

> When my father was dying, this year, one man came in and dug his garden; another loaded and delivered a lorry of sleepers for firewood; another came and chopped the sleepers into blocks; another – I don't know who, it was never said – left a sack of potatoes at the back door; a woman came in and took away a basket of washing.
>
> *(Williams 1989 [1958]: 9)*

The structure of feeling that was being made so evident in Cambridge was one that could include these neighbourly practices *only* as outmoded residues surviving in the present, in a world where *neighbour* simply designated proximity, rather than living obligations and networks of care.

But I think 'structures of feeling' (as a device for understanding historical change) began to become evident to him in 1945 when he returned to Cambridge at the end of the war. Upon arriving back he remembers that 'the student culture had altered. There was a lot more religion about [...] There was no longer a conscious left presence' (Williams 1981: 61). In Cambridge he met up with his friend and fellow socialist Eric Hobsbawm (whom he had known at the start of the war) and they agreed 'that we were in a different world' (Williams 1981: 61) and that the people around them 'just don't speak the same language' (Williams 1983 [1976]: 11). In 1945, that meant that the shared language of leftist political commitments was no longer 'near at hand', no longer part of the assumed resources for talking about the present and the future. In his book *Keywords* he explains what people mean when they say 'we just don't speak the same language': they mean 'that we have different immediate values or different kinds of valuation, or that we are aware, often intangibly, of different formations and distributions of energy and interest' (Williams 1983 [1976]: 11).

It is worth staying with some of these words: 'energy', 'interest', 'intangible', 'values' and 'immediacy'. On the one hand, Williams seems to be claiming that at the level of intuitive life (the world of cultural reflexes, the world of meaning that is nearest to hand) something has fundamentally altered. As far as this goes it is not impossible to talk the language of pre-war politics, but you can't be guaranteed an immediate comprehension and you might need to explain and qualify the terms and values you are using. On the other hand, and in a more intangible way, something has altered at the level of what we could call abstract form: direction of interests, distributions of energy. It is a common enough response to reply to enquiries about how you are feeling by saying that you 'feel a bit flat' or that you 'feel up for anything', or by saying 'that you can't seem to settle on something', and it is this arena of feeling that for Williams is crucial to a 'structure of feeling'. In *Politics and Letters* he continually describes cultural situations and his relation towards them in terms of energy. Energy, for Williams, is always about focus, distribution, concentration – it always contains a social attitude. Thus in the immediate post-war years, after a number of political and literary projects had collapsed, he writes that 'the experience confirmed the pattern of feeling I had found in Ibsen. For a period I was in such a state of fatigue and withdrawal that I stopped reading papers or listening to the news' (Williams 1981: 77). But this feeling shouldn't be construed as pessimistic or depressed: for Williams it meant a refocused energy, one that wasn't socially expansive but concentrated on understanding and working through cultural change. In clarifying the reference to Henrik Ibsen, he writes: 'In his plays, the experience of defeat does not diminish the value of the fight. That was precisely the personal "structure of feeling" within which I lived from '45 to '51 at the deepest level' (Williams 1981: 63).

While the first published use of the phrase 'structures of feeling' occur in the early to mid-1950s, he probably started thinking about 'feelings' as an approach for practicing cultural history and criticism in the mid-1940s when he was writing about Ibsen. In looking back at that moment in Cambridge he states that there he 'found the new alternative sub-culture, which in English but also in Anthropology was the group around F.R. Leavis' (Williams 1989a: 11). Cambridge English in the 1930s and 1940s was dominated by the figure of Leavis and the journal he edited, *Scrutiny* (see Mulhern 1979 for an exacting critical account of the journal as a cultural formation). Within this context, the word 'feelings' is part of a lexicon of terms that wants to treat novels and poems as part of a world of experience. Thus, writing in 1932 in *New Bearings in English Poetry*, Leavis can describe T.S. Eliot's poetry as a form of writing 'that expresses freely a modern sensibility, the ways of feeling, the modes of experience, of one fully alive in his own age' (Leavis 1972 [1932]: 61).[9] Here 'feelings', 'sensibility' and 'experience' are either synonymous or cognate terms. For Leavis, one of the ways of valuing literature is to see it as a distillation of experience, and therefore a successful poem could be described as articulating (in a literal rather than a judgemental sense) 'refined' feelings, precisely because the task that literature undertakes is to refine or distil experience.

It is part of a common understanding of Williams' 'structures of feeling' project (one that is encouraged by Williams in his writing) that it combined Leavis' approach to literature with an adherence to Marxism. It is tempting to see this 'Left Leavisism' (Eagleton 1988: 7) as establishing an equation whereby the word 'feeling' drives the Leavis side of the equation, while 'structures' points us to a Marxism that could be attentive to structuring activities such as the division of labour. My sense, however, is that the word 'feeling' in the phrase points to a much more diverse set of concerns that were pertinent to both anthropology and the study of literature at this time (and within the limited milieu of Cambridge), and named phenomena that purposefully expanded the meaning that Leavis gave the term. This is not to say that Leavis wasn't also informed by more anthropological discussions of feeling and experience; for instance, when, in the 1960s, he edited two anthologies made up of selections from *Scrutiny*, he chose to begin the first volume with a long review by Q.D. Leavis (from 1943) of a biography of A.C. Haddon, the man who established anthropology at Cambridge early in the twentieth century (Leavis 1968 [1943]).[10]

'Cambridge English', as it came to be known, might have been heavily associated with Leavis, but it was underwritten by the 'practical criticism' established at Cambridge by I.A. Richards. For Richards, 'feeling' was a key term for analysing all utterances (alongside 'sense', 'tone' and 'intention'); it named the utterance's attitude towards what it was referring to. For Richards, 'feeling' is 'some special direction, bias, or accentuation of interest towards' the content and references of an utterance: it is that aspect of an utterance that demonstrates 'some personal flavour or colouring of feeling; and we use language to *express* these feelings, this nuance of interest' (Richards 1976 [1929]: 181, emphasis in original). 'Nuance of interest' suggests that feelings name the particular shape that a desire or a demand may take: its strength (or weakness), its focus (or diffusion), its density (or delicacy). Just to show how extensive is the range of phenomena that could be included as a feeling, Richards explains: 'under "feeling" I group for convenience the whole conative-affective aspects of life – emotions, emotional attitudes, the will, desire, pleasure-unpleasure, and the rest. "Feeling" is shorthand for any or all of this' (Richards 1976 [1929]: 181). The conative-affective aspect is that animated realm of life (all our volition, propulsion, attraction and repulsion) that is not governed by rationalised thought. It is, in other words, the world least available to being represented as ideas, arguments and thoughtful reflection.

The realm of feeling is an aspect of life that, within the reflexive world of intellectual writing, is often more gestured at than directly attended to. It is an aspect of life that Williams sometimes called the 'lived', an arena that he is constantly scrabbling around to find the right word for:

> The lived is only another word, if you like, for experience: but we have to find a word for that level. For all that is not fully articulated, all that comes through disturbance, tension, blockage, emotional trouble seem to me precisely a source of major changes in the relation between the signifier and the signified, whether in literary language or conventions.
> *(Williams 1981: 168)*

This is, in some regards, Williams extolling a form of vitalism that he sees as animating the living world of social communication and practice as well as literary forms. In choosing the term 'feeling' over the word 'experience', Williams is making a strategic move to avoid what he saw as the pitfalls of 'these great blockbuster words like experience' that 'can have very unfortunate effects over the rest of the argument' (Williams 1981: 168). The unfortunate effects included the privileging of particular subjectivities (whether these belong to the critic or the poet) who could be considered professional distillers of the 'lived', but also the way that 'experience' often suggests phenomena that *had* occurred (and had been reflected on) rather than something that was ongoing, and existing in pre-articulated states.

But it is the anthropological context that shows us how 'feelings' can be used, not simply as a way of attending to drama and literature, but as a way of pursuing cultural politics more systematically than via Leavis' approach. The term 'feeling' would have had a particular resonance within anthropology at Cambridge in the 1930s and 1940s, and would, importantly, have signalled a specific ambition for anthropology. Anthropology was first established at Cambridge in 1908 in the wake of the university-backed anthropological expedition to Torres Straits, organised and directed by A.C. Haddon in 1898–1899. This expedition is often understood as the first instance of intensive and wide-ranging anthropological fieldwork, a moment when the ethnographer left the colonial veranda, so to say, to go in search of 'native' culture. What also characterised the Torres Straits expedition was the range of approaches it deployed: psychology, biology, physical anthropology, ethnography, geography and so on. It became the basis for what at Cambridge became known as the intensive study. By the 1930s, however, Cambridge was not the centre of anthropological innovation in Britain. By this time, Cambridge often operated as a training college for colonial administrators, while the more innovative fieldwork was being conducted under the directorship of Malinowski at the London School of Economics, or by the social anthropologists at Oxford. It was precisely in this context that a younger generation of anthropological concerns were circulating in Cambridge.

And it is here that the word 'pattern' becomes a vital term for naming the role of feelings in culture. In his 1961 book *The Long Revolution*, Williams claims that some form of pattern recognition forms the basis of cultural analysis:

It is with the discovery of patterns of a characteristic kind that any useful cultural analysis begins, and it is with the relationships between these patterns, which sometimes reveal unexpected identities and correspondences in hitherto separately considered activities, sometimes again reveal discontinuities of an unexpected kind, that general cultural analysis is concerned.

(Williams 1992 [1961]: 47)

The Long Revolution offers two analyses of structures of feeling. The first is concerned with the literature of the 1840s and in the way that attitudes and behaviours towards the poor are articulated in the novels of the period; the second is concerned with 'Britain in the 1960s' (the book was written in 1959) and is an attempt to extrapolate changing structures of feeling in Britain within social institutions (schools, universities, trade unions, political parties and such like), within work relations (the rise of managerialism, for instance) and within everyday life (the extension of consumerism, the growth of media consumption and so on). I will return to this analysis later; for the moment I want to give a sense of the descriptive language that Williams employs in these and other analyses. In many ways it could be described as 'social formalism', thus he isn't necessarily concerned with the explicit content of an argument, but in its 'approaches and tones' (indeed 'tone' is an insistent descriptor in Williams' approach). Some of the 'feeling' words connect to behavioural attitudes ('thrift', 'sobriety', 'piety', 'pathos' and so on). Other words connect to a sense of the tempo of change and the orchestration of energies ('pulse', 'rhythm', etc.). And some words suggest, metaphorically, some hard-to-pin-down atmosphere or mood ('colour', 'tone' [again], 'flavour', etc.).

This vocabulary is close to the language that anthropologists, particularly Ruth Benedict and her associates (and in the context of Cambridge, Gregory Bateson is the crucial champion of Benedict's work) used in their 'pattern' analyses. In her work in the 1930s, Benedict sought a synthetic, comparative approach to the study of culture that looked for particular configurations of what she called 'the emotional background' of a culture and the observable rituals, forms of behaviour, which were the privileged phenomena for anthropological concern at the time. Culture, for Benedict, was a gestalt form that configured beliefs and behaviours against affective and emotional conditions and traditions. This emotional background was sometimes referred to by Benedict as 'ethos', a term that was also deployed and elaborated by Gregory Bateson in his 1936 book *Naven* (1958 [1936]). An ethos might include tacit understandings that allow a statement to be understood as a joke rather than as a serious opinion; it might include shared sentiments that will be oblique or obscure to an outsider while requiring no reflexive attention on the part of an insider; it might signal those cultural forms that get called manners, mores or 'appropriate' behaviour. In Benedict's analyses the emotional background or ethos is pushed to the foreground and used to characterise a particular society: 'I have called the *ethos* of the Pueblo Apollonian in Nietzsche's sense of the cultural pursuit of sobriety, of measure, of the distrust of excess and orgy' (Benedict 1932: 4, emphasis in original). Thus 'ethos' was the 'emotional patterning characteristic of the culture' and a crucial element in 'fundamental and distinctive cultural configurations that pattern existence and condition the thoughts and emotions of the individuals who participate in those cultures' (Benedict 1934: 55).

When Bateson started out in the early 1930s to undertake fieldwork with the Iatmul people in New Guinea, he had a vague but ambitious project in mind:

> I was especially interested in studying what I called the 'feel' of culture, and I was bored with the conventional study of the more formal details. I went out to New Guinea with that much vaguely clear – and in one of my first letters home I complained of the hopelessness of putting any sort of salt on the tail of such an imponderable concept as the 'feel' of culture. I had been watching a casual group of natives chewing betel, spitting, laughing, joking, etc., and I felt acutely the tantalizing impossibility of what I wanted to do.
> *(Bateson 1972 [1941]: 81)*

Analysis is left with spitting, laughing, joking, but the project is always of understanding how such practices are part of a whole way of life that has a distinct tonal range, a definite set of attitudes, of feelings, of moods and manners. Or at least the project is always attempting this understanding.

For Bateson, the word 'feel' was crucial, not because it pointed to emotions or affects, or manners and attitudes, but because it didn't really point anywhere at all. Bateson used words like 'feel', 'stuff' and 'bits' as placeholder words: 'these brief Anglo-Saxon terms have for me a definite feeling-tone which reminds me all the time that concepts behind them are vague and await analysis' (Bateson 1972 [1941]: 84). In other words, one of the points of using a word like 'feeling' rather than, say, 'affect' would be that it was less able to determine the sorts of phenomena that it might uncover and disclose. In this we could say that 'structures of feeling' was not simply a phrase that sought to attend to culture in solution rather than as precipitate, but that the phrase itself was designed to refuse, or at least delay the sort of precipitation that results from all analysis. For Bateson, 'feel' could only be a beginning, to be swapped for more complex and precise designations of cultural process, and it was here that Ruth Benedict provided the tentative solution to Bateson's initial quest.[11] The fluidity of the term 'feeling' alongside the search for substantial patterns and structures is one of the reasons that Williams hung on to the phrase 'structures of feeling' even though it was constantly critiqued (by people close to him) and was for him, as we saw at the start of this chapter, an unsatisfactory phrase. In many ways, I think this dissatisfaction was important. The phrase sat on the side of the empirical, not in some naïve anti-theoretical manner, but as part of a commitment to a radical empiricism that always moves towards the pulsing, populated world even if it recognises that there is no untroubled access to such a world. In other words, 'structures of feeling' names a *theoretical* commitment to the priority of corporeal, telluric life.

Such an approach to the study of culture takes us close to the concerns of 'Cambridge English'. To get a sense of the feel of culture (to register the ethos of a culture, in other words) required ethnographers in the field to practise a form of practical criticism. They had to be able to attend to utterances and practices of an unfamiliar culture in a similar way to how Richards attended to a poem, by being attuned to the 'sense, feeling, tone, and intention' of the utterance: to develop an ear for a culture, so as to be able to recognise irony, jokes, teasing, self-deprecation, emotional force, as well as lightness, triviality and so on. Such an anthropology was emphasising the practical in practical criticism.

The path from ethos to structures of feeling, from Benedict and Bateson to Williams, is not a straightforward one and includes aspects of discontinuity as well as continuity. The continuity is evident when, for instance, Williams describes structures of feeling as 'characteristic elements of impulse, restraint, and tone; specifically, affective elements of consciousness and relationships: not feelings against thought, but thought as felt and feeling as thought: practical consciousness of a present kind, in a living relationship to continuity' (Williams 1977: 132); this has the same sense of knotted gestalt that is evident in the work of Benedict and Bateson. But there are also differences and discontinuity.

It seems clear that Benedict and Bateson were more interested in the stabilities of cultural forms than in their radical mutability. When Benedict describes a cultural ethos as Apollonian or Dionysian, what she has in mind is a distinct taxonomy of 'emotional backgrounds' that could allow her to compare and contrast cultural forms (which would include critiquing, as we shall see, the rivalry at the base of North American competitive capitalism). Bateson, who defines an ethos as 'a culturally standardised system of organisation of the instincts and emotions of the individuals' sees his project as uncovering a distinct typology of ethoses:

> The ethos of a given culture is as we shall see an abstraction from the whole mass of its institutions and formulations and it might therefore be expected that ethoses would be infinitely various from culture to culture – as various as the institutions themselves. Actually, however, it is possible that in this infinite variousness it is the *content* of affective life which alters from culture to culture, while underlying systems or ethoses are continually repeating themselves. It seems likely – a more definite statement would be premature – that we may ultimately be able to classify the types of ethos.
>
> *(Bateson 1958 [1936]: 118)*

Williams does have some sense that, at least on one level, such large-scale 'structures of feeling' are indeed operative and can tell us something about the character of a society (its commitments to competitive individualism, for instance, or the structural dominance of a class system). But in general, Williams is much more interested in the sorts of incremental changes that gather around a generation, or a community, or a class.

Benedict's work was essential for the 'structures of feeling' project that Williams had set himself and in many ways it is unthinkable without it. It is here that Williams' so-called 'left Leavisism' is better understood as the deployment of Benedict's 'patterns of culture' approach now directed at industrial, capitalist culture and its histories of structural inequalities (in this sense, 'patterns of feeling' might be the more complete way of saying 'structures of feeling'). Williams' politics is not necessarily an addition to this approach; it is, rather, part of the reason for his attraction towards it. Benedict's approach, for instance, led her to denounce the configuration of US capitalism and its 'emotional background', as it is represented and explored in a book such as *Middletown*, as fundamentally wasteful and inefficient (and thereby failing on its own terms) (Benedict 1934: 247, 273). Thus Benedict's evaluation of North American culture is aimed at its orchestration of attitudes and energies, rather than at a moral condemnation of its hypocrisies or hierarchies. Williams' debt to Benedict is profound; it is what allows him to write about 'cultural form' as well as 'structures of feeling'.[12] And because it is so fundamental, it often goes under-acknowledged by Williams. But in the early years her work is a constant reference: for instance, in his discussion of how to analyse a world made up of 'newspapers, magazines and best-seller fiction, advertisements and propaganda' as well as 'broadcasting and the cinema; architecture and town planning' he insists on one specific reference:

> There is one book among many works of anthropology which seems to me so distinguished that it cannot wisely be omitted from an essential reading list in this field; Ruth Benedict's *Patterns of Culture*. Her book provides the method of comparative social evaluation which is necessary both to give the work of cultural analysis full scope and to keep it relevant.
>
> *(Williams 1993 [1950]: 178)*

For Williams, an attention to cultural feelings takes Richards' practical criticism into the living world of industrial capitalism through Benedict's insistence on ethos. 'Feelings' becomes a word that allows him to be sensitive and attentive to attitudes and attunements (practices of generosity, of neighbourliness, for instance) as well as to what could be called the energies of culture: the rising and falling quota of hope, of political fatigue, the amount of energy that can resource projects of collective action, and so on.

Feelings and material culture

One of the reasons, I think, for revisiting the link between anthropology and cultural studies is that anthropology has never had a particular stake in privileging the complex representational forms that are often the mainstay of humanities research (novels, plays, commentaries) and which cultural studies inherited from its roots in the study of English literature, not least from Raymond Williams. For anthropology (or the type that Benedict and Bateson pursued at least), 'a whole way of life' is not just found in foundation myths, rituals or beliefs, or in cultural objects and practices, but in the ways these exist within 'functioning wholes'. Thus, for Benedict, objects and beliefs have to be seen *in situ*:

> We still know in reality exactly nothing about them [cultural objects and practices] unless we know the way in which the arrangement of the house,

the articles of dress, the rules of avoidance or of marriage, the ideas of the supernatural – how each object and culture trait, in other words, is employed in their native life.

(Benedict 1932: 2)

Williams, of course, also maintained the importance of 'a whole way of life' as the crucial context and ambition of any analysis. Yet while Benedict and Bateson undertook their fieldwork within living culture, Williams' field was the *longue durée* of industrialised change that stretched from the seventeenth century to the late twentieth. Because the analyses of structures of feeling are concerned with the historicity of experience they are in one important sense always grammatically in the present, even if that present is in the eighteenth century.[13] But this does mean that while the carriers of structures of feeling within a current moment might be informal and ephemeral culture, 'carried' primarily by living (and unrecorded) speech and everyday social practice, this is not possible to recover when that moment is located in the past. 'Once the carriers of such a structure die,' Williams wrote in *The Long Revolution*, 'the nearest we can get to this vital element is in the documentary culture, from poems to buildings and dress-fashion, and it is this relation that gives significance to the definition of culture in documentary terms' (1992 [1961]: 49).[14] Quite rightly, Williams is less remembered for his commentary on dress-fashion and building than he is for his accounts of poetic and dramatic cultures. Yet there are telling moments within his work – often these are autobiographical moments – where description of dress, of places (the tea rooms of Cambridge, for instance), and the lives conducted within buildings (in chapels, factories, universities and railway signal boxes), combine with feelings sustained by material forms, and with Williams as a living witness and carrier of specific feelings.[15]

In a conversation conducted in 1959 between Williams and the literary and social critic Richard Hoggart, the pair discuss 'working-class attitudes' (and 'attitudes' is very much a 'structure of feeling' word), particularly in terms of the difference between the densely populated urban world of Leeds where Hoggart grew up (an industrial and commercial centre in northern England) and the Welsh village of Pandy where Williams lived. Williams describes how class feelings among labourers and miners in Wales didn't take the form of a sense of inferiority. Such feelings were sustained not simply by self-belief but by a whole panoply of material forms including clothing:

> I remember the men at home – a whole attitude in a way of dress. Good clothes, usually, that you bought for life. The big heavy overcoat, good jacket, good breeches, leggings, then a cardigan, a waistcoat, a watchchain, and all of it open, as a rule, right down to the waist. Layers of it going in, and of course no collar. But standing up, quite open. They weren't, really, people with a sense of inferiority.

(Hoggart and Williams 1960: 27)

'A whole attitude in a way of dress' might be a useful way of locating structures of feeling within relays of material culture and social conventions that aren't the usual evidential basis for social attitudes and structural sensitivities. Clothing or crockery or furniture are difficult to see as determining and sustaining carriers of feelings in themselves, which is why Williams treats them (as Benedict might) within a larger sense of practice and practical consciousness: it isn't simply the wearing of a good quality jacket, waistcoat and cardigan; it is a certain *practical* bravura in wearing these in a way that wasn't 'buttoned up' (in both a literal sense and a metaphorical sense of not being tentative, inward, cagey). The modern sense of 'having attitude', meaning not being passive or compliant, is enacted in this example of garment-wearing a century before the modern sense of the word 'attitude' had currency.

In the same discussion, Williams mentions how his father had a feel for democratic practice, and that this disposition was the product of non-conformist religious institutions (the tradition of attending chapel):

> Well, the self-government tradition in the chapels disposed many people to democratic feeling; feeling, really, rather than thinking. Someone like my father who grew up in a farm labourer's family, outside the tradition that brought conscious trade union attitudes, still got, I think, the feelings that matter.
>
> *(Hoggart and Williams 1960: 27)*

For Williams, a democratic feeling is a crucial aspect of a progressive cultural politics. And you can see a crucial aspect of the politics of a 'structures of feeling' approach when you recognise that a democratic impulse might be more important as a feeling than as a thought, or rather if it isn't felt, if it isn't lived as a felt thought, it can just produce the gestures of an ersatz and empty impulse that results in democratic-seeming phenomena like 'staff satisfaction surveys' that, instead of teaching democratic feelings, primarily teach us how to submit to bureaucracy.

In his analysis of the structures of feeling circulating in Britain in 1960, Williams is prescient in his sense of the way that a smokescreen of 'consultation' and feedback is used to mask a savage authoritarianism:

> This is the real power of institutions, that they actively teach particular ways of feeling, and it is at once evident that we have not nearly enough institutions which practically teach democracy. The crucial area is in work, where in spite of limited experiments in 'joint consultation', the ordinary decision process is rooted in an exceptionally rigid and finely-scaled hierarchy, to which the only possible ordinary responses, of the great majority of us who are in no position to share in decisions, are apathy, the making of respectful petitions, or revolt.
>
> *(Williams 1992 [1961]: 312)*

This aspect of an undemocratic 'felt culture' is a crucial aspect of the structure of feeling of neoliberalism, where a constant demand to 'feed back' and to 'share best practice' is a condition of unconstrained submission to administration.[16]

Structures of feeling, however, don't have to have an explicit socio-political form such as a pathos towards suffering, or a submission to bureaucratic networks. They can also feature much more indefinite and diffuse sensual forms. At the start of *The Country and the City* from 1973, Williams offers his own feelings towards the city and the country. The city for Williams is full of ambivalent feelings. On the one hand, the city can be seen as an obstacle to progress: he has, he writes, 'known this feeling' when 'looking up at great buildings that are the centres of power'. On the other hand, his overarching feeling towards the city is a 'permanent feeling' 'of possibility, of meeting and of movement' (Williams 1993 [1973]: 6). A feeling of possibility strikes me as a very different kind of feeling than a 'democratic' impulse, or a sense of self-respect. It suggests energy, a sense of a rhythm, an unknown form of practice that could erupt at any time. It sits on the side of the emergent, or the pre-emergent, whereas the democratic feeling that his father had sat more precisely on the side of the residual, a form that was being steamrolled into oblivion by anonymous bureaucratic forms.

In his description of feelings in relation to the country, Williams is at his most evocative, describing not an idyll but a dense network of sensual triggers and conflicting sentiments:

> It is the elms, the may, the white horse, in the field beyond the window where I am writing. It is the men in the November evening, walking back from pruning, with their hands in the pockets of their khaki coats; and the women in headscarves, outside their cottages, waiting for the blue bus that will take them, inside school hours, to work in the harvest. It is the tractor on the road, leaving its tracks of serrated pressed mud; the light in the small hours, in the pig farm across the road, in the crisis of a litter; the slow brown van met at the difficult corner, with the crowded sheep jammed to its slatted sides; the heavy smell, on still evenings, of the silage ricks fed with molasses. It is also the sour land, on the thick boulder clay, not far up the road, that is selling for housing, for a speculative development, at twelve thousand pounds an acre.
>
> *(Williams 1993 [1973]: 3)*[17]

Feelings can't be contained by positive or negative evaluations; instead they exist in 'whole ways of life' that feature speculative financial development alongside 'women in headscarves' and men with 'their hands in their pockets'. Attitudes clash, sensual forces connect the 'heavy' smell of silage with the 'sour' earth. This is a structure of feeling that is a feeling for community, and nature, amid the threat of developers.

But if structures of feeling can contain sensorial description and collective memory, if they can include bodily attitudes and 'fellow feeling', if they can register practical consciousness and material politics, is the phrase just too vague to be useful? Is an approach to 'structures of feeling' simply an invitation to register cultural forms beyond the ideational, beyond the ideological? Is it simply a provocation that petitions for fuller descriptions of our collective lives, lives lived across landscapes and cityscapes, across institutions and informal gatherings, among furniture and clothing, sounds and smells?

Configurations of feeling are not carried by words alone. The material world of things undergoes all sorts of re-accentuation and re-attunement. For instance, the pine kitchen table, once only found in working-class houses or in those kitchens where only servants worked, became in Britain and elsewhere in the 1960s and beyond an essential element of a more informal domesticity for the 'new middle classes' who were also re-accentuating words such as 'freedom', 'liberty' and 'community', in new directions. And kitchen tables connected to other relays of clothes, music, food, chairs, greetings, names, books, forms of relaxation, sayings, and on and on and on.[18] They also disconnect: a second-hand pine table is neither an oak dining table nor a Formica-covered table. Williams prioritised language and dramatic forms as his documentary evidence of the past in his works of literary criticism: in the realm of feelings that he describes in his personal testimony we are shown a more physically sensual world of clothing and community, food and furnishings.

In many ways, the world of clothing and furnishings might offer a different sensitivity for registering changes in 'structures of feeling' than that found in language and dramatic forms.[19] As Williams seems to suggest in *Keywords*, semantic shifts and semantic struggles are usually slow, accumulating over decades and centuries. Clothing, food and furnishings, on the other hand, are much closer to the world of commerce, and much more sensitive to the vagaries of taste, as well as directing and giving form to such changing tastes. They are syncopated to much faster rhythms. Of course, in some ways I'm setting up a false alterative here: the worlds of novels and films, for instance, rely heavily on conjuring mood and feeling precisely through their particular use of clothing, architecture, furnishings, food and so on. But it is worth noting that the material forms (from vocabularies, through genres, to fashions) convey changes to feelings with different degrees of sensitivity and that it is the orchestration of these together (in dissonant harmonies) that sustain patterns of feeling.

Many of the most exciting writers in the current 'turn to affect' in the humanities are also literary critics who acknowledge their relationship with Williams' attention to structures of feeling. Some of the best work in this area recognises the way that Williams' project was purposefully open to include more phenomena than those covered by the terms 'emotion' and 'affect'. Sianne Ngai, for instance, has a wonderfully compendious grasp of the range and ambition of Williams' use of the term 'feeling':

> Williams is not analysing emotion or affect, but, rather, strategically mobilizing an entire register of felt phenomena in order to expand the existing domain and methods of social critique ... His primary aim is to mobilize an entire affective register, *in* its entirety, and *as* a register, in order to enlarge the

scope and definition of materialist analysis. This is something quite different from the goal of offering a 'materialist analysis' of affect itself.

(Ngai 2005: 360, emphasis in original)

Such an assessment is based on the openness and vagueness of the term 'feeling'. It is this openness that is important, and one way of continuing and extending its use is to direct it towards new objects of attention. And this might mean reconnecting with its roots in anthropology and the social sciences more generally. I also think that those who study material culture and design could usefully employ 'structures of feeling' to describe the energies and tones that attach to our material worlds.

Williams' phrase has often functioned as a sort of flag of convenience for any number of different projects. Champions and critics alike have sometimes sought to give it a more precise and evaluative role than it has across Williams' work. In this, I think that commentators such as Andrew Milner, who claims, in an otherwise superb article, that 'structures of feeling' are always counterhegemonic, miss something crucial in the ways that cultural feelings can be residual or dominant as well as emergent, and that patterns of feeling may be an articulation of an emergent extension of a current hegemony, a new addition to undemocratic culture, for instance (Milner 1994: 55). It is true that Williams had blind-spots, and as many critics have noted, these tend to be gender and ethnicity. As with class, an analysis of structures of feeling that is alert to gender and ethnicity will need to face the problem that characteristic elements of a structure of feeling might often include racism and misogyny as overarching structural elements, while particular sets of 'feelings' may be mainly 'felt' by women, say, or by non-whites.

For others, Williams' phrase is just not theoretically rigorous. For Lawrence Grossberg, the term 'structures of feeling' is never adequately theorised by Williams (Grossberg 2010: 317). But what if this inadequacy was a crucial element of its flexibility, requiring it to be theorised anew each time it was deployed to apprehend the empirical as a whole way of life? What if theorising tended towards culture-as-precipitate and that what was required was a concept phrase that insisted on the culture-as-solution of the empirical? Such a concept phrase might, I think, look a lot like 'structures of feeling', which might be a way of pursuing a theory of the waywardly empirical.

Stimmung: mood and attunement

The previous discussion of Raymond Williams and 'structures (or patterns) of feeling' has, I hope, provided some of the methodological and theoretical coordinates for my descriptions of mood and feeling in Chapter 1 and for subsequent chapters. I am keen that so far in this book the following (at least) is clear: cultural feelings are neither internal, subjective states of affairs, nor are they ethereal atmospheres that exist outside of history. My aim has been to argue that feelings and moods are embodied and embedded in practices and habits, in routines and procedures that often have both a linguistic and a material support (sometimes more one than the other). That is also to say that changes in patterns of feeling are constituted by changes in material habits just as much as by changes in expression that can be seen in alterations in literary and dramatic conventions. In this section, however, I want to take this a step further by describing the use of the term '*Stimmung*' within the work of the German philosopher Martin Heidegger. What Heidegger offers the exploration of cultural feelings is an insistence that something like 'feeling' is constitutive of what it is to be in the world. If Williams insists that it is through patterns of feelings that we can see social changes taking place, then Heidegger offers us the insight that *Stimmung* (translated as attunement and mood) is how the world is to us. Without *Stimmung* there is no world for us, or not a world that can matter for us.

The broad project that Heidegger was involved with in the 1920s and that culminated in his extraordinary book *Being and Time* is an attempt to provide an ontological description of what it is to live (to be) in a world at a particular time and place. Rather than being interested in 'being' (*Sein*) in the abstract, he was interested in the concrete actuality of Being-here or there (*Dasein*); that is, he was concerned with 'being' as an insertion into world-hood or world-ness. What Heidegger is not asking is 'how do we make sense of the world?' Rather, he is concerned with 'how is the world *for* us so that sense could be something that we can make with it?' His strategy is usually to take everyday words and allow them to provide the foundations for such an inquiry. So while he may use a philosophically technical word such as 'ontology' to describe his enquiry, he will populate his ontological investigation with words like 'thrown' (*Geworfen*), 'care' (*Sorge*) and 'mood' (*Stimmung*) as well as his own neologisms, which are often assemblages of ordinary words, such as 'there-being' (*Dasein*). So 'thrown' is used to insist that we are always finding ourselves in already constituted worlds: we find ourselves in the midst of things (as in the Latin phrase *in media res*). 'Care' (or concern) is used as a foundation term for describing how the world matters to us. As we shall see, Heidegger often comes perilously close to forms of tautological description (which may well be his particularly insistent rhetorical form) such that what presents itself to us 'mattering' (our matters of concern) can only do so because we are concerned with things that matter.

It is not my intention to try and characterise and describe the philosophical edifice produced by Heidegger and its position in philosophical thought: greater minds than mine have dedicated their careers to just such an endeavour. Nor do I intend to enter into a critical encounter with the notoriety surrounding his deplorable actions during the period of National Socialism within Germany. Here I am interested in his work in as much that his use of *Stimmung* offers a specific dimension for understanding cultural feelings, and provides one of the most ambitious incentives for placing cultural feelings at the forefront of investigation. My use of Heidegger, then, is unapologetically instrumental in the sense that I have a particular task for him to perform, one that he is supremely well-suited for. There are, however, fundamental difficulties to be born in mind when approaching Heidegger in translation, and in having to use English language equivalents for Heidegger's German.

Stimmung *as fundamental orientation*

We can get a sense of why *Stimmung* would be important both for Heidegger and for my project of exploring cultural feelings when we realise the broad plasticity of the term, and the way that it seems purposefully to bridge the sense of intimate feelings and more general social and public feelings. *Stimmung* draws on the words *Stimme* (meaning voice) and *Stimmer* (meaning tuner: *Stimmgabel* is a tuning fork) to give the word a musical quality that leads to one of the ways it has been translated into English as 'attunement'. *Stimmung*, however, is usually translated as 'mood' with the same connotations as the English word, in that it can describe somebody feeling happy or sad, being in a 'bad mood' or euphoric, or somewhere in between. But if that suggests an interior or subjective state, it is clear that for Heidegger *Stimmung* is always leaning towards a much more collective experience. And *Stimmung* also echoes with a much more public world of sentiments and sensibilities: *Stimmabgabe*, for instance, means 'voting' (literally to deposit your voice) and *Stimmungsbarometer* is a barometer of 'public opinion' (or public feeling). If we thought of *Stimmung* as something like the feeling of social weather, we wouldn't be far off the mark. And while the most vivid weather (and the weather most remarked on in news media) is often extreme (floods, storms and so on) there is never a condition where weather is absent: it wouldn't make sense to be told that today there is no weather. In the same way, there is never a condition of mood-less-ness.

Heidegger in a sense trusts vernacular expressions to register something of what it is like to be in the world. If he had been an English speaker and living today he would, no doubt, have been interested in everyday phrases such as 'How's it going?' and 'How are you doing?' If he had been less of a scholarly recluse with a love of forests he might have enjoyed phrases like 'What's happening?', 'Where's it at?' or even 'You feel me?' It is in the spirit (if not the letter) of Heidegger's thought to recognise something profound in the literal wording of a phrase like 'How's it going?' where neither the 'it' nor the 'going' are given a specific referent. When we meet someone and ask 'How's it going?' we are saying something like: 'What is the situation [it] like?' 'What sort of energies [goings] are circulating in it?' We say 'How's it going?' precisely because we are saying something different from 'How are you?' or 'How do you feel?' We are looking at a situation that isn't internal to the subject but is felt by a subject in an environment, one where we are often surrounded by other subjects.

In German, in Heidegger's day, people said 'Wie befinden Sie sich?' which is usually translated as 'How are you?' but which literally means 'How do you find yourself?' and for Heidegger it was the 'finding' (the '*befinden*' or the 'to be situated') that was crucial. This 'finding ourselves' is for Heidegger a foundational condition for our being-in-the-world, and Heidegger turns this into a 'state' for which he coins the term *Befindlichkeit* (literally 'the state in which one may be found'). One set of translators have translated this as 'state of mind'. The problem here is that 'mind' suggests cognition and consciousness, whereas clearly there are a whole range of states that we might find ourselves in that are much more to do with our conative-affective register (we may find ourselves depressed, depleted, unsettled, anxious, 'ready-for-anything', bored, bubbling with life and so on). And clearly for Heidegger the conative-affective register is the important one. For Heidegger, *Befindlichkeit* is the ontological condition of Being. And here is where we can find most clearly Heidegger's tautological arguments. Heidegger writes: 'what we indicate *ontologically* by the term "state-of-mind" (*Befindlichkeit*) is *ontically* the most familiar and everyday sort of thing; our mood, our Being-attuned (*die Stimmung, das Gestimmtsein*)' (Heidegger 2008 [1927]: 172). Recognising that 'state-of-mind' is inadequate, another set of translators have translated *Befindlichkeit* as 'attunement', which is also a way of translating *Stimmung*.

The tautological aspect of Heidegger is, I think, actually quite useful. I think Heidegger is saying that an essential condition of our existence is that we exist as attuned beings, and that this is a very ordinary condition that we see all the time because we are always attuned in some way or another. And we are never not attuned. *Befindlichkeit* is the broad condition of attunement, our constitutive ability to be disposed; *Stimmung*, in contrast, is the actual attunement, out real dispositions. Reading Heidegger can be a frustrating experience because it can seem simultaneously profound and banal. But it is worth sticking with precisely because it puts cultural feelings at the basis of our being-in-the-world.

In his lectures that he gave a couple of years after the publication of *Being and Time*, Heidegger clarifies what it means to treat *Befindlichkeit* as our ontological condition. He is puzzling about the way that something that seems as personal as our mood (our irritability, for instance) is an aspect of our social existence with others:

> A human being who – as we say – is in good humour brings a lively atmosphere with them. Do they, in so doing, bring about an emotional experience which is then transmitted to others, in the manner in which infectious germs wander back and forth from one organism to another? We do indeed say that attunement or mood is infectious. Or another human being is with us, someone who through their manner of being makes everything depressing and puts a damper on everything: nobody steps out of their shell. What does this tell us? Attunements are *not side-effects*, but are something which in advance determine our being with one another. It seems as though an attunement is in each case already there, so to speak, like an atmosphere in which we first immerse ourselves in each case and which then attunes us through and through [...] It is clear that attunements are not something merely at hand. They themselves are precisely a fundamental manner and fundamental way of being, indeed of being-there [*Da-sein*], and this always directly includes being with one another.
>
> *(Heidegger 1995 [1929–1930]: 66–67)*

We have all had that experience of being 'brought down' by another's mood, or 'buoyed along' by another's good humour. It is this everyday mundane experience that shows Heidegger that mood is not something that sits inside us, so to say, but is the condition of our being with others in the world.

We can see how important (and socially significant) mood can be in these moments of change (the bringing down, the buoying up) but for Heidegger we can only recognise the constitutive aspect of mood when we can attend to the fact that there is never a lack of mood (which would be as unthinkable as there being a lack of weather) and when we can recognise the moodfulness (and importance) of mundane moods. For Heidegger it is because we mistake mundane moods for a lack of mood that gives them their power: 'precisely *those* attunements [or moods] to which we pay no heed at all, the attunements we least observe, those attunements which attune us in such a way that we feel as though there is no attunement there at all, as though we were not attuned in any way at all – these attunements are the most powerful' (Heidegger 1995 [1929–1930]: 68, emphasis in original). What Heidegger is pointing to is both the invisibility of what we could call 'mood norms' and their constitutive power. In *Being and Time*, Heidegger emphasises what we could think of as 'minor moods':

> Both the undisturbed equanimity and the inhibited ill-humour of our everyday concern, the way we slip over from one to the other, or slip off into bad moods, are by no means nothing ontologically, even if these phenomena are left unheeded as supposedly the most indifferent and fleeting in Dasein. The fact that moods can deteriorate and change over means simply that in every case Dasein always has some mood. The pallid, evenly balanced lack of mood, which is often persistent and which is not to be mistaken for a bad mood, is far from nothing at all. Rather, it is in this that Dasein becomes satiated with itself.
>
> *(Heidegger 2008 [1927]: 173)*

I will, at times, need to come back to these moods that appear least emphatic (it will become a focus for the next chapter). They have already been important in the previous chapter when I was considering the mood that could be found in a science lab, for instance. Indeed, often our workplaces have these low-intensity moods that veer from 'inhibited ill-humour' to 'undisturbed equanimity'. We could also say that a condition for a particular mood becoming part of a dominant structure of feeling is often on condition that it is un-emphatic. For instance, a mood of low-level anxiety, coupled with a fatalistic sense of 'social reality', was often the dominant feeling associated with the Cold War, rather than a state of unfettered panic.

For now, however, it is worth noting two things. The first is that by looking at changes in mood (from pallid irritation to anger, for instance) we recognise quite how fundamental mood is, precisely because there is never a condition of no-mood. The second point (closely aligned with this) is epistemological. If there is never a lack of mood, and if mood is the condition for our being-in-the-world and how that world discloses itself to us, then are we forever determined by mood? If I am in an irritable mood, isn't the world going to be different than if I am in a curious mood? Is what we might call 'objectivity' (or perhaps more correctly, the *feeling* of objectivity), for instance, something like the mood of 'equanimity'? In this we might also recognise a politics to mood, a sense that how the world matters to us is going to have something to do with the way that the world is disclosed to us as a matter of concern. In this, we might also ask ourselves: what moods should we champion as being the most productive or critical? What moods are our 'mood norms' and what does this tell us about the world as it is? But before we can address these questions, we need to look at some of the critical problems that have been identified around Heidegger's ontology of mood.

The problems and potential of Stimmung

In his important commentary on the first 'division' of *Being and Time*, the philosopher Hubert Dreyfus points to a problem that we have already encountered in our discussion of 'structures of feeling': namely the lack of specificity for feelings and mood:

> *Stimmung* seems to name any of the ways Dasein can be affected. Heidegger suggests that moods or attunements manifest the tone of being-there. As Heidegger uses the term, mood can refer to the *sensibility* of an age (such as romantic), the *culture* of a company (such as aggressive), the *temper* of the times (such as revolutionary), as well as the *mood* in a current situation (such as the eager mood in the classroom) and, of course, the mood of an individual. These are all ways of finding that things matter. Thus they are all ontic specifications of affectedness, the ontological existential condition that things always already matter.
>
> *(Dreyfus 1991: 169)*

For Dreyfus this reveals a problem with Heidegger's approach while also allowing Dreyfus to clarify a general condition pertaining to mood, whether on the level of sensibility or the mood of an individual.

The problem with Heidegger's use of *Stimmung* is that he starts out by using the most personal aspects of mood; for instance, grief. At this level, it is hard to really see the way that mood can help us understand how cultural feelings can establish our 'being-in-the-world' *together*. Heidegger's examples of the way that one person's jubilant mood affects everyone in the room as a contagion could actually be read as the domination of the group by one charismatic figure. Dreyfus asks: 'How can you and I be said to be open to the same situation if what each of us is in is threatening to me and exhilarating to you?' (Dreyfus 1991: 169). If mood is what saturates a situation then we are going to need more nuanced ways of describing mood for situations of conflict and struggle, i.e., for those very moods that might be central to the world of competitive capitalism and its structured inequalities. Dreyfus' critique is aimed at two ways of clarifying Heidegger's work. The first suggests that unlike Heidegger we should start our understanding of *Stimmung* not by emphasising the most intense, personal moods (like grief) but by seeing *Stimmung* in terms of the most collective, historical and social moods, the ones that we could also identify as 'cultural feelings' or 'cultural sensibility'.

> If Heidegger had started his discussion of affectedness with cultural sensibility rather than individual mood, he could have avoided this possible Cartesian misunderstanding. Cultural sensibility is a mode of affectedness that is public and is prior to mood in that it governs the range of available moods.
> *(Dreyfus 1991: 169)*

'Affectedness' is Dreyfus' translation of the neologism *Befindlichkeit*, and by linking it to cultural sensibility he is suggesting ways of making Heidegger's work not just more understandable but also useable as a philosophy of historical and social experience (i.e., as something useful to a 'cultural feelings' project).

We could think of examples that could make this clearer. For instance, at various times during the Cold War (when things were hotting up, so to say) there would have been moods of palpable anxiety that would have been circulating, such as at the time of the Cuban Missile Crisis in 1962 when it looked as if the world was about to enter into a third world war. But if that was a recognisable and vivid mood of international political anxiety, we could say that across the decades of the Cold War a low-level (and heavily normalised) anxiety existed around possible nuclear war. Such anxiety would have meant that the world 'disclosed itself' to us in quite particular ways (as precarious, for instance) where certain things mattered less than others. But we could also point to other 'sensibilities' that circulated at the same time: for instance, it was during the same years as the Cold War that house-buying rose exponentially in the United States and United Kingdom. Does this seem to contradict Heidegger? If the mood was one of 'anxiety', where the world disclosed itself to us precariously, then would we be attuned to house-buying? What we need is a more complex way of understanding mood as an orchestration of cultural feelings, that could negotiate 'house-buying' and 'nuclear anxiety' as a generalised *Stimmung* where social subjects were retreating from the public world of feeling and bedding down in a smaller, less anxious world of domestic control (including, importantly, owning property). And in this way we could answer Dreyfus' concern that if one person finds a situation threatening and another finds it exhilarating then we need to be able to name that mood or cultural feeling in a way that can describe the 'collective nature of a conflict'. Indeed, I would suggest that just such a mood often permeates urban space, and simultaneously can make it uncomfortable for one group (vulnerable young people, women, the elderly, etc.) while making it exhilarating for others (large groups of revellers, for instance).

But the second point that Dreyfus wants to take from Heidegger is that even when we are thinking about scenes of intensely felt personal moods (grief, for instance, or depression) we haven't simply left the world of social and historical experience. I might, for instance, be in a mood of apprehension and this would mean that I'm attuned in particular ways (perhaps generally suspicious, fearing the worst and so on). But I'm only apprehensive because apprehensiveness is near at hand: it is an available mood. At times it might be a mood that is almost unavoidable (Chapter 3 will be particularly concerned with this). For Heidegger, mood is always generated in our mingling with others: my grief, my apprehension is in response to what others have done, or what has been done to others. Mood in one sense is always part of our social experience and even those moods that make us antisocial are still social and historical. This requires us to think of moods as being available and never entirely the property of a subject. Heidegger is clear that whatever else a mood is, it is not something that bubbles up from inside of us:

> A mood assails us. It comes neither from 'outside' nor from 'inside', but arises out of Being-in-the-world, as a way of such Being. But with the negative distinction between state of mind [*Befindlichkeit*] and the reflective apprehending of something 'within', we have thus reached a positive insight into their character as disclosure. *The mood has already disclosed, in every case, Being-in-the-world as a whole, and makes it possible first of all to direct oneself towards something.*
> (Heidegger 2008 [1927]: 176, emphasis in original)

Being 'in love' or 'in grief' sometimes seems to emanate from somewhere inside us: and we often use the word 'soul' to name this place. Yet it is often at just these moments that seem to mark our moods out from those around us that we are often most aware of our cultural connectivity. When I'm in love, I hear the clichéd words of those love songs as describing my condition; when I'm mourning I am alert to the general pain that grief causes in others. It is when my mood is of 'undisturbed equanimity and the inhibited ill-humour' that I fail to recognise the collectivity of grief and love.

For Heidegger, *Stimmung* is always historical and social because it is available. We could say the same about cultural feelings more generally: when we are caught up in a world of feeling we are caught up in a determinate cultural world precisely because that feeling or mood is available for us to feel. Some moods and feelings might be generally available across a number of cultures and over a long period, while others may mark a particular epoch and milieu. And it isn't hard, I don't think, to imagine cultures dominated by certain moods that are quite distinct from those that are circulating around us at the moment.

One of the best descriptions of Heidegger's understanding of mood is offered by Charles Guignon:

> Our moods modulate and shape the totality of our Being-in-the-world, and they determine how things can count for us in our everyday concerns. Heidegger's point is that only when we have been 'tuned in' to the world in a certain way can we be 'turned on' to the things and people around us. Moods enable us to focus our attention and orient ourselves. Without this orientation, a human would be a bundle of raw capacities so diffuse and undifferentiated that it could never discover anything. What we *do* encounter in our

> attuned situatedness is not just worldhood, but rather a highly determinate cultural world.
>
> *(Guignon 1984: 237, emphasis in original)*

This to me gets the sense of importance that Heidegger accredits moods with. Moods are what prepare us as social beings: they govern how the world discloses itself to us as something that we are concerned with. I think Guignon's hippy phrasing gets it right: this is about being 'tuned in' and 'turned on', and I think we can actually use this as an example of a particular mood that circulated among many involved in the counterculture in the 1960s. To be tuned in and turned on was to be concerned with things and people (with the peace movement, the anti-Vietnam War protests, the drug culture and so on). It was also to be alert to some things more than others: to be alert to music more than the long progressions of a career; to some forms of political expression and not to others (to the sit-in and the demo, rather than the long struggles of the labour union movement). As Jonathan Flatley suggests, 'mood is an important concept [...] as a kind of state of readiness for some affects and not others' (2008: 17). It is, potentially at least, determinedly political.

We could say, then, that mood is the form that attention takes. It is the way the world presents itself to us as 'matters of concern' and matters to ignore. It is always involved in the distribution of the sensible, in the parcelling out of attention and concern. It directs attention and it inevitably (but more indirectly) distributes resources. Mood, as an analytic invitation, has the distinct advantage in that it allows us to attend to the world of affect, to the world of sensation and the senses, and to the world of perception, simultaneously. It is a way of showing how cultural feelings are orchestrated in such a way that they seem to be intimate and internal yet connect us to our available social feelings. These available moods and feelings are always social and political: they can include feelings and moods of xenophobia and cosmopolitanism, of social optimism and political despair. What sorts of moods do we want to help develop? What sorts of moods would be most productive to fostering a deeply ordinary democratic ethos?

Affect theory

In the past 20 or so years, an orientation towards affect has characterised some of the most interesting work within the humanities and social science. For the editors of *The Affect Theory Reader* (Gregg and Seigworth 2010), the crucial year that marked the emergence of a sustained and consolidated interest in affect was 1995, the year that Eve Kosofsky Sedgwick and Adam Frank published their essay on the psychologist Silvan Tomkins (in Sedgwick 2003: 93–121) and Brian Massumi published his essay on 'The Autonomy of Affect' (Massumi 1995). It becomes clear, however, even with just a cursory glance at these two essays, that 'affect' as a concept is hardly something that appears 'out of nowhere' in the mid-1990s. First of all, the affect theory that emerges at this time draws on a long lineage of writers going back to (at least) the seventeenth-century philosopher (and lens grinder) Baruch

Spinoza. Second, the mid-1990s affect theory can be seen as continuing a concern that had been central to feminism, namely the continued critique of disembodied rationalism by insisting on life as enfleshed and entangled in material force-fields that produce various social differences, which are intimately lived. Third, that while 'affect theory' was being produced by humanities scholars (in the main), it was keen to enlarge the range of resources for talking about affect and this meant drawing on the biological sciences, neurology and psychology (all of which had been undertaking longstanding research projects around affect), and constructing diverse historical archives relevant to an understanding of affect as part of a vital current of life.

For the psychologist Silvan Tomkins (and for most others working in this field), the 'primary affects' designate a set of forceful qualities that exist in a range of intensities. These consist of interest-excitement (the former term designating the lower intensity affect, the latter the higher), enjoyment-joy, surprise-startle, distress-anguish, fear-terror, shame-humiliation, contempt-disgust, and anger-rage (Demos 1995: 218–219). Much of the work around affect for the humanities and social sciences has been directed at the way that affect circulates to exacerbate and undermine the unequal orchestration of social difference or the way it is mobilised at particular moments in the name of 'security' or other governmental concerns.[20]

Since 1995 the literature around affect theory has grown enormously and 'affect theory' now exists as an invitation to consider affect as a base materialism for understanding the economy, capitalism, debt, nationalism and so on.[21] Affect theory is also a major approach within disciplines across the humanities and social sciences, from geography to film studies.[22] This is not the place to try and offer an adequate account of such work nor is it my intention to add to the debates that would argue about the much-debated 'autonomy' (its autonomy from social and cultural determinisms) of affect, or about the value of neurologically oriented accounts of affect.[23] In many ways this book is only an oblique contribution to affect theory. Its primary loyalty is to cultural feelings, and this means that I'm more interested in the sustained and maintained feelings and moods that characterise a historical situation or a social milieu than I am in the more flighty and less predictable world of affect, when 'affect' is characterised as a 'vivacious' phenomena, for instance (Massumi 2015: viii). Of course there is a huge amount of crossover between feeling, mood and affect and I have learnt a great deal from 'affect' work. And there are numerous different approaches to affect and some of these seem eminently suitable to the sort of approach I am trying to foster here (which is why I will go on later in this section to concentrate on the work of Lauren Berlant).

In one sense I share many of the interests that are accorded to those involved in charting affect. For instance, I would agree with Margaret Wetherell's assessment of affect as an optic for addressing social processes:

> How do social formations grab people? How do roller coasters of contempt, patriotism, hate and euphoria power public scenes? The advantage of affect is that it brings the dramatic and the everyday back into social analysis. It draws

attention to moments of resentment, kindness, grumpiness, ennui and feeling good, to the extremities of distress that can result from ill use, and to the intensities of ecstasy. Interest in affect opens up new thinking about nebulous and subtle emotions like *schadenfreude*, or mixed and ambivalent phenomena such as reluctant optimism, intense indifference, or enjoyable melancholy.

(Wetherell 2012: 2)

I particularly like this insistence on ambivalent and ambiguous feelings that we can only seem to name by invoking oxymoronic phrases that seem to articulate contradictory conditions like 'intense indifference'. This attention to affect and emotion – that is concerned with the way that social processes are lived – seems to be precisely in line with an approach to cultural feeling that I want to promote.

A good deal of affect theory is aimed at building an understanding of the human subject as an organism embedded in networks that are both historical and neurological:

In affective practice, bits of the body (e.g. facial muscles, thalamic-amygdala pathways in the brain, heart rate, regions of the prefrontal cortex, sweat glands, etc.) get patterned together with feelings and thoughts, interaction patterns and relationships, narratives and interpretative repertoires, social relations, personal histories, and ways of life. These components and modalities, each with their own logic and trajectories, are assembled together in interacting and recursive, or back and forth, practical methods. Pattern layers on pattern, forming and re-forming. Somatic, neural, phenomenological, discursive, relational, cultural, economic, developmental, and historical patterns interrupt, cancel, contradict, modulate, build and interweave with each other.

(Wetherell 2012: 13–14)

While such neuro-cultural overlays are deeply fascinating, they are not a primary concern for *Cultural Feelings* mainly because the intention of this book is to trace the realm of feelings as they circulate within culture, rather than try to explain the specific experience of being a human creature entangled in complex social and cultural networks that are simultaneously biological, social and political.

Attention to affect can describe a register of feeling that is particularly concerned with the dynamic energy that Williams sees as a key element of 'structures of feeling'. Thus, if a general concern with feeling tends to be attentive to moods and atmospheres of optimism or hostility, say, then affect theory is useful for staying alert to the peculiar rising and diminution of energy that accompany such feelings. As Jonathan Flatley suggests:

Affects are always amplifying, dampening, or otherwise modifying some other affect, or drive, or perception, or thought process, or act or behaviour, resulting in a well-nigh infinite number of combinations between different affective microsystems and their feedback mechanisms in interaction with their environments.

(Flatley 2008: 16)

Such sensitivity to the liveness and lived-ness of affective life should allow for nuanced historical accounts of actual instances of culture within patterns of feeling. And this sensitivity would be as much alive to the blockages of energy, to the flattening of affect, as to the more spectacular irruptions of affective life. And this is where the work of Lauren Berlant is, I think, exemplary.

Berlant and the historical sensorium

There are many reasons for singling out Lauren Berlant's writing for contributing to the task of attending to cultural feelings. During the past 30 years she has been developing a writing practice that is uncommonly attentive to the broad 'feel' of cultural texts: their tones, moods and attachments. And as result of her writerly 'ear' for cultural feelings she has fashioned an extraordinarily rich descriptive vocabulary for attending to them. Reading her work, then, is never just a case of being confronted with a theory or a set of interpretations: it is, primarily, a sensitising encounter with a world of passions, affects and atmospheres. This is, I think, its essential pedagogy. The second reason for picking out Berlant among the myriad of 'affect' writers is that she is peculiarly attentive to minor moods, deflated feelings and blocked responses. She doesn't feel drawn to the spectacular vivacity of affect but opts instead for its drone and drag. The third reason (and of course she is far from alone in this) is that she has purposefully pursued the invitation that Raymond Williams' work set out with its concern for 'patterns of feeling', and has pushed this into new arenas of analysis and description.[24] Last, but by no means least, Berlant names as her object of analysis (or objective for analysis) the 'historical sensorium'. To my mind this seems an endlessly suggestive phrase for naming the condition of cultural feelings as it establishes a conative-affective register of interests, sensations, pulsions, energies, senses and so on, that take definite shape, colour, tone and texture in our social and cultural life.

In her brilliant *Cruel Optimism* she describes her project in the following terms:

> My aim is to construct a mode of analysis of the historical present that moves us away from the dialectic of structure (what is systemic in the reproduction of the world), agency (what people do in everyday life) and the traumatic event of their disruption, and toward explaining crisis-shaped subjectivity amid the ongoingness of adjudication, adaptation, and improvisation.
>
> *(Berlant 2011: 54)*

We can immediately hear a shift in gears, from a set of fixed positions (agency versus structure and back again) to something more fluid, more dynamic, where adjectives and nouns become activated as verb forms, and start becoming processual, start describing the business of negotiating and adapting.

Her critical practice doesn't pursue a 'critical position' but instead seeks out what she calls 'crisis ordinariness'. What this means is that she finds 'criticality' not in theory, but out there in the living world among social life often when it is lived out within traumatic circumstances. 'Critical ordinariness' is Berlant's way of addressing the 'traumas of the social that are lived through collectively and that transform the sensorium to a heightened perceptiveness about the unfolding of the historical, and historic, moment' (Berlant 2008b: 5, note 8). In *Cruel Optimism* (and we should note how this phrase also refers to a situation of contradiction) she is particularly concerned with the 'cruel' attachments people make to optimistic invocations of the 'good life', invocations that are structurally fated to fail them: 'Why do people stay attached to conventional good-life fantasies – say of enduring reciprocity in couples, families, political systems, institutions, markets, and at work – when the evidence of their instability, fragility, and dear cost abounds?' (Berlant 2011: 2).

Here her goal is to apprehend a historical sensorium that could be seen to sustain this situation within recent decades, and to this end she scours literature (from populist to avant-garde), television, film and video for 'the historical sensorium that has developed belatedly since the fantasmatic part of the optimism about structural transformation realised less and less traction in the world' (Berlant 2011: 3). It is a historical project that is aimed at the contemporary world (the US since 1990) and in this spirit she names the 'affect' that she finds the 'Post-Fordist affect'. By this she names the period when manufacturing gave way to service industries across many so-called 'First World countries' towards the end of the twentieth century and the way that this coincided with what she describes as 'frayed fantasies': 'the fantasies that are fraying include, particularly, upward mobility, job security, political and social equality, and lively, durable intimacy' (Berlant 2011: 3). In Britain, this is also seen as part of the longer history of the way that the post-war settlement and consensus around welfare and social fairness gets reneged upon in the final third of the twentieth century. For Berlant: 'Post-Fordist affect here designates the sensorium making its way through a post-industrial present, the shrinkage of the welfare state, the expansion of grey (semi-formal) economies, and the escalation of transnational migration, with its attendant rise in racism and political cynicism' (Berlant 2011: 19).

Berlant's project is aimed at charting the historical sensorium (which is really another name for 'patterns of feeling' as they are materialised in sensorial forms) across recent decades. In this she follows the ambition of Raymond Williams' approach to patterns of feeling rather than the more theoretical work of someone like Massumi. Indeed, this is something she is clear to stress:

> In the contemporary world of affect-talk, affective tendencies often refer to an assessment of intensities, and that linkage leads back to an image of the subject's ordinary life as a melodramatic stage, a scene in which feeling states find their true expression in expansive bodily performance. In contrast, Williams' model places the historical present in the affective presence of an atmosphere that is sensed rather than known and enacted, a space of affective residue that

> constitutes what is shared among strangers. It indicates a collective experience that mostly goes without saying of something about belonging to a world.
>
> (Berlant 2015: 194)

For her (as for Williams) affect and feelings are 'ordinary', deeply ordinary. And like Williams, it is a way of addressing the close at hand but under-articulated aspects of social life. For Berlant, this aspect is another name for intuition: 'In the model I'm putting forth intuition is the subject's habituated affective activity, the sensorium trained to apperceive the historical in the present by a whole range of encounters and knowledges, not just memory' (Berlant 2008b: 5, note 7).

The historical sensorium operates at the level of conative-affective register – the register of all that can't be incorporated in conscious cognition and reflexive reason. Such a register requires attention not just to a range of affects and feelings (such as 'cruel optimism') but also to a host of different ways of perceiving the world (modes of attention), different states of being (different ways of finding yourself, in a more Heideggerain language). So mood matters for the historical sensorium: it matters not simply as a shock of affect emanating from a political and historical event (the sub-prime banking crisis, for example) but also as the waves of responses that could include a myriad of forms of attention.

> It is true that under the pressure of an intensified, elongated present moment where affective, experiential and empirical knowledge norms seem in disarray there develop states of sociopathic disavowal and ordinary compartmentalization. See the sub-prime banking or 'climate change' crisis, for example. See systemic racialized, gendered, sexual and regional class inequalities whose evidence in ordinary subjectivity shifts between foreground and background. Being overwhelmed by knowledge and life produces all kinds of neutralizing affect management – coasting, skimming, browsing, distraction, apathy, coolness, counter-absorption, assessments of scale, picking one's fights, and so on.
>
> Indeed, most social life happens in such modes of lower case drama, as we follow out pulsations of habituated patterning that make possible getting through the day (the relationships, the job, the life) while the brain chatters on, assessing things in focused and unfocused ways.
>
> (Berlant 2008b: 5–6)

In her careful address to the minor keys of attention, to the 'lower case drama' of everyday life, Berlant offers a productive approach to the world of cultural feelings that are often characterised by the impossibility of direct response. How, for instance, would you *directly* respond to the low, long drone of anxiety of nuclear war? Would this stop you planning your weekly shopping or developing plans for your retirement? And yet to assume that it doesn't produce responses would also be a nonsense. And it is in being able to work across 'lower case drama' as a complexity of responses that can address different crises (and the frayed promises that they trample on) that Berlant offers cultural feelings an exemplary practice.

A large part of this exemplary practice is a writing style that as Gregory Seigworth comments:

> eschews any linear or multi-linear discourse of vectors, lines, and articulations and chooses to speak instead of saturations, magnetizations, tonalities, and resonances, of affective attunements and attachments (as well as austerities, demagnetizations, dissonances, stuckness, unattachments): because this is, in fact, the place – naïve melodies and all – where we dwell (flourishing and not).
>
> *(Seigworth 2012: 351)*

The place of the everyday is laminated in overlapping layers that rarely result in confrontation or dramatic dénouement. Part of the ongoingness of everyday life is the way that conflicts and contradictions (between fear of nuclear war, say, and having to get the kids' food on the table) are endlessly negotiated as part of the wear-and-tear of daily life, rather than as dramatic confrontation.

Like Williams, Berlant is primarily a literary and drama historian and critic, who, again like Williams, constantly steps out of such disciplinary enclaves to write about the life that sometimes informs literature and drama. Indeed, her approach to the literary taxonomy called 'genre' purposefully challenges any finite boundary we would want to draw between 'real life' and 'fiction':

> A genre is an aesthetic structure of affective expectation, an institution or formation that absorbs all kinds of small variations or modifications while promising that the person transacting with it will experience the pleasure of encountering what they expected, with details, and general about the subject. It is a form of aesthetic expectation with porous boundaries allowing complex audience identifications: it locates real life in the affective capacity to bracket many kinds of structural and historical antagonism on behalf of finding a way to connect with the feeling of belonging to a larger world, however aesthetically mediated.
>
> *(Berlant 2008a: 4)*

It is clear for Berlant that we live genres just as much as we read them or watch them on the screen. These bundles of promises, that are reneged or not, ruined or not, burnished or not, bridge the way that cultural feelings find their place in how you find yourself. They are the subject that this book addresses.

Notes

1 As a way of de-masculinising the phrase, I will mainly use the phrase 'patterns of feeling' in this book, but I will do this once I have rehearsed the genesis of the phrase 'structures of feeling' and its specific use by Williams.
2 These clarifying tools are most succinctly introduced in his essay 'Base and Superstructure in Marxist Cultural Theory' (Williams 1980: 31–49), and elaborated on in *Marxism and Literature* (1977).

3 While the book is co-authored, it is made up of two distinct parts. The first part 'Film and the Dramatic Tradition' was written by Williams, and the second, 'Film and its Dramatic Techniques', by Orrom. In an earlier book, *Drama from Ibsen to Eliot*, Williams uses the phrase 'community of sensibility' in what feels like a rehearsal for the more expansive phrase 'structures of feeling' (Williams 1964 [1952]: 31).
4 At roughly the same time, Henri Lefebvre (in 1956–1957) wrote a similar definition of everyday life: 'Everyday life, in a sense residual, defined by "what is left over" after all distinct, superior, specialised, structured activities have been singled out by analysis, must be defined as a totality' (1991: 97). A similar sense of everyday life as something that often gets remaindered by the social investigation designed to apprehend it is also evident in Michel de Certeau's *The Practice of Everyday Life* (1984). Thus we could suggest that, on one level at least, there is a family resemblance between the terms 'structures of feeling' and 'everyday life'.
5 This doesn't mean that artworks are simply reflections of lively feeling; they are also, for Williams, the conveyors of feelings: 'the new work will not only make explicit the changes in feeling, but will in itself promote and affect them' (Williams and Orrom 1954: 24).
6 Though he uses the phrase 'a whole way of life' throughout his early work, it is given pride of place in his essay 'Culture is Ordinary' (first published in 1958), which can be read as a statement of purpose to combine an anthropological understanding of culture with careful attention to representational forms (Williams 1989b: 3–14).
7 I discuss Rancière's phrase in Highmore (2011: 44–53).
8 Autobiographical material is scattered throughout Williams' oeuvre but can be found in its most sustained form in Williams (1981). For biographical studies see Inglis (1995) and Smith (2008).
9 For an excellent account of the way that the term 'experience' is used at this time see Middleton (2016), who also uses this quotation from Leavis.
10 Other evidence of F.R. Leavis' interest in anthropology and sociology could include his constant reference to (and promotion of) Robert and Helen Lynd's *Middletown: A Study in Modern American Culture* (1929).
11 In a footnote (Bateson 1958 [1936]: 112), Bateson acknowledges his indebtedness to Ruth Benedict. In 1932, when Bateson was in New Guinea (with Margaret Mead and Reo Fortune), he read *Patterns of Culture* as a draft manuscript: see Lipset (1982: 137).
12 'Cultural form' is the critical unit of analysis in Williams' 1975 book on television (1990 [1975]).
13 For a discussion of the differing availability of structures of feeling in the past and present see Williams (1981: 162–164).
14 Social media and instant messaging will likely alter our historical access to ephemeral communication. As yet it is too early to say what kind of historical process it could make accessible, and what sort of digital methods will be needed to draw out changes in the structures of feeling that such communication can reveal.
15 Perhaps the most obvious place that Williams articulates autobiographical structures of feeling is in his novels (e.g., Williams 2006 [1960]). For a relevant account see Di Michele (1993).
16 Universities, for instance, could be extraordinary sites for learning democratic feelings (for all of those concerned, not just students). The actuality is somewhat different.
17 The 'may' in the first line refers to the may tree, which is a common name for the hawthorn tree that flowers in the month of May.
18 The historian Raphael Samuel had a strong sense of the way 'structures of feeling' in the 1980s, at the time of Margaret Thatcher, were sustained as much by kitchen design as by an ideology of 'Victorian values' – or to be more precise that 'Victorian values' were *enfleshed*, so to say, in kitchen designs and not by parroting Thatcherite beliefs (Samuel 1994).
19 As one example from hundreds of possibilities, see Auslander (1996).

20 For instance, Ahmed (2004, 2010) looks at the way affect circulates as an aspect of racism and nationalism and how it is used as an assertively normalising stricture within the governance of 'well-being'. Other classic investigations would include Massumi (2005) on the colour coding of threat as an attempt to deploy fear as part of national security, as well as the various studies by Protevi (2009) and Probyn (2005).
21 For work on economics and affect see Deville and Seigworth (2015), which is the introduction to a special issue of *Cultural Studies* on the topic of debt, credit and everyday life. See Konings (2015) for an affect-oriented account of capitalism. For an anthology of affect writing that demonstrates the varied ambition of such an approach see Gregg and Seigworth (2010).
22 For examples from geography see Anderson (2009, 2014), Edensor (2012), and Thien (2005) (for a sceptical review). For examples from film studies see Brinkema (2014) and Singh (2014). The literature within affect-centred disciplines such as psychology, psychiatry and psychoanalysis is too numerous to mention, but as a general overview of affect within Freudian psychoanalysis, Green (1999 [1973]) is indispensable.
23 A general understanding of these arguments could be quite quickly arrived at by reading Massumi (1995) and Sedgwick and Frank's 1995 essay on affect (in Sedgwick 2003: 93–121), followed by the critical intervention of Hemmings (2005). This could then be followed by reading Damasio (2000, 2004), Leys (2011a, 2011b), Altieri (2012) and Connolly (2011).
24 Other writers who have also pushed a 'structures of feeling' agenda into new realms would include Ngai (2005, 2010, 2012), Woodward (2009), Stewart (2007) and Flatley (2008).

3

MORALE WORK

(Experience feeling itself)

> And here again the dominant note of the time is heard – problems revealing themselves and experience feeling itself.
> *(Sansom 2010 [1947]: 29–30)*

There are no moods, patterns of feelings, or atmospheres *in general*. In other words, there are no moods and feelings outside history. We may use the word 'disquiet' to describe all sorts of uncanny feelings and forms of disquietude over time, yet there is only ever this or that disquietude that emanates from and is felt in these circumstances. Feelings and moods are tied to practices and habits, to institutional regimes, to styles and genres, and these habits and conveyors of feeling change over time. Some are more stable and longer-lasting than others, grounded by well-established institutions and practices; some are fleeting, tied to specific circumstances. There are no moods and feelings that are independent of their mediations. And because patterns of feeling are conveyed and sustained by mediations in their socially material forms (from longstanding social conventions to fads and fashions), they have different durations, different geographies and different intensities.

As a way of developing these claims, this chapter – and all the chapters that follow – pursues a concern with specific patterns of feelings and moods that are in all cases historical. But 'historical' is as much a question as a solution, and it is a question that is always partly a question about the present. We live history and we live 'our' history, but what history is this? Which histories impinge on the present, which historical feelings resonate and circulate now? In what follows, I look at patterns of feelings that seem to be very specific to a distinct period of time (in this instance, the Second World War). Other chapters concern patterns of feeling that are linked to an ongoing condition ranging over a relatively long period of time, for example, the time of mass-migration, from post-war Commonwealth migration and on into a future of unknown (but globally increasing) migrations. Sometimes, however, it isn't time but space that characterises a pattern of feeling. Sometimes moods and atmospheres seem to congregate in and cling to a particular kind of landscape, a specific and changing geography. Other less-sustained moods have an iridescence to them that belongs both to a time and a place that seems to be short and local but can also resonate beyond their initial sites. If the history of patterns of feelings is also a history of changing levels of energy and enthusiasm, it might be that an ecology of moods would recognise longer periods of relative atmospheric stability with irruptions of energy that have long 'tails' in the landscape of mood.

While certain patterns of feeling seem to belong to a particular time that is in some sense 'finished' (again, the example could be the Second World War) it is clear that feelings don't always remain in their 'proper' place. Nostalgia, as a particular mood-form, demonstrates the portability of certain feelings and atmospheres. Nostalgia, as a form of sentimental memory that carries over an excess of feeling into the present and the future, is a constant aspect to the patterns of feeling that have characterised twentieth- and twenty-first century Britain. 'Nostalgia', it is often claimed, is about remembering the past as *it never really was*. Because nostalgia is never simply 'remembering' but also registers a melancholy desire for an out-of-reach and an out-of-time past, it is a particularly powerful feeling, and one that has increasingly infiltrated our sense of our contemporaneity, our sense of the present. Within our various presents are a myriad of unfinished pasts that live among us as a material culture of retro designs, as history lessons (learnt at school, or learnt from TV dramas, or from a host of other sites), as political narratives (idealising 'Victorian values' or warnings about the miseries of another 'Winter of Discontent') to a sustained nostalgia industry that can cater for your particular nostalgic world (radio stations dedicated to 1980s pop, TV channels showing old movies from the 1940s or sitcoms from the 1970s). The past, it seems, is both unruly and capable of being managed to affect certain kinds of feelings today.

My focus in this chapter is the Second World War, and particularly with what was called 'Home Front Morale'. To start here is to enter a particularly congealed historical scene. The 'spirit of the Blitz' is a frequently evoked call to national identity, to ideas of national character ('stiff upper lip', 'keeping your chin up'), and to the values of equanimity in the face of crisis. It is a moment so threaded through with ideas of patriotic fervour and peculiar forms of melancholic longing that it is impossible to treat as if simply belonging in the past. Yet the intense concentration on Home Front Morale (as an identifiable concern of governments, of civic institutions and of the general public) was primarily confined to the war years (although there was general concern with 'fatigue' from rationing and austerity in the post-war years). In this chapter I am centrally concerned with what could be called 'mood management' and the orchestration of feeling during a time of incessant physical threat and intense national anxiety.

Snapping out of it

Towards the end of Humphrey Jennings' 1943 film *Fires Were Started* (Figure 3.1), we see an auxiliary fire crew return to their depot after a night spent trying to put out a raging fire. The fire has engulfed a warehouse in a London dock. The blaze was started by the Luftwaffe's incendiary bombing campaign and the conflagration was in danger of spreading to a munitions ship moored nearby. The fire-fighting crew managed, over the course of the night (and of the film), to stop the fire spreading, but in the process one of them, Jacko, is killed. We see them the next morning, tired and dirty, lying on their cots. One of them reads some lines of poetry: it is clear that they are in a defeated, disconsolate mood. Jacko's loss is a palpable presence in the room and you can feel a sense of morbidity and melancholic reminiscence descending on the crew like a pall. The team leader is having none of this. He shouts angrily at them, 'snap out of it chaps'. And they do.

In 1943, the 'snapping out' of moods, particularly those associated with morbid feelings of melancholic despondency or debilitating anxiety, was a national concern. It had been since before the war began. National mood had a name in Britain in the early 1940s; it was called morale, or more elaborately Home Front Morale. In late 1940, the year before the United States of America entered the war, George Orwell was asked by the left-wing US magazine *Partisan Review* to comment on the 'general mood, if there is such a thing, among writers, artists and

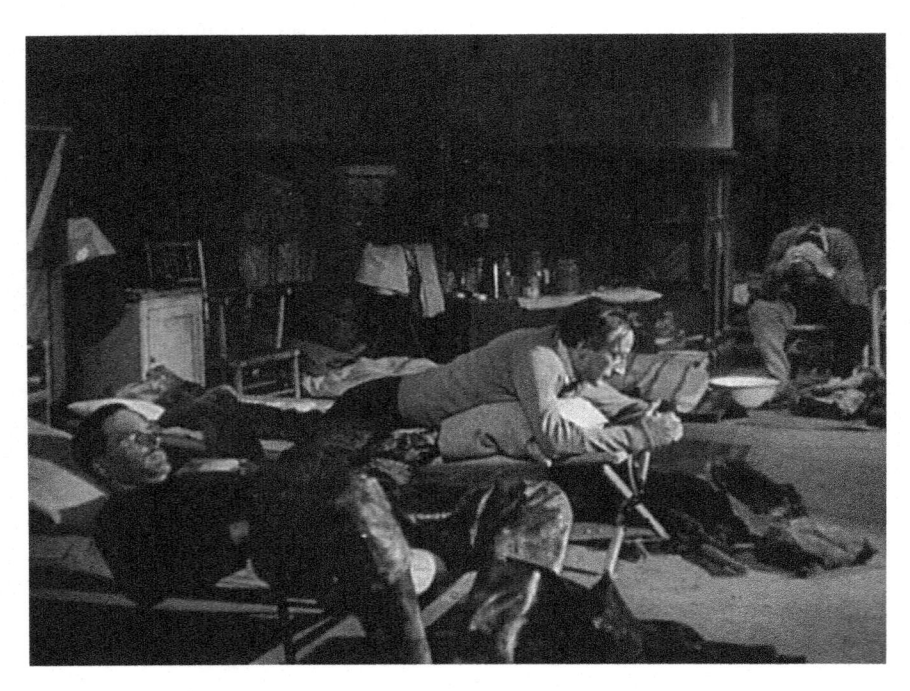

FIGURE 3.1 Humphrey Jennings, *Fires Were Started*, 1943.

intellectuals' in Britain (Orwell 1970a: 67). That was the year when Britain, and particularly London, received consistent and systematic aerial bombing. In reply to *Partisan Review*, Orwell published his first 'London Letter' (the first one is dated 3 January 1941 and they continued until 1946) and rather than limiting his appraisal of mood to sundry intellectuals, he gave a general sense of the moods affecting different constituents, classes and regions (albeit in a fairly piecemeal fashion – it was a letter after all). Looking at Orwell's language, we get a sense of what morale and mood meant at the time; he writes of 'readiness' and 'determination', but also of 'fermenting grievances'. Positive moods for pursuing war aims seem to be attentive and forward-looking (moods of alertness and perseverance), while less positive moods for a civilian population look backwards ('fermenting grievances' are moods remembering past hurt).

Prior to the outbreak of war between Britain and Germany in 1939, the British government put considerable energy into estimating the effects of a war that was inevitably going to be pursued via systematic aerial bombardment of civilian populations. In anticipating the results of bombardment on Britain (but this invariably meant focusing on London as the obvious strategic target) various military experts, medical practitioners and politicians imagined an outcome that included social breakdown in the form of rioting and civilian surrender, mass psychological collapse, the production of an ungovernable homeless population, huge increases in communicable diseases due to lack of sanitation and so on. Winston Churchill, speaking in the House of Commons in November 1934, claimed:

> We must expect that, under the pressure of continuous air attack upon London, at least 3,000,000 or 4,000,000 people would be driven out into the open country around the metropolis. This vast mass of human beings, numerically far larger than any armies which have been fed and moved in war, without shelter and without food, without sanitation and without special provisions for the maintenance of order, would confront the Government of the day with an administrative problem of the first magnitude.
>
> *(Churchill, cited in Titmuss 1971 [1950]: 9)*

If the breakdown of social order could be imagined as a result of a newly destitute population, the effect of bombing on the collective psyche would be similarly catastrophic:

> In the middle of 1938 a number of eminent psychiatrists from London teaching hospitals and clinics formed a committee to consider the mental health services in time of war. A report was drawn up and presented to the Ministry of Health [...] It was suggested that psychiatric casualties might exceed physical casualties by three to one. This would have meant, on the basis of the Government's estimates of killed and wounded, some 3–4 million cases

of acute panic, hysteria and other neurotic conditions during the first six months of air attack.

(Titmuss 1971 [1950]: 19–20)

As a result of such reports specialist hospitals (called 'Neurosis Centres') were built on the peripheries of major UK cities (Jones et al. 2004).

In the months leading up to war and during the war, 'nerves' and 'morale' were seen as the central elements of the way that the fight was being conducted and named the effects and affects it was having on the domestic front. Would a civilian population, untrained and inexperienced, be able to hold its 'nerve' in the face of bombardment? Would mass neurosis be the outcome? How could a population withstand such concerted aggression aimed at a domestic situation, and how could they develop a resilience towards it? The discourse of nerves was everywhere. In the language of the psychological experts, the war was treated as a 'war of nerves' (MacCurdy 1943: 9). In the language of advertising, ingredients in drinks could be 'nerve restoratives' (phosphorous, vitamin B and calcium), producing the 'sound sleep' that is the necessary 'wartime tonic'. Crispbreads could provide 'lightweight meals for ironclad nerves', while cocoa drinks could be 'rich in nerve-strengthening substances'.[1]

Advice about how to deal with nerves and how to respond to constant bombardment was an urgent concern, and answers came in thick and fast. In the second month of the Blitz, *Picture Post*, the popular photo-magazine, sought to answer the question 'Should We Feel Fear?' by asking an anonymous psychologist her or his opinion. The question was framed explicitly as a patriotic question: the 'should' was a judgement that was tied to the question of morale. The answer, it seemed, required a civilian population to negotiate their fear in subtle and careful ways. Those who felt no fear at all were the ones most likely to 'snap' (snapping 'into it' rather than 'out of it', so to say) and examples were given of burly policeman suddenly fainting from months of nervous trauma. What was required was to acknowledge your fear: 'it is the refusal to acknowledge the existence of fear that sooner or later leads to some explosion of feeling' (Anonymous 1940: 37). 'Explosions of feeling' were not conducive to the war effort, not just because they might render the subject incapacitated, but because feelings are contagious. Acknowledgement of fear, then, required some form of containment against that contagion (and exacerbation) of fear:

> At the same time, while we should recognise our fears, we should keep our fears to ourselves during the actual moment of danger to avoid disturbing others. For this reason soldiers will tell you that during their first bombardment they noticed that their hands were trembling. This is what happens when morale is good. The fear is acknowledged to oneself, but automatically kept in check. So, during air raids, be frank with yourself. But don't show fear to others.

(Anonymous 1940: 37)

But this negotiation of fear required getting the tone of your response right: too much fear and a morbid mood could spill over into your general milieu, but not enough fear could be equally damaging. As one respondent enquired, what do you do about those more pugnacious responses to bombardment? Writing about an uncle of some friends, a correspondent asks what to do about someone:

> who does not feel fear at all, but thinks that air raids are a game between himself and the Germans, and sits in an armchair shouting 'Rotten shot!' when they fall close. When his own windows and ceiling were blown in, he rushed into the garden, shouting at the sky, 'Well played, sir!' Now he is living with them [the correspondent's friends] and he makes them all more nervous than air raids, particularly the baby.
>
> *(Picture Post, 19 October 1940: 5)*

Morale, as a negotiated response to aggression and its anticipation, was both a tonal question (how to gauge the right mood) and a practical question (what do you do with your fear?). And because this was a war between nations, such questions were immediately of political concern and required government leadership. But it also required knowledge: what affected morale? How could it be strengthened and how could it be known? If morale is about nerves and resilience, how could a government know if it was affecting morale in an adverse or in a productive manner? One of the first things that 'morale workers' did was to recognise that morale wasn't primarily a subjective, internal state, but was about a collective and practical response to threat. As a director of the Home Intelligence Division (HID) put it, morale must be 'ultimately measured not by what a person thinks or says, but by what he [*sic*] does and how he does it' (Taylor, cited in McLaine 1979: 9). But if this solved the question of how morale could be measured (if there was a general willingness among the population to participate in social activities that would further national war aims then this would register strong civilian morale), it didn't necessarily help to explain some of the fluctuations in civilian morale, nor how information and propaganda could mobilise morale, nor how morbid moods and melancholic feelings could be 'snapped out of' at will.

A war barometer

Humphrey Jennings' film work is important to this chapter both as an example of morale work and because it shares an ethos with other sorts of morale work that were taking place elsewhere during the war. The avant-garde sociological movement Mass-Observation, which was founded by Jennings and others in early 1937, became a central component of morale investigation, and it devised mechanisms and tools for tracking morale in relation to such ambient phenomena as rumour, superstition and mood. When Mass-Observation was first established, it saw its task as producing 'meteorological stations from whose reports a weather-map of popular feeling can be compiled' (Mass-Observation 1937: 30). At the beginning of the war it declared that 'one of the vital needs now in this war is that the Government should be fully aware of all the trends in civilian morale. They need an accurate machine for measuring such trends; a war barometer' (Mass-Observation 2009 [1940]: v). Weather (as we have already seen) has been an insistent metaphor for describing mood, atmosphere and cultural feelings, both in the work of Mass-Observation and more generally: it gives a material sense to the metaphor, insisting that there is always something there (sometimes imperceptibly – there is never an absence of weather) and something that infuses an entire situation.

Mass-Observation's work was the inspiration behind the establishment of the Home Intelligence Division (HID) mentioned above, which was part of the Ministry of Information (MOI).[2] If the MOI were responsible for propaganda, the HID (often using the services of Mass-Observation) provided a feedback loop reporting on how well a particular propaganda campaign was going. It also took on the task of being the 'war barometer' that Mass-Observation had asked for by constantly sampling public opinion from across the UK (opinions either directly solicited or purposefully 'overheard' at bus queues and shop counters by a network of 'listeners'). The HID was the brainchild of Mary Adams and was set up as a way for government to monitor public opinion and public mood. Adams had experience working in educational broadcasting at the BBC and was also sympathetic to the work of Mass-Observation. For Adams the role of the HID was 'to provide an assessment of home morale. For this purpose, it is necessary to study immediate reactions to specific events as well as to create a barometer for the purpose of testing public opinion on questions likely to be continuously important, e.g. pacifism' (Addison and Crang 2010: xii). You can, of course, hear the meteorological language of mood in her vocabulary. To this end, Regional Information Officers and the volunteers that they recruited were instructed to get a sense of the mood of their region by eavesdropping when they were out and about, and by asking regular associates what they thought and felt. Adams often employed Mass-Observation for more systematic tasks; for instance, in the study of pacifism or in gathering information about the effectiveness of a particular policy or propaganda campaign.

Between 18 May 1940 and 27 September 1940, the Home Intelligence Division reported daily to the ministry and to government (after that its reports were delivered weekly). Reading these reports, you get a sense of the population as some sort of complex organism reacting and responding to both world events (and their mediations) and to local circumstances. For instance, Adams writes on Saturday 25 May: 'There is definite evidence of increasing confusion. Today the strongest optimists (working-class men) are often qualifying their remarks with slight suspicion or doubt about the way things are developing. There is public uneasiness: a fortnight's waiting filled with troughs and peaks of depression and optimism is now beginning to produce bewilderment and disquiet' (Addison and Crang 2010: 31). On Monday 9 September (in the midst of the Blitz): 'In the areas which have been most heavily raided there has been little sign of panic and none of defeatism, but rather of bitterness and increasing determination to "see it through"' (Addison and Crang 2010: 407).

Morale work   **61**

Many of these mood reports mention specific rumours that were circulating. For instance, on 18 May we find out that in Bristol: 'Many rumours of air raids occur from time to time; one has it that all areas of the South East coast will be raided to drive people over to the South West [i.e., to Bristol] where they can be bombed collectively' (Addison and Crang 2010: 9). Rumours were a clear source of disquiet and the response of Adams and others to this were clear: the radio and the press should be used to immediately quash rumours by providing information related to the rumour (even if such information showed the public the strength of the Axis campaign). But if the response to misinformation seemed to be straightforward, there were other problems to do with civilian mood that were more problematic: what could you do about the attrition of morale that might come from a longer period of waiting for bombing, or through the actual horror of being bombed?

One of the first feedback 'barometer' tests the HID carried out involved the poster campaign that took the form of a number of implicit commands: 'YOUR COURAGE, YOUR CHEERFULNESS, YOUR RESOLUTION WILL BRING US VICTORY' (Figure 3.2). The poster was part of a campaign that included the much better-known (but never actually used during the war) poster 'Keep Calm and Carry On'. The posters were a simple design of white lettering on a red background with the image of a stylised crown at the top of the poster.

FIGURE 3.2 Propaganda image from the Ministry of Information. Topical Press Agency/Stringer.

Adams commissioned Mass-Observation to survey opinion as to how the poster was being received. From a survey of more than 1,000 people Mass-Observation found that the posters were unnoticed by the vast majority, and where they were noticed and were remembered they were consistently criticised as being vague blandishments or simply patronising. Much was made of the fact that the poster asserts that YOUR courage will bring victory to 'us': this was generally interpreted to mean that the public (the 'masses') will bring victory to the ruling elite (Mass-Observation 2009 [1940]: 92–98). *The Times* condemned the poster campaign as 'the insipid and patronising invocations to which the passer-by is now being treated' (cited in McLaine 1979: 30).

But if, on reflection, people found that the message linguistically reinforced a division of elites and mass ('us' versus 'you'), the more general reaction was simply that the posters had no power to affect its audience. Or rather, while 'other people' might be affected, the 'intelligent reader' (i.e., the person being questioned) is going to remain untouched: 'really no intelligent person can take any notice of them'; 'I suppose trusting souls are brightened by the few kind words'; 'it doesn't affect me personally' (Mass-Observation 2009 [1940]: 90). This response demonstrated an implicit understanding that morale, as a cultural feeling, can't simply be orchestrated by command: what was needed was practice. One of the most insistent complaints about the propaganda and the information was that it was too vague and abstract. The reports coming in from the Regional Information Officers, based as they were on overheard conversations as well as informal questions, was that people 'would welcome instructions about what to do or how to act, providing these were of a *definite* nature' and 'the public would like some sort of instructions about what they are expected to do in the present state of crisis' (Addison and Crang 2010: 8, emphasis in original).

If patronising blandishments didn't work, there was still a need for something that could address the increasingly unstable morale of the population. Adams recognised this as a problem, and one that required addressing in an aesthetic register. On Friday 24 March 1940 she wrote:

> London continues to have a lower morale than the provinces. Londoners are more mobile, more subject to news changes by placards and evening editions. This London situation requires attention since the first real shock is likely to fall on London. London therefore needs a firmer and more stable background tone instead of a less-integrated and more changeable emotional tone.
>
> *(Addison and Crang 2010: 25)*

I think by using the term 'tone' here Adams is invoking precisely the terrain that is covered by Heidegger's *Stimmung* (mood and attunement). The task of morale work wasn't simply to find a social tone that could fit with an enthusiastic prosecution of war (that is the 'cheerfulness' that is experienced as patronising, and the wayward enthusiasm of the uncle who shouts 'good shot' when a bomb lands on him), it was to find a *stable* and *practical tone* that could defeat persistent and debilitating anxiety through habits of the sensorial body that would also be habits of mood.

Morale as mood habit

How could we describe what is happening at this historical moment, in terms of feelings, moods and mediations? I think one way of describing it would be to say that we are seeing a civilian population learning what to feel in response to the anticipation and the actuality of a systematic and anonymous violence falling from the sky. This is a population learning feelings and responses that would somehow be adequate to the new circumstances, or at least not totally inadequate. What I think is also being witnessed is a pedagogic situation where the conveyors of learning include a range of state-sponsored texts and practices (pamphlets on bomb shelters, propaganda films [both newsreel and dramatic], new rules about lighting and so on) *and* the phenomenal learning that inevitably accompanies new experiences. This phenomenal form of pedagogy (the 'university of life', the 'school of hard knocks', to trade in some relevant clichés[3]) often seems to find itself bracketed out of accounts of morale as a form of governance, and yet it could be considered to be the test of social practice that is the fate of all learning.[4] The test of social practice is the actualisation of a pedagogy that emerges in experience and as a frame of experience. It is the place where governmentality has its bite (or not) and where this bite isn't always to the same degree, isn't always deep and isn't always conclusive. As we have already seen, state-produced propaganda isn't fed to a submissive and malleable population who might lap up blandishments about courage and cheerfulness. Any account of morale work needs to have a sense of the provisional and improvised nature of real-life responses to events (to war, privation, threat) that are likely to have corrosive and unstable effects. Accounts more amenable to the dialectics and dynamism of experience can be found within the landscape of morale work itself.

Many of the characters in Jennings' *Fires Were Started* were serving firefighters (trained both in fighting fires and snapping out of unproductive moods) and one of them was the writer William Sansom. At the end of the war when there was time for reflection, a number of writers (novelists, academics, poets) began to write about the experience of aerial bombardment.[5] In Sansom's extraordinary 1947 account of the Blitz (originally titled *Westminster at War*, now published as *The Blitz: Westminster at War*) he writes about the buildings and streets that were bombed, and explains the sequence of events that established the organisations that attended to fires, to unexploded bombs, to destitute families and to badly damaged buildings. Unlike so many books that were written about the Blitz it is neither a dry (triumphalist or not) recollection of facts, nor a dramatic retelling of events through the lives of particular individuals. Instead it is an account of collective action and collective sentiment, as a 'body' of people learn how to respond to aerial bombing in a densely populated city. It is filled with description but the description is not filtered through the prism of the self: there are no vying egos and no individual consciousness invades the scene. Instead the book describes practices and perceptions of an anonymous collectivity. And in this it is a model of how cultural feelings can be written as neither internal emotion, nor as external ideology, but as something quite different.

Writing about the forms that attention took during the years of the Blitz, Sansom describes:

> a time of raised eyes and apprehension, of ears opened to the lance-like descending whistle of high explosives (a sound that made the sky seem so very high and wide) and the dull smothered boom that had shattered some house somewhere away out in the darkened streets.
> (Sansom 2010 [1947]: 32)

Here anxious apprehension is feeling, but not feeling that is interior to the subject; instead it is materialised as part of the new situation, where daily attunement is to a sonic field that is perceived with anticipation (the whistles of incoming bombs) and geographical understanding (the dull thuds and booms of the explosion giving a sense of distance and proximity). Feeling is there in the material practices (in the descending of bombs and the noises that they make), the habits of perception (listening, looking) and in the alterations to the collective sensorium (to a world of noises and sights that has been fundamentally reconfigured in a landscape of deathly anticipation and preparation).

Initially the descriptions in the book seem as if they are describing subjective experience until you realise that there is no subject *of* the experience. Or rather, the descriptions reveal themselves as subjective in a peculiarly objective form: they are the sensorial experience of a collectivity undergoing nightly bombing and adjusting itself, learning to start the day again each day knowing full well that the night will bring further carnage:

> The morning streets had an unreal air; the City continued about its business, there was an atmosphere of normality in the traffic and the people going to work; but the undertone whispered, the memory of the firebells and the ambulances of the night, the sharp smells of burning and the poison of plaster-dust, the knowledge of the stretcher and the shroud.
> (Sansom 2010 [1947]: 38)

Here it is the 'undertone' that is the active subject, and this undertone is embedded in the sensorial environment. This is a way of writing that is highly attuned to mood and feeling. And it is also, and this is crucial, attuned to the way that feelings and moods change and fold back on themselves (certain moods are peculiarly self-conscious, while others are peculiarly self-obliterating) and are held, not by consciousness but by the actuality of the world: it is the acrid smell of burning that holds the memory-mood of the night before.

Where Sansom's writing is particularly productive for understanding the world of feelings that circulate around morale work is when he describes the process by which a body of people become newly attuned to their dynamic situation. He describes how citizens involved in fighting fire and clearing up bomb damage have to deal with 'pieces of flesh' – anonymous human flesh that was the gristly result of bomb blasts – that war workers had to catalogue in record books and that had to be disposed of with a degree of reverence. It is a macabre situation that no one is prepared for (and that no one could abstractly prepare for). In many ways, the whole of the Blitz was similar to this experience: it was unknown, uncharted and always at the very edge of human endurance. How could a group of civilians go about dealing with a situation where a bomb had broken through the water supply and the gas supply, where a group of people were trapped in a space that was gradually filling with water, and where an unexploded bomb was precariously positioned (Sansom 2010 [1947]: 31)? His formulation, which I have used as my epigraph and subtitle for this chapter, is 'here again the dominant note of the time is heard – problems revealing themselves and experience feeling itself' (Sansom 2010 [1947]: 29–30). It is a condensed and complex formulation: experience feeling itself. It is neither a moment of revelation, nor the self-conscious act of reflection (what could be described as self-reflexive-ness). It is something more dynamic, something caught up in the vital moment, where 'feeling out' a scene (a scene that includes your fragile body as one of many fragile bodies) is a constant process of sensing and acting, where 'trial and error' (where the stakes are as high as they could be) produced provisional practices and habits that will need to be constantly renewed in the face of new circumstances.

This is to put mood and feeling on the side of process rather than on the side of product (where a mood or a feeling might be seen as an end result). It is also to recognise that morale work is a day-to-day activity, and that during the Blitz it was a continual ongoing process that could be described as pedagogical. What was crucial for both ordinary firefighters and for the morale workers who were part of the HID was to find a way of 'experience feeling itself' that could offer new habits that could accommodate daily life as catastrophe. As the HID was finding out, what morale needed wasn't encouragements to feel cheerful, but mechanisms for practice, for 'feeling useful', for doing something, and for not getting pulled into the bleak void that was opening up in human experience.

In this, Sansom is describing the pedagogic condition of Home Front Morale in a way quite similar to that in which the psychologist William James described the relationship between habit and learning. In 1882, James gave a number of talks to teachers showing them how a psychologist understands the role of the pedagogue and warning them that psychology won't provide a pedagogic programme. He offered them a synoptic definition of the pedagogic: 'Education, in short, cannot be better described than by calling it *the organization of acquired habits of conduct and tendencies to behavior*' (James 1962 [1899]: 15, emphasis in original). Instilling habits of conduct and tendencies of behaviour wasn't simply the job of producing 'docile bodies' that would willingly acquiesce to any demand the teacher made; rather it was a more complex process of establishing repertoires of reactive possibilities that would include practical activities as much as intellectual judgements and beliefs.

66 Morale work

The Jamesian pedagogue has the task of preparing the child for the unforeseen as much as for what is foreseeable and desirable. Thus:

> You should regard your professional task as if it consisted chiefly and essentially in *training the pupil to behaviour*, taking behavior, not in the narrow sense of his manners, but in the very widest possible sense, as including every possible sort or fit reaction on the circumstances into which he may find himself brought by the vicissitudes of life.
>
> The reaction may, indeed, often be a negative reaction. *Not* to speak, *not* to move, is one of the most important of our duties, in certain practical emergencies.
>
> (James 1962 [1899]: 13–14, emphasis in original)

James invokes a social world of uncertainty and ultimately of emergencies, the greatest of which is undoubtedly war. What James was imagining was a human subject that wouldn't be unnerved by life's vicissitudes and emergency circumstances. For this James recognises that one habit that needs to be instilled is the habit of dehabituation: 'do every day or two something for no other reason than its difficulty, so that, when the hour of dire need draws nigh, it may find you not unnerved and untrained to stand the test' (James 1962 [1899]: 38).

Morale work then, rather than working to establish a set of feelings (cheerfulness, for instance) was charged with the pedagogic task of preparing people how 'not to feel', or how to flatten the monstrous affects that were in circulation. Such pedagogy was being conducted informally, 'on the fly' so to say, in the field of civilian bombing, where the teachers were as likely to be falling masonry and bomb blasts as any official fire expert. More generally though, morale workers had to prepare a civilian population for war on the Home Front, so that they could greet catastrophe with a degree of nonchalance that wouldn't be lack of fear but would be a form of practical consciousness that was aimed at getting people to 'keep on keeping on' (Orwell 1970b: 435). If it included self-reflection, it wasn't the sort of self-reflection that could encourage introspection (melancholic or otherwise): far from it, it was a self-reflection aimed at finding productive ways for 'experience feeling itself' so as to produce new habits.[6] James, of course, had no expectation of a war that would include the dropping of high explosives on a civilian population. Given such a 'practical emergency', the importance of a population not becoming 'unnerved' and the importance of instilling 'negative reactions' to circumstances (including subduing panic reactions to bombing) was clearly a pressing concern in 1940.

Listen to Britain: attention, anticipation, practice

When the American commentator Quentin Reynolds intones at the end of *London Can Take It!* (dir. Jennings and Watt 1940) that 'there is no panic, no fear, no despair, in London Town', he is asserting a wish. The film was destined for the US and designed to solicit help, and for that particular task, mood (optimism, steely determination and so on) was an essential currency. Earlier in the film we see Londoners preparing for another night of bombing, 'the greatest civilian army ever to be assembled' is seen 'going home to change into the uniform of their particular service' (Hodgkinson and Sheratsky 1982: 128–131). We see a giant poster above what looks like a shop (or it could be a theatre); it says 'CARRY ON LONDON AND KEEP YOUR CHIN UP!' The film is doing mood work; it is asserting a resilient population carrying on under duress (keeping its chin up). The poster is attempting to instil a moodful habit, but it belongs to a pedagogy of paternalism, rather than the Jamesian pedagogy that emerges in later films (in this it works in a similar way to the poster campaign that extols a population to be cheerful). And I think that it is precisely this *assertion* of mood (*be* cheerful, *don't* panic, *don't be* frightened) that is rightly seen as ineffective and patronising (for a home audience), and is replaced by a pedagogic form that performs mood as a repertoire of responses.

'Experience feeling itself' is not something that just takes place out in the field of battle (which were also the streets of London, Coventry, Cardiff, Belfast, Glasgow and so on). It could also take place in the field of film propaganda. Between *London Can Take It!* and *Fires Were Started*, Jennings produced (along with Stewart McAllister) the film *Listen to Britain*, which was finished in 1942.[7] I want to treat this film as an example of a particular cultural feeling materialised, and one that was particularly adept at the pedagogic work of preparing a civilian population so that they could learn the habit of 'snapping out of it'. The film was made under the Crown Film Productions for the MOI, and it was partly designed for a US audience as encouragement for help with the war effort. It is a montage film without any voice-over commentary (which was distinctly unusual within the documentary conventions of the time). It also evoked the ethos of the HID, which prided itself in 'listening to Britain'. It is as much about sound as it is about images, which is also made clear by the title. It is a film where the audience is positioned so as to 'listen' to the sounds of Britain during wartime, but it is also, and perhaps more emphatically, a film that presents us with people listening, or of sounds being listened to (or of sounds intended to be heard but where the image of hearing is missing). It is then primarily a film about attention, about bodies oriented towards sounds, sounds that bring comfort and anxiety. It is, if you like, the representation of 'experience feeling itself'.

It was initially thought of as an utter failure by people within Crown but seems to have been recognised by cinemagoers, at least in Britain, as directly connecting to their experience of the Home Front. For instance, Helen de Mouilpied, who worked within the film programming department of the MOI, recalled that:

> All sorts of audiences felt it [*Listen to Britain*] to be a distillation and also a magnification of their own experiences on the home front. This was especially true of factory audiences. I remember one show in a factory in the Midlands where about 800 workers clapped and stamped approval. Films got very short shrift if they touched any area of people's experience and did not ring true.
>
> *(Mouilpied, cited in Chapman 1998: 170)*

Given that even today the film looks like an experimental film poem, this seems to register a particularly positive response to the film by the people the film depicts. The film has a double invitation to listen: we as an audience are invited to listen in to Britain as it gets on with the business of war work, but we are also invited to watch and listen as Britain goes about listening. The first thing I want to register is the oddity of this film: to pay attention to the paying of attention turns out to be a peculiar affair. For the most part we cannot tell, for instance, if people are attentive. So we see people listening to a concert, but we don't know if they are really attentive or if they are thinking other thoughts. For the most part, listening is something that continues alongside other activities: women listen (and show their listening by singing along) to 'workers' playtime' radio broadcasts in the armaments factories while they operate the machinery that produces the munitions; or by the mass-whistling that accompanies a show by Flanagan and Allan. In this sense, a lot of the time it simply doesn't matter if people are listening or not. What matters is that listening doesn't jeopardise the ability to function. Morale, if we recall, was to be measured not by what someone thinks but by what they do and how they do it.

I want to suggest two 'listening' activities that the film encourages as a form of mood, or as a form of attention associated with morale-mood. One is that morale-mood requires a form of alertness that requires a 'listening out for' but not a form of contemplative 'transport' (as in losing yourself in the music or being transfixed by messages on the radio). The second is the role of memory: reminiscences are fine but they must be managed. Your morale-mood can allow for the memory of loved ones fighting elsewhere, or for a home left behind (we hear Canadian soldiers singing 'Home on the Range'), but they must be followed quickly by activities. I want to signal this by two very short sequences.

The first seconds of the film initiate what will be a consistent manoeuvre throughout the film. We see trees move in the wind, we see wheat swaying in the breeze and we see Spitfire planes flying in the sky. The first shots then are classic English pastoral and to follow this with industrial machinery is consistent with Jennings' aesthetic. It is in one sense a poetic juxtaposition of 'England's green and pleasant lands' with the machinery of war. But what seems more unusual, and is a procedure followed throughout the film, is the way in which sound is used in an anticipatory way. We hear the massive rumbling of the aeroplanes before we have any sight of what is causing this deafening noise. And when we see them pass we see a group of 'land girls' momentarily look up and then carry on with collecting a harvest (Figure 3.3). We then see the formation of spitfires followed by soldiers watching them in camouflaged dugouts. The soldiers are following them with binoculars. And as the aeroplanes fly by, and as the soldiers watch the planes, the harvest is being brought in. Each is attentive to what is to hand. Those working the land might be momentarily distracted by the planes, but only for a moment. In one sense it registers the sonic recalibrations described by Sansom, the listening out for whistles, but here the listening has become managed: experience has felt itself, and produced a habituated response of nonchalant alertness. Those whose business it is

FIGURE 3.3 A land army at work, from *Listen to Britain*, dir. Humphrey Jennings and Stewart McAllister, 1942.

to listen out scour the skies; those whose task is to feed a population listen momentarily and then 'keep on keeping on'.

The film is constantly about attention, about orientation, about concentration. But it is also about temporality and this is written into the very form of the anticipatory structuring of sound and the visual delay in picturing the sound-generating object. This provides a forceful push forward: an orientation of preparation. The sound in the film is the substantive sensory motor: it is insistently foregrounded and small sounds are amplified (distant motorised sounds 'appear' very close, sounds of clattering feet take on machinic dimensions, etc.). The pastoralism of much of the imagery is laced with industrial sounds, and yet while the presence of industrial/military/musical sounds is pervasive, so too is the business of getting on with what is to hand (the war work of the Home Front). All is foreground: all is background. This is the *musique concrète* of total mobilisation where landscape and tradition are part of that mobilisation while remaining 'nationalist' and 'pastoral'.

The second sequence I want to point to juxtaposes children in a playground (the material future, so to say) and a lone woman indoors making tea. We first see the woman but the sound we hear is of the stamping and clapping that is the sound of the children (they are playing a sort of mass form of the 'one potato, two potato' game that involves clapping each other's hands and stamping their feet as they stand in pairs). We then see a long shot of the playground. The woman moves to the

70 Morale work

window and looks out and we see the children playing. Then back to the woman who glances at a photograph of a man in uniform: the sound continues with the children as we linger on the photograph. Then back to the children, this time in close-up (Figure 3.4). The sound of the children's phenomenally loud clattering feet and slapping hands turns into a loud deep rumbling. We next see armoured carriers driving through the village. Reminiscence is a minor note in the business of moving forward, of preparing the future (food, children, schooling, soldiering). So the sense of readiness, of attunement to the future might well be seen to be the 'object of this film'. The film could then be seen as a phenomenological investigation of anticipating attention and the way to proceed in the business of getting on. It is an unemotional mood, but a mood nonetheless.

At a symbolic level, *Listen to Britain* provides us with a semiotic avalanche of Englishness (and sometimes of Britishness more generally), seen as embedded in a pastoral setting, in the ritual games of children, and in a national and European culture. This is juxtaposed with another semiotic layer that is constantly threaded through the scenes: this is the total mobilisation of war. But if we shift away from the symbolic level to look at the sensory work of images and sound, we see a phenomenal situation where sound is constantly foregrounded and is always in advance of its visual referent. We hear before we see. The world at hand is the world of practical considerations: providing sustenance, delivering information, playing, looking

FIGURE 3.4 Ritual play in *Listen to Britain*, dir. Humphrey Jennings and Stewart McAllister, 1942.

out for enemy aircraft. It is, if you like, the phenomenal pedagogy, demonstrating the kind of attention required to avoid morbid attitudes so as to 'keep on keeping on' during a time of extreme danger.

The following year Jennings made the film where we see the distraught fireman (including William Sansom) 'snapping out' of their disconsolate moods. To treat *Listen to Britain* as providing the conditions for such snapping out is, of course, to cede far too much power to propaganda. The success of *Listen to Britain* was down, I think, to the way that it found a phenomenal form for a way of feeling that had been learnt on the job (in the factories, in the bombing raids, in the farms). In *Listen to Britain*, Jennings' subject is the sensorial recalibration of the environment during wartime. His topics are not straightforwardly emotional: they are instead the field of perception at a time when anxious anticipation could descend into self-absorption. We see a world of feeling that shows another sort of absorption, one absorbed in the activity of keeping on keeping on.

The Blitz spirit

Much of the historical work concerned with morale and the British Home Front during the Second World War has been focused on trying to assess the actuality of reactions to the Blitz.[8] Was the general population generally stoical and courageous in the face of aerial bombardment as was insistently proclaimed by both official account and various journalistic reports? Or was this a myth produced at the time to yield the sort of behaviour that it was asserting (a form of self-fulfilling prophecy)? Films and posters, newspapers and newsreels, information leaflets and training manuals were all mobilised for the purpose of morale at a time when it was a criminal offence to circulate reports or statements 'likely to cause alarm or despondency' (Sinfield 2000: 84).[9] Given such a situation, it would be hard not to imagine that the historical record has been fatally skewed simply because the fact that what is available from newspapers and official documents has already involved the production of positive morale and cultural feelings designed to help the war effort.

But the work of exploring cultural feelings has other questions to attend to. Rather than just ask whether people felt despondent when faced with bombing, we need to ask what cultural forms (of experience feeling itself) were available for such experiences to be fully articulated. Morale work was in the business of promoting certain sorts of cultural forms and, alongside this, of rejecting other cultural forms. I think one of the first cultural forms to be obliterated (an early casualty of war, so to say) was exactly the sort of cultural form that could wrestle with emotions and reactions, and the sort of existential crisis that the world was going through. As far as this goes, it might very well be that people were undergoing massive psychological breakdowns, but that the cultural forms that could discuss them were momentarily unavailable (or their availability was unacceptable and unpatriotic).

The following account of psychological breakdown comes from the autobiography of a man whose role during the war included directing an art college that had been redirected to focus on war work. He provides this account of his psychological breakdown:

> Amongst the maze of houses and bombed wreckage in the East End it was hardly possible to find our way through in the black-out. However, Tommy knew his London very well, and thought that if he went up a side street which seemed very quiet, we could work back on to the main thoroughfare and get down to Ilford. It was a very, very quiet street. A warden shouted, 'You bloody fool, where the hell do you think you're going?' and stepped out to stop us [...] A landmine had entangled itself in a small tree growing in the pavement beside the road. It was fixed on a very slender branch and, as it waved in the wind, the two points of the detonator just missed touching the pavement. One extra gust of wind and the bomb would surely slip and the street would go up in the air.
>
> (Johnstone 1980: 193)

In the next paragraph we get a sense of the corrosive and accumulative effects of such 'routine' experiences.

> Then, between bombs and worry about my wife and daughter in America, I collapsed. William Ritchie put me in hospital at Galashiels and it was not until eleven months later that I was allowed to return to Camberwell on the strict understanding that I was not to remain in London at night.
>
> (Johnstone 1980: 194)

And that is pretty much that. No self-reflection. No account of what happened in the hospital, or how he recovered from this breakdown. And this within a literary form (the autobiography) singularly available for just this kind of introspection. This, I think, is the other side of Home Front Morale work. If the major work of morale was to produce the 'conditions of feeling' that could cope with constant catastrophe, it actively removed the conditions of feeling that could narrate the moment when morale no longer worked, when the soul collapsed.

The 'myth of the Blitz' is not, to my mind, a product of propaganda informing history (or it is not primarily that). People did collapse, riots did occur. Where the myth lies is accounting for the labour of morale. Where an ordinary patriotism morphs into an ideology of racism is where accounts of morale are explained by reference to national character. To explain morale in terms of national character is not only to invoke a racist disposition, it also undersells the extraordinary work of producing cultural feelings at a moment of crisis. The real myth of the Blitz can be summed up in such sentiments as these:

> British morale springs from within, and not from without. That which is phenomenal in British history is the extent to which a people, insular, uninterested in domination and expansion, have yet spread the pattern of their

thought and rule over the world. The magic of their success is their faith in their own way of life, their incredulity when confronted with the customs of other people. Their will to resist has nothing to do with theories, and little connection with causes; it is the resistance of their whole nature, their whole history, the whole pattern of their culture, against any attempt to impose on them the behaviour of another nation.

(Spender 1945: 38)

If the study of cultural feeling can do anything, it can stop us believing that cultural practices and feelings 'spring from within' as if they are part of a national chromosome. It was not national character that produced the conditions that allowed civilians to maintain adequate Home Front Morale, it was the day-to-day labour of morale work, which included 'experience feeling itself' and producing new routines and habits, and new mediated forms of communication such as Jennings' film work.

Notes

1 Advert copy is taken from *Picture Post* magazine, 28 September 1940, 18 January 1941 and 7 December 1940.
2 A history of the HID can be accessed through the following books: James Hinton's *The Mass Observers* (2013) provides an excellent account of Mass-Observation's activities during the war and their involvement with the HID; Ian McLaine's *Ministry of Morale* (1979) is excellent on situating HID within the larger workings of the Ministry of Information; Robert Mackay's *Half the Battle* (2002) offers a more culturally nuanced account of the story told by McLaine. Paul Addison and Jeremy Crang's edited collection *Listening to Britain* (2010) is an excellent sample of the reports that the HID produced.
3 To my mind, clichés always represent arenas of life that are worth investigating rather than modes of expression that need to be either avoided or critiqued. The cliché is often a short-cut into everyday life and represents some of our most condensed and knotted forms of common knowledge.
4 I'm thinking particularly of analyses inspired by Michel Foucault's approach, with the primary example being Nikolas Rose's *Governing the Soul: The Shaping of the Private Self* (1989). This is an excellent book, with much to recommend it, yet its perspective is unrelentingly from the point of view of the discursive mechanisms of institutions (and it assumes that this intentionality is both effective and constitutive of subjects).
5 As I mentioned in the preface, I am, in this book, focused primarily on Britain for my case studies (though hopefully without any sense of jingoism!). It would be interesting to extend the discussion by looking at other national contexts, and then to see these within a larger history of aerial bombing that is part of a world history. I think an initial sense of this could be seen through the work of writers such as Sloterdijk (2009), Lindqvist (2012 [2001]), Schivelbusch (2001) and Sebald (2004). Like many with my national background and from my generation (a child in England in the 1960s and 1970s), I grew up among adults for whom the Blitz was a material experience, and yet my cultural reference points for the Second World War were either war comics and war movies (and these never represented civilian populations) or non-British literature, particularly Kurt Vonnegut's 1969 novel *Slaughterhouse Five* (2000 [1969]) about the firebombing of Dresden and Günter Grass' 1959 novel *The Tin Drum* (2010 [1959]) set in Danzig (later Gdansk) chronicling, in a fabulist manner, the rise of Nazism in what was a semi-autonomous state.

6 One new habit might be described as being to 'keep calm and carry on', which was the slogan of a poster produced as part of the same campaign as the poster I discussed earlier in this chapter ('YOUR COURAGE ...'). The 'Keep Calm and Carry On' poster was printed but never used (it was going to be rolled out at times of aerial bombing). My argument would suggest that a cultural feeling (or morale work) that could resist panic and produce purposefully 'carrying on' moved from the world of instruction to a world of demonstration and habit.
7 The critical literature around Jennings is not extensive. For a selection see Jackson (1993, 2004), Jennings (1982), and Hodgkinson and Sheratsky (1982).
8 A general review of this material can be found in Shapira (2013) and Jones et al. (2004). Both of these texts take as central the work of Angus Calder (1971) and then his qualification crucially titled *The Myth of the Blitz* (1992). Historical work around the Blitz seems unlikely to end anytime soon. Some of the best recent work follows the early example of Tom Harrisson's *Living through the Blitz* (1976) and give ordinary people the chance to speak. I'm thinking of Bell (2011), Hinton (2010) and Levin (2016) as relatively recent examples. My sense of the Blitz is that the general level of courageous nonchalance has undoubtedly been exaggerated and this was a product of morale work both at the time and subsequently. On the other hand, I find it hard not to simply sit in awe as I think of domestic households in Britain, Germany, Japan and elsewhere dealing with such malignant forces raining down on them from the air: to carry on carrying on seems heroic indeed.
9 In this respect, there is an enormous repository of materials that were never used during the war because they fell foul of the censor's red pencil. Arthur Marwick's *The Home Front: The British and the Second World War* (1976) makes use of a vast number of photographs that were never published during the war precisely because they might not be conveying the right feelings and moods.

4

BOMBSITES AND PLAYGROUNDS

(A wrecked, indifferent calm)

> We take our wilderness where we go.
> *(Macaulay 1958 [1950]: 155)*

A child, alone or with others, stands amid rubble. A boy, a girl, a group of kids of indeterminate age, scattered among bricks, window-frames and half-collapsed walls. Huddling around a fire, kids holding pieces of wood, ready to throw them on the fire or turn them into weapons. A group of children on a patch of waste-ground, staring out at the camera, staring at us, the viewers: they scowl, or look disdainful, or simply carry on indifferent to the attention aimed at them. You can't tell from the clothes that they wear when all this is meant to be: the ragamuffin garb is loosely 'post-war'. You can't tell from the rubble what has caused the wasting of this ground: Luftwaffe bombing or local government redevelopment. It could be the 1960s or the 1970s, or it could be the 1940s or 1950s. Rubble and ruin has a timeless look to it.

Waste-ground has been a central motif within the social imaginary of post-war reconstruction in Britain. It constituted an affective landscape that played host to a mood-world that was sometimes morose or despondent, sometimes indifferent or disdainful or preoccupied, sometimes resilient or defiant, sometimes joyful and exuberant, and sometimes resigned. Often the figuring of waste-ground offered an assemblage of mixed moods. The human figures that populated this ruined landscape were cast as performers for an atmospheric orchestration: they were the youthful hordes that could be framed as a cause-for-concern (potential or actual), or, more threateningly, as a major-social-problem. Whether it was the juvenile delinquent intent on bringing civilised society to its knees, or the child-we-feel-general-concern-for (as gleeful rapscallion or doleful child-in-need), it was the juxtaposition of figure and landscape that did the affective work. The landscape literalised a set of analogies for damaged youth, as well as being a material space fashioned from the aggressions of warring nations and from the dreams of those wanting to build the 'new Jerusalem' on the plains of urban Britain. In part this social imaginary is still with us in nightmare fantasies of roaming hordes of youthful 'hoodies'. The cultural landscape, however, has shifted; the high-density estates of Glasgow, Manchester and London are now the more insistent backdrop.

Cultural feelings, then, are not just attached to historical moments (for instance, the Blitz); they can also congregate around certain sites and spaces, around particular landscapes. This, of course, is not to escape history. The reasons that a set of feelings concentrate around a landscape of ruin and dereliction are very much to do with historical process of decline and fall, rebirth and progress. Ruin often signals, for a particular group, the passing of one historical period and the implicit emergence of something new. Thus, the ruined castle could signal to Victorians in the nineteenth century the end of a pre-modern social world to be replaced by something new, rational and modern. In the twentieth century, however, such historical process seemed much less secure, much less straightforwardly linear. And in the second half of that century, the image of the derelict waste-ground was an image of space that was often distinctly 'out of time'.

The ruined urban townscape, particularly as it appeared in the 1960s and 1970s, pointed simultaneously to the past and the future. On the one hand, the bomb damage inflicted during the Second World War was still a feature of many British towns and cities. It was a memory cast in stone, albeit cast in a scattered and capricious fashion; it was an insistent reminder of a recent past. On the other hand, the 1960s and 1970s was a period of intense urban refashioning, of razing the past and building ambitious urban conurbations that were refashioning and reconceiving the urban landscape. On top of this, or alongside it, was an amorphous fear that nuclear war was an imminent possibility. Nuclear anxieties were consolidated and amplified by the exponential build-up of weapon systems during the Cold War, by various moments of nuclear brinkmanship (for instance, the Cuban Missile Crisis), and by a number of seemingly inevitable accidents at nuclear power plants (Windscale, Three Mile Island and so on).[1] The patch of waste-ground, then, wasn't something that could feature as part of a picturesque aesthetic from the past, where the image of ruin could evoke a previous era of myth and legend. But nor was it in any way straightforwardly an image of a nihilistic future. The landscape of ruined urbanism articulated a set of feelings that were contradictory and ambivalent: of fragility and strength, of permanence and impermanence, of innocence and guilt. The images looked forward in time to inevitable devastation, while looking back to the still-warm memories of recent destruction. And yet these desolate landscapes were often the bare canvases for future urban schemes: for road-building and housing estates, for shopping complexes and new industries. The juxtaposition of this cleared landscape with children playing further deepened the ambiguity: here was new life, filled with energies and hopes. Promises were scattered on this desolate landscapes, like seeds on bare earth. These images conjoined feelings of hope strangled at birth with the triumph of sheer life flourishing in a desert.

Image-repertoire of ruin and youth

The prevalence of images, films and descriptions of ruined urban landscapes with a scattering of youths loitering or playing could be seen as part of what Roland Barthes called an image-repertoire. Image-repertoire is the name that Barthes and his translators give to the psycho-semiotic idea of the Imaginary (*L'Imaginaire*) and for Barthes it is an archive of cultural gestures that are imbedded deep in our cultural imaginations, feelings and actions, as well as being available (and unavoidable) in a corpus of films, photographs, novels and so on (Barthes 1979). The image-repertoire is the world of cultural apperception supported by a series of pictorial and descriptive conventions, which while they allow for a good deal of variation also share a family resemblance. It would be wrong, I think, to assume that an 'image-repertoire' exists primarily in a visual register: some of the most powerful aspects of it might be connected to sound (the sound of laughter mixed with sirens, for instance), and smell (cement dust and burning wood, perhaps). In this case study, I'm particularly interested in the image-repertoire of post-war Britain that fashions the moods and feelings of redevelopment from wrecked landscapes.

Take, for example, Figure 4.1. It shows us a scattered group of young children on a piece of waste-ground around some derelict buildings. We know from the legend attached to the photograph that the ground has been laid waste by the 'benevolent' planning of local councils rather than by the malevolent force of aerial bombardment. And yet the landscape could as easily be the cleared remains of bombing. In some ways, this distinction is not of overriding importance in the image-repertoire

FIGURE 4.1 Slum clearances, Gorbals, Glasgow, 1960s. © Nick Hedges and Birmingham Central Libraries' photographic archive.

of post-war waste-grounds: one of the functions of this particular genre of image is to fold together bomb damage and redevelopment into a single continuum. The image genre seems to say: it is all, in one way or another, damage. The image of children standing about on waste-ground like this is a mainstay of 'caring' photojournalism from before the war and on into the post-war period. It carries on until about the early 1980s, which is roughly when bombsites stopped being a presence within the British urban landscape (often visible as a space around ruined churches or as informal car parks).

Images such as Figures 4.1 and 4.2 fed the photo magazine industry that emerged with magazines such as *Picture Post* (1938–1957) and then later with the colour supplements that were founded in the 1960s as part of British national newspapers' weekend provision (the *Sunday Times* launched its colour supplement in 1962 and the *Observer* in 1963). These magazines mixed socially concerned photojournalism (often using grainy black and white film stock and aimed at the problems of youth, poverty and urban degradation) with the imagery of aspirational lifestyle (nearly always using colour photography and showing images of food, fashion, interiors, holiday and the latest consumer durables). The depiction of kids-on-waste-ground also fed a post-war sociology that echoed some of the concerns of photojournalism. This urban sociology often articulated a leftist social attitude, which was often focused specifically on the fate of young people in urban space, and was consistently anchored by black and white images of kids standing among rubble (see, for instance, Ward 1978). The conventions of picturing such waste-ground were fashioned by the presence of bombsites within the urban landscape (which often resulted in

FIGURE 4.2 Children play on the site of demolished houses in Byker, Newcastle. Photograph: Trinity Mirror/Mirrorpix/Alamy.

juxtapositions of the built and the unbuilt, of ruined housing juxtaposed with monumental industry and so on), and on the presence of bombsites within literary and visual cultural forms (novels, films, poetry and so on) (see Mellor 2011).

This seam from the image-repertoire didn't generate a single meaning: indeed 'meaning' seems an inadequate term for considering the significance of this corpus of images. Perhaps their most important and powerful feature was that they seemed quite capable of carrying opposing social atmospheres and explanations on their backs. This was a set of descriptions that could act as atmospheric evidence for culturally conservative feelings that would claim that 'core' social values were in decline and that the root cause of the 'youth problem' was the lack of family discipline, the increase in divorce rates, the new air of permissiveness and so on, but it could also support a more radically democratic critique that could point the finger of blame at instrumentalist governance that was keen on reproducing the conditions for capitalist expansion and was indifferent to the complex requirements of adolescence. It is this ability to vacillate between quite different and conflicting social moods that make this seam from the post-war image-repertoire so important for the period and for the emotional situation of redevelopment and the so-called post-war settlement that materialised in such socially liberal and optimistic formations as the Welfare State.

In an essay from 1996, the Italian Marxist Paolo Virno set out to analyse the emotional tonalities that emerged in the 1980s and that characterise the conditions of possibility for social and political activity in Italy in the last decades of the twentieth century. For Virno, analysing the emotional situation is not a marginal activity; it does not mean attending to surface articulations of a more profound materiality of the social world to be found elsewhere. For Virno the 'emotional situation' constitutes 'modes of being and feeling so pervasive as to be common to the most diverse contexts of experience' (Virno 1996: 13). In Italy (and elsewhere) in the 1980s and after, a set of emotional modes constituted the conditions for productive life (rather than just the effects of that production): these included fear and anxiety built around precariousness of employment; forms of opportunism and cynicism that directed market expansion; experiences of teleology and belonging that had become bereft of content; and a number of other fears and anxieties. In a way that continues the tradition of analysis associated with Walter Benjamin and Raymond Williams (with a dash of Jean-François Lyotard thrown in), Virno puts experience and feeling at the centre of his political economy. In Virno's terms, what is essential is grasping the ambivalence that circulates around a feeling like job-fear and its attendant mutability: 'we need to understand, beyond the ubiquity of their manifestations, the *ambivalence* of these modes of being and feeling, to discern in them a "degree zero" or neutral kernel from which may arise both cheerful resignation, inexhaustible renunciation, and social assimilation on the one hand and new demands for the radical transformation of the status quo on the other' (Virno 1996: 13, emphasis in original). In other words, the aim is not to grasp a mode of feeling that animates a collective mood that can then be read politically; rather the task is to grasp the range of vacillating feelings that are politically ambivalent and connect these back to underlying social forms and forces (Virno's 'neutral kernel') that drive the specific contradictory affects of the mood-world (its ability to animate critical and affirmative responses). For Virno this is the world of productive labour relations (often of a particularly immaterial kind) and work-life attitudes – and it is also an emotional situation.

While Virno writes to pursue a conjunctural analysis of contemporary production and the relationships between work and non-work, here I am more interested in a set of feelings that circulated in the immediate post-war period (that period's pattern of feeling) and that animated ideas about urban landscape, children, play and – by inference – the idea of the Welfare State as a social and political project. This pattern of feeling is, I think, one that predates the emergence of a neoliberal conjuncture (which is to a large degree the phenomena that Virno is describing), but it is also a set of feelings that feeds into a neoliberal mood-world and does something to legitimate it. One way of restating this is to say that the conjuncture that surrounds and grounds the post-war settlement (and the Welfare State) was animated by internal conflicts and that these conflicts underwrote the emergence of a new conjuncture (neoliberalism) as a legitimate or necessary social formation. Or to put it slightly more succinctly, the social and political instabilities within the mood of the post-war settlement were used in a particular way to legitimate the late 1970s conjuncture that we call neoliberalism. Virno's sense of the importance of ambivalence is crucial for understanding this – although I'm less convinced that it is possible to separate the husks of ambivalence from a supposed kernel of neutrality (but that is not an argument I will pursue here). The emotional situation that I want to take as my subject is that which is materialised by the image of the bombsite-as-playground.

Figures in a landscape

One of the most affecting descriptions of bombsites in London is to be found in Rose Macaulay's 1950 novel *The World My Wilderness*. The novel's protagonist is a teenage girl called Barbary Deniston and much of the book is taken up with her life in London after the war, among the bombsites around St Paul's Cathedral. She spent the war years in Occupied France with her mother and mixed with young resistance fighters – the *Maquis*. After the war, Barbary's mother sent her away to England to live with Barbary's father, his new and pregnant wife and their child. But rather than hanging around the emotionally austere household of her father's new family, Barbary instead frequents the bombsites with a *Maquis* friend and gets to know the various spivs, deserters, shoplifters and damaged souls that can be found there.

The novel has a strange and compelling mood. On the one hand, it is a modern gothic tale, with the bombsite figured as an abysmal milieu alive with moral vacuity and restless despair. So when Barbary escapes from a family holiday in Scotland to return to her bombsites, she 'was going back where she belonged, to the waste margins of civilization that she knew, where other outcasts lurked, and questions were not asked' (Macaulay 1958 [1950]: 82). At another point she meets a disturbed vicar lurking in a bombed-out church and is told by another clergyman, that: 'he often wanders about the ruined churches, looking for his own. His church was bombed in 1940; he was trapped in the wreckage for two days; he could scarcely move, and the flames raged round him. He hasn't, of course, been the same since [...] He thinks he's in hell and can't get out' (1958 [1950]:124).

On the other hand, Macaulay's novel is a consideration of action, memory and the perspicacity and usefulness of psychoanalysis. Given that the book is primarily about a young woman (Barbary) whose parents had divorced (a fairly major event back in the London of the 1940s), who is deeply attached to her mother but who has been rejected by her, and who has witnessed traumatic war activities (some of which she has been complicit in), the novel ruthlessly refuses to grant Barbary the sort of psychical interiority that is granted to other characters in the book. We never perceive the world of the novel from within the emotional economy and ecology of Barbary: we never really know how she feels and we are never given any explanation for why she acts the way she does or why she feels the way she does (whereas, for instance, the actions of her brother, a fairly minor character, are discussed within his interior conversation as relating to his narcissistic masochism). The book explicitly refuses a psychoanalytic explanation of Barbary's woes, and explicitly rejects the 'talking cure' that is offered (Barbary's uncle is a psychoanalyst and offers to counsel her when they are in visiting him in Scotland), which might have offered some respite to the ailing soul of Barbary. The novel levels its critique of psychoanalysis at the inadequacy of an approach that is centred on talk: Barbary has little to say and her past actions do not constitute a discursive form. Barbary is clearly not brimful of anxious content: indeed, it may well be that Barbary is suffering from emptiness – a directionless emptiness – a wilderness. And this is where the equivalence exists between the physical wilderness of the bombsite and the wilderness that is Barbary: 'the maquis is within us, we take our wilderness where we go' (Macaulay 1958 [1950]:155).

It is worth offering some of the flavour of Macaulay's novel by quoting a more extended description of the bombsites from the novel. This is the bombsite ready to welcome Barbary when she returns from Scotland:

> The maze of little streets threading through the wilderness, the broken walls, the great pits with their dense forests of bracken and bramble, golden ragwort and coltsfoot, fennel and foxglove and vetch, all the wild rambling shrubs that spring from ruin, the vaults and cellars and deep caves, the wrecked guildhalls that had belonged to saddlers, merchant tailors, haberdashers, wax-chandlers, barbers, brewers, coopers and coachmakers, all the ancient city fraternities, the broken office stairways that spiralled steeply past empty doorways and rubbled closets into the sky, empty shells of churches with their towers still strangely spiring above the wilderness, their empty window arches where green boughs pushed in, their broken pavement floors – St Vedast's, St Alban's, St Anne's and St Agnes's, St Giles Cripplegate, its tower high above the rest,

the ghosts of churches burnt in an earlier fire, St Olave's and St John Zachary's, haunting the green-flowered churchyards that bore their names, the ghosts of taverns where merchants and clerks had drunk, of restaurants where they had eaten – all this scarred and haunted green and stone and brambled wilderness lying under the August sun, a-hum with insects and astir with secret, darting, burrowing life, received the returned traveller into its dwellings with a wrecked, indifferent calm.

(Macaulay 1958 [1950]: 94–95)

The bombsite becomes a sequence of lists of what has been lost and what has been gained. It is a post-Blitz audit of the bombsite as the concrete embodiment of what Nietzsche referred to (in quite a different context) as the revaluation of all values (*Umwerthung aller Werthe*) (see Nietzsche 1968 [1901]). In the bombsite, what was once seen as timeless and monumental has turned out to be ephemeral and easily destroyed (buildings, businesses, societies, churches, age-old beliefs); what was seen as unimportant and incidental now appears timeless, reliable and eternal (weeds and wildflowers springing up out of rubble). Children's play will also become part of this reversal and will appear newly important in this 'wrecked, indifferent calm'. We should be sensitised to the idea that 'a wrecked, indifferent calm' doesn't refer to a state of relaxation or ease. It should, instead, alert us to the way that the shocked nonchalance of the Blitz experience is now concretised in these spaces where an idea of civilisation as a 'natural' property of certain cultures (of Europe, of Britain, of the West) has been abandoned.

The wrecked space of the bombsites constitutes an emptying out of content. It is a wilderness in a sense that it is empty (what was there has been desolated) and in the way that it has become uncultivated and returned to the forces of nature. One of the rhetorical ploys of the novel is to materialise the equivalence between Barbary and the bombsite. The novel does this partly by treating the bombsite-wilderness as a metaphor (and one with obvious Christian resonances) for her situation: she is out in the wilderness, away from her mother. But a much more material equivalence is fabricated by drawing constant connections between the bombsites and Barbary (and by inference other war-children) in that both have been 'emptied' of moral content (though, importantly, for Barbary and others this is a situation of never having been filled in the first place) and both have been given over to the forces of nature. One of the best contexts for reading this aspect of Macaulay's depiction of bombsites is, I think, to connect it to the various figurations of bombsites that were appearing within sociology, psychology and social work during the war and directly after it, and to set this alongside those working on progressive playground education.

Junk playground and moral landscapes

In the image-seam that I have started to excavate, two elements are clearly at stake: the child and the environment. It might seem unsurprising then that their combination should resonate with debates that were (and still are) at the crux of the modernising project; namely debates about the relative determining power of nature (the child's) and the nurturing environment (or lack of it). Within the context of the particular assemblage of child and bombsite, these debates took on a specific identity around delinquency, aggression and the benefits of certain forms of play.

The transformation of bombsites into playgrounds was one way of addressing the presence of this particular waste-ground in the city. Bombsites weren't just a reminder of recent traumas and unleashed aggression; they were (at least within the image-repertoire) sites of present-day moral as well as physical danger. In Macaulay's novel, the bombsite is the site of the ruined architecture of the church: the bombsite offers us organised religion as an archaeological find. But it is also where spivs and army deserters live. Towards the end of the novel, Barbary is persuaded to undertake a shoplifting spree. When returning with her 'loot' she is stopped by a policeman (who had been asked to keep an eye out for her) and decides to run away. This action provokes the dénouement of the novel: in attempting to escape the police she runs into the bombsite and ends up falling from one of the many half-destroyed buildings. The danger of moral corruption is enacted as physical danger, as one action (shoplifting) leads to another (a life-threatening fall).

The theme of moral corruption is a central component within the bombsite imaginary. In a very different vein, the Ealing film comedy *Hue and Cry* from 1947 is a light-hearted thriller for adolescents and centres its narrative on the warren of London bombsites. These provide a landscape for children's gangs and secret societies, and while 'the Blood and Thunder Boys' (the main gang of children who frequent the bombsites in the film) are in the end a force for good (they foil the criminal gang), it is also clear that the bombsites allow for all sorts of morally ambiguous activities (symbolised by the reading of comics and other 'unsavoury' and corrupting literature).

When in 1946 Lady Allen of Hurtwood – who had been an influential campaigner for children's progressive education during the war and after (Allen and Nicholson 1975) – suggested, in the pages of *Picture Post* (Allen of Hurtwood 1946), that Britain's bombsites could be turned into adventure playgrounds for disadvantaged children, more was at stake than the quick and cheap transformation of bombsites into something useful. Crucially the bombsite needed recoding as a place for moral fortitude rather than a place of festering turpitude and moral degeneracy. Offering the example of a 'junk playground' in Copenhagen (set up as part of a social housing scheme) Lady Allen claimed that the bombsite playground could become a space that could actually stop children from becoming delinquent rather than a specific breeding ground for delinquency:

> Juvenile delinquency and the death of young people in road accidents both arise, in part at least, from the inadequate and unimaginative manner in which local authorities try to meet the need for creative play [...] His [the Borough Engineer's] paradise is a place of utter boredom for the children, and it is

little wonder that they prefer the dumps of rough wood and piles of bricks and rubbish of the bomb sites, or the dangers and excitements of the traffic.
(Allen of Hurtwood 1946: 26; see also Maxwell 1948)

The adventure playground would offer minimal adult supervision (the adventure playground worker was a social worker who was trained never to answer the young people who used the playground in the negative), and would re-aim the seductive 'wild' energies of the bombsite in the direction of cooperative play and project-based creativity (the building of 'houses', 'tinkering' with engines and so on). As Roy Kozlovsky in his very useful review of the adventure playground movement in Britain and its forerunner in Denmark describes it: 'the permissive atmosphere in the playground provided a safe and creative simulation of lawlessness, where children could regain the trust in society through their engagement with a play leader who acted as their advocate and took their side' (2008: 175).

A more radical suggestion for the bombsites had been issued in 1944 by the Austrian social worker and pacifist Marie Paneth who had been working with 'delinquent' children in London's semi-destroyed East End (see Kozlovsky 2008). Paneth embodied the progressive social worker, the one who doesn't tell the children that they aren't allowed to do things. Instead she envisaged a space where they could 'be allowed to make great mistakes there, and be messy and unjust and have trouble with it' (Paneth 1944: 58). Her account of working with 'slum urchins' in a 'condemned street' where more than 100 children lived is given in her book *Branch Street: A Sociological Study* (Paneth 1944: 5, 7). It is an extraordinary book charting the fortunes and failures of her permissive attempts to give the children of Branch Street the space for what today might be called self-actualisation. In the language of Paneth's time, she was according them respect and giving them responsibility. She and her co-workers used one of the derelict houses as a club house where the children were encouraged to paint or engage in other creative occupations. The story Paneth tells is of her unswerving (and sometimes unnerving) belief, not in the children's goodness, but that their violence was masking other possible ways of living. And it is a story of violence: 'Dirty, wet canvas was slung into our faces when we passed them, they spat at us and tried to hurt us and showered gross indecencies at us with wild laughter. There was no stopping them' (Paneth 1944: 12).

Paneth's approach was to refuse the guiding principle that 'delinquent' children needed paternalistic discipline. Her idea was that aggressive children should be allowed to be aggressive, and that in having this permission the aggression would be seen by the children as a form of performance and one that would come to seem unnecessary and overly stagey. For Paneth, the bombsites should be given to the children: they would become the legal and economic landlords of that space. As real custodians they could use them how they liked and could grow food on the sites to earn extra money. Like Lady Allen, Paneth recognised these repurposed bombsites as potential prophylaxes against delinquency and against the political project of Nazism:

> It [the bombsite] is a damaged bit. Its very existence is a reminder of damage and destruction. A sore spot and harmful to all of us. But it could be put to good use even before the war is over. It seems to me it could have a very healing effect if one were allowed to build upon the very spot where damage had been done. Perhaps it would save the community from some of the criminals of the future generation, and would make a few happier people. We should always remember that the horde which Hitler employed to carry out his first acts of aggression – murdering and torturing peaceful citizens – was recruited mainly from desperate Branch Street youths, and that to help the individual means helping Democracy as well.
>
> *(Paneth 1944: 120)*

But, and here is the difficulty, the repurposing of bombsites brings with it no guarantee of efficacy; indeed, the power of the bombsite as a disordering of value was such that its negative force would always be in competition with this healing purpose.[2]

Two years prior to Paneth's sociological study of a street full of troubled and troubling youth, Dorothy Burlingham and Anna Freud, who had been running the Hampstead Nurseries, published their findings on the effects of aerial bombing on children. What was crucial to Burlingham and Freud's study was that a sentimental understanding of the effects of war on children had to be jettisoned:

> General sympathy has been aroused by the idea that little children should thus come into close contact with the horrors of the war. It is this situation which led many people to expect that children would receive traumatic shock from air raids and would develop abnormal reactions very similar to the traumatic or war neurosis of soldiers in the last war […] So far as we can notice there were no signs of traumatic shock to be observed in these children.
>
> *(Burlingham and Freud 1942: 28–29)*

In place of a sentimental assessment of the effects of war on children, Burlingham and Freud find something much more malevolent at work:

> Instead of turning away from them [incidents of wholesale destruction] in instinctive horror, as people seem to expect, the child may turn towards them with primitive excitement. The real danger is not that the child, caught up all innocently in the whirlpool of war, will be shocked into illness. The danger lies in the fact that the destruction raging in the outer world may meet the very real aggressiveness which rages in the inside of the child.
>
> *(Burlingham and Freud 1942: 31)*

War and the bombsites it produces are amplifiers of something essential to early childhood. Here the equivalence between child and bombsite resonates across the shared aggressions and violence that is the core of both. The wild wilderness of the bombsite is also the wild nature of the child. In terms of debates about the determining impact of nature and the environment on children, Burlingham and Freud offer us a child whose natural state is partly violent rage and where the environment offers opportunities for this to be legitimated and socially extended. In developmental terms, war prolongs early childhood into adolescence and beyond:

> Under the present war conditions two factors combine to make children at the nursery stage more aggressive and destructive than they were found to be in normal times. One factor is the loosening of early repression and inhibition of aggression, due to the example of destruction in the outside world. The other is the return to earlier modes of expression for aggressive tendencies. The bigger child then becomes as unrestrained in this respect as he has been in his earliest years. Like a small toddler he will again be loving and affectionate at one moment, enraged, full of hate, and ready to bite and scratch in the next. His destructive tendencies will turn equally towards living people and towards lifeless objects.
>
> *(Burlingham and Freud 1942: 71)*

The potential juvenile delinquent who might be seen to haunt the real-and-imagined waste-ground of post-war redevelopment is partly this perpetual toddler driven by ungovernable violent urges. While Burlingham and Freud are trying to explain the continuity of toddler characteristics in adolescents by recourse to socio-historical circumstances and its effects on some children (their nurseries and care homes looked after children whose parents were undergoing psychological breakdowns), they also impute the idea that these youths are somehow naturally violent. This sense of urban youth as naturally violent (or as violent when found in an urban environment) works across the twentieth century and is particularly powerful in relation to the 'juvenile delinquent' and its cognates – 'hooligans', 'thugs', 'muggers', 'hoodies' and so on (Mass-Observation 2009 [1949]; Hall et al. 1978). Within this image-repertoire, the waste-ground is the natural habitat of the 'slum urchin'.

Placed together, the image of untamed urbanism (waste-grounds, bombsites, street corners) and adolescent youth generates a composite image that unsettles the promise of unfettered progress. You can get a sense of this when you see how infrequently you find such images in the development literature that was produced in anticipation of post-war redevelopment. On the cover of Ralph Tubbs' *Living in Cities* (1942), a book published the same year as Burlingham and Freud's study of young children in wartime, there is a tableau of four images. The first is titled 'long ago' and is an aerial photograph of an ornate church with flying buttresses. The second is titled 'yesterday' and shows industrial chimney stacks and a polluted urban landscape. The third is 'to-day' and shows a bombed-out street with people walking in the road. The final image is 'to-morrow', and has a question mark attached to it: instead of an urban scene we see an architect or planner's hands, a set square and a ruler. Inside, this tetraptych format is repeated. There is a photograph of women and children sheltering in Piccadilly Circus underground tube station; a photograph of a fiercely burning warehouse; an image of smouldering ruins being hosed down; and finally a picture of soldiers clearing the rubble. The legend attached to this final image is: 'what is the future to be?' While it is often usual to represent and imagine the future through the figure of the child, *Living in Cities* is adamant through exclusion: the future of the city will not include children's rights to urban space.

As Anthony Vidler has recently argued, the architectural reconstruction of Britain was built by veiling the anxiety of war and the continued threat of catastrophe (Vidler 2010). By turning their back on the recent historical past and palming off any troubling doubts about the project of endless expansive progress onto troublesome figures like the delinquent, those invested in the future-as-progress could sleep well at night. The scapegoat is the denizen of bombsites as playgrounds (Figure 4.3). Instead of explanation, we have an anxious mood made concrete because (according

FIGURE 4.3 Boy destroying piano, Wales. © Phillip Jones Griffiths 1961.

to this pernicious image-repertoire) urban blight isn't the result of uneven development but of street-corner-kids; it isn't corporate interests and underinvested social amenities that destroy cities but waste-ground ragamuffins. The fate of such sleight-of-hand is to offer legitimation to a new conjuncture that is happy to watch the Welfare State disintegrate on the basis that it is already ruined by the 'natural' hordes of 'benefit-cheats', 'the idle', 'the chav' and any other heir of playground-bombsites that can be conjured by the fetid imagination of the reactionary press.

Ruins and cultural politics

The image of children playing within ruined landscapes has had a compelling hold on the post-war imagination, partly because it brought together a powerful combination of debates and concerns that worried at the core of how society could be conceived, and partly because it could feed a range of fantasies (both wishful and fearful) about the direction in which it was heading. These images could, for instance, hold out the promise of children's resilience in the face of so much adult destruction and symbolise, to the viewer, the new post-war generation who will build on these ruins. But it could also quite easily resonate with the possibilities of future catastrophes including the growing anxiety around nuclear devastation. It is an image that encourages fantasy because it is, in so many respects, an unmade and unfinished image. Once the waste-ground has been built on, we are faced with the necessary banality of reconstruction (in its obvious actuality, in its taken-for-granted-ness). But in its pre-realised state it can point forward to many unmanageable and different possibilities from the utopian to the chronically dystopian.

While images of ruins, of course, are not limited to the immediate post-war years and aren't limited to Britain, post-war Britain seems to have given rise to a literature of the ruin (Edensor 2005; Farley and Roberts 2011; Hatherley 2011; Wright 2009 [1991]; and with a different purview Woodward 2002). The longer history of ruination and modernisation would have to include two of the most often quoted passages of leftist cultural and political analysis. Karl Marx and Frederick Engels in a famous passage from the 1872 *Manifesto of the Communist Party* claimed that 'uninterrupted disturbance of all social conditions, everlasting uncertainty and agitation distinguish the bourgeois epoch from all earlier ones' and result in a condition where 'all that is solid melts into air' (Marx and Engels 1968 [1872]: 38). Marx and Engels, of course, had little way of anticipating the aerial bombardments that have since become central to modern warfare, but there is hardly a more literalising example of turning solidity into air. In a similar vein, in 1941 Walter Benjamin characterised modern progress (for progress read 'capitalist modernising') as a destructive force that will be recognised by the angel of history: 'Where a chain of events appears before *us, he* sees one single catastrophe, which keeps piling wreckage upon wreckage and hurls it at his feet' (Benjamin 2003: 392, emphasis in original).

These are powerful images to throw in the face (and at the feet) of modernisation understood as beneficial progression, even if they have lost some of their bite through constant reuse. The endless catastrophe that Benjamin writes of at the end of his life was being simultaneously actualised as the waking nightmare of National Socialism, which through Benjamin's melancholic gaze seems less like errant behaviour and more like the logical culmination of a long history of barbarism. As Marx and Engels were writing their manifesto they (and Engels had insider knowledge on this) were witnessing the despoiling of nature in the guise of the total mobilisation of industrial production. Between the *Communist Manifesto* and Benjamin's final texts, the catastrophic reality of aerial bombardment, which had for a long time been imagined, had finally been demonstrated (Lindqvist 2012 [2001]; Mackay 2002; Sloterdijk 2009). In Benjamin's 'On the Concept of History' – in which he envisages the angel of history watching the wreckage gather at his feet – he obscures something of the political lesson that could be drawn from such a conceptualisation. One of the thoughts that didn't make it into the final published version of 'On the Concept of History' went as follows: 'Marx says that revolutions are the locomotive of world history. But perhaps it is quite otherwise. Perhaps revolutions are an attempt by the passengers on this train – namely, the human race – to activate the emergency break' (Benjamin 2003: 402).

The image of dereliction and children accompanied a post-war building programme that sought to encase the ethos of optimism and progress in glass, steel, brick and concrete. In Virno's terms, the emotional situation surrounding reconstruction and the image of children on bombsites is the vacillating of optimism and pessimism, and of resignation and refusal. It is a mood-world whereby optimism is constantly struggling with its opposite. The picture of bombsites is the antidote to a dream of unfettered post-war redevelopment whether in its welfare guise or as corporate culture: it doesn't invalidate it, nor critique it, but it tugs at its hubris and provides a mood-world that refigures social optimism as a gleeful hurrying towards a future that might inevitably end in entropic disaster. It is hardly surprising, then, that in Macaulay's novel, Barbary's mother echoes almost word for word the thoughts of the cyberneticist Norbert Weiner when she says: 'we shall all go down and down into catastrophe and the abyss. We must snatch what good we can on the way' (Macaulay 1958 [1950]: 70).[3]

Violence and aggression may well be part of nature: our most cherished institutions of civilisation might crumble into dust and be replaced by a rapacious crop of buddleia. How do we envisage the future when this might be our continual present? The desire to shape a generation of children so that they could 'make something of themselves' might well be a desire that is built, if not on sand, then on a blasted earth, built in the feeling-space of waste-ground. In Wiener and Macaulay's words, the incentive to practise is not to imagine a future that is in some sense perfection realised, but to gather moments of dignity and goodness from the messy business of catastrophic history. A cultural politics might be glimpsed here, one that isn't searching out new ways of re-enchanting itself but one that in the name of pragmatism is prepared to pursue a melancholic quest without the guarantee of the promise of a utopian future (Clark 2012). The bombsite offers us an image of children looking back at us, questioning us about our desire to mould them for the future. Perhaps if we are to be true to the history that the bombsite invokes, we need to return this gaze with something a little closer to productive and purposeful (but not indulgent) melancholy: something like Paneth's unsentimental hope in the face of relentless aggression.

Coda: landscapes of obliterated pasts

The image of large swathes of derelict landscape had a life beyond images of impoverished and improvised children's playgrounds. In the mid-1970s the comedy writers Dick Clement and Ian La Frenais revisited their comedy series from the mid-1960s *The Likely Lads* (BBC 1964–1966). The original series was based around two young factory workers (both worked in a small electronics factory) and was based in the north-east of England (in and around Newcastle). Both lads had been to school together and while they were both leading working-class lives, one – Bob (played by Rodney Bewes) – had aspirations to join the expanding middle classes, while the other – Terry (played by James Bolam) – is happy for his life to continue as it is. Both are grown-up children. By the end of the original series, Bob had decided to join the army but had been rejected (due to having flat feet) while Terry, who never wanted to join up, has successfully managed to have an army life on the basis that he wanted to show solidarity with his friend.

The new series *Whatever Happened to the Likely Lads?* (BBC 1973–1974) catches up with the two friends nearly ten years later. By this time the aspirational Bob has managed to achieve an approximation of a middle-class life: he has bought an 'executive home', he has his own office and he is engaged to be married to the more solidly middle-class Thelma (played by Brigit Forsyth). Terry has just left the army to return to the north-east. The comedy plays on the different expectations that the two men now have, against the backdrop of their shared past (in this respect Thelma is the foil in the show, vigilantly having to stop Bob constantly sliding back down the social ladder to his working-class roots). The new series established the differences between Bob and Terry in its title sequence: Bob's montaged sequence shows a modernised Newcastle of tower blocks, private cars, executive homes and modernist civic architecture; Terry by contrast is shown waiting for a bus while reading a newspaper, and his sequence includes terraced housing (some of which is in ruins) and dockyards.

In the fourth episode of the new series, Bob takes Terry out for a Sunday morning drink at the pub. They have some time to kill before the pub opens so they go on a tour of their old haunts. Bob warns Terry that things have changed significantly. They drive past streets and streets of back-to-back terraced housing and Bob informs Terry that it will all be pulled down in the next year or two. He takes Terry up to the top of what looks like a new shopping complex and multi-storey carpark. He asks Terry if he knows where he is; Terry isn't entirely sure. They are, Bob informs Terry, on the site of Newcastle's premier music venue, the Go Go (the nightclub has been razed to make way for the new, or in Terry's words – 'the Go Go, gone?'). A world of music, shared memories and nights out has been buried under a future made out of what seems like a concrete sarcophagus of modernist design.

FIGURE 4.4 What is left of 'Saturday morning pictures' from *Whatever Happened to the Likely Lads?*, Series 1, Episode 4 'Moving On'.

From the town centre to the pub they pass by derelict houses ('this was Saville Street') and desolate landscape of waste-ground ('that was the market'). 'Saturday morning pictures' (Figure 4.4) is nothing more than a ruined skeleton. The old fish and chip shop that they used to go to is still left, but as a solitary building (it was obviously part of a terraced row) in a desert of rubble.

What Bob is showing Terry is the future as it is being built. What Terry sees is the past being destroyed. Neither the past nor the future have won out. The new hasn't quite been born, and the old hasn't quite been obliterated. The waste-ground is the interregnum – the transition between one social orchestration and another, between a future cast as a technological democracy where everyone 'can' achieve social mobility (though proportionally few actually do achieve this) and a past, for an industrial working class and its vibrant culture of neighbourhoods, public houses and revelry. The waste-ground is neither one thing nor the other: as a space it holds time in abeyance. It is a site ripe for projecting fears and hopes on to, for casting dreams and burying memories: it holds the foundations of a future that might be better or might be worse, but one that will grow out of a past that it cannot help but obliterate. As a place of cultural feeling, it often lives on the edges of representation. But as a mood-space that shows us a present where the future is always an interregnum that is unstable, often fatally flawed, it is a central cultural feeling of our modernity.

Notes

1 For an overview of the world of Nuclear Fear as a realm of living representation see Weart (2012). The effect of nuclear war was given one of its most affecting accounts in John Hersey's widely available *Hiroshima* (1946). Nuclear anxiety was a sustained anxiety across the post-war decades, saturating some lives, rising and falling in relation to political circumstances, and a focus of protest (see, for instance, Thompson and Smith 1980). The link to wartime Blitz was maintained by information leaflets with instructions for protection against nuclear attack that looked almost identical to those that were circulated during the Second World War (see Civil Defence Handbook 1963).
2 Paneth's book records a number of successes but is also honest about the dangers of its own approach: a number of times the communal club house is totally ransacked and everything in it destroyed.
3 The cyberneticist Norbert Weiner wrote in a book first published the same year as *The World My Wilderness*: 'In a very real sense we are shipwrecked passengers on a doomed planet. Yet even in a shipwreck, human decencies and human values do not necessarily vanish, and we must make the most of them. We shall go down, but let it be in a manner to which we may look forward as worthy of our dignity' (Wiener 1954 [1950]: 40). This is a feeling formation that exists across very different articulations, here literature and mathematics.

5

CITY OF STRANGERS

(Qualities of disappointment)

> And then you become settled and then you too become part of the strangeness.
> *(George Lamming in the film* The Nine Muses*)*

A few months before he died, my neighbour George invited me inside his house for some beer. His wife had died the previous year and the house was fairly gloomy. But this had less to do with his grieving, and more to do with George's fading eyesight. He wasn't sad; he was a Jehovah's Witness. We had chatted in the past and I had occasionally helped him with his shopping. A couple of years before, when he had heard that I was ill in bed with a throat infection, he had knocked on my door with some medicine. It was amazingly effective. His was an easy-going evangelism, which communicated his belief through thought, word and deed. But when he asked me in for a drink he had other things on his mind besides God. It must have been the late 1990s and he wanted to tell me about his coming to Britain in the early 1950s. He recognised, quite rightly, that the details of that migration might have been less than clear in the mind of his white neighbour.

In the early 1950s, George was doing fairly well: he was married and was working as the head barman in a fairly wealthy golf club on the outskirts of Kingston, Jamaica. He had skills and he had a social position. Jamaica at that time was still part of the British Empire (it achieved independence in 1962) and to be Jamaican in the 1950s was to have the same rights as any other British citizen. George's schooling had been thoroughly British: like anyone else growing up in what was then called the West Indies, George was taught English history, English literature and an imperialist version of geography, and consequently he knew England from the inside. Like most other West Indians, he *felt* British: he had to come to England to feel Jamaican, and to feel West Indian.[1]

George and his wife were persuaded that life in Britain would afford them better opportunities, better prospects, than life in Jamaica. Perhaps they would come to England and work for five or ten years and then return to Jamaica. As was often the practice with this wave of migration, George would come to England first and once he was settled and making money his wife would come and join him. When he had saved up the considerable amount of money for the one-way fare, he came to Bristol, in the south-west of England. He came without savings (he had invested his money on the fare) and the labour exchange made him take the first job that was offered to him. In George's case this meant working at the Clift House Tannery on Coronation Road, where animal carcasses were skinned and processed for shoe leather, and where the smell on a summer's day can still make you retch.

Indignities characterised George's migration to Britain, but on that evening of reminiscences what seemed to sting George the most was the feeling of never actually arriving at the metropolitan and imperial 'centre' of the land he had set sail for. From the docks to Waterloo, across London to Paddington and out to Bristol Temple Meads railway station in Bristol, George saw nothing of that Imperial City that he had read about in school: no Houses of Parliament, no Tower Bridge or Buckingham Palace, no Mall or Regent Street, or Piccadilly. What he saw was just endless rows of the backs of terraced houses and their measly yards: insistent and repetitious. The promise of the imperial 'motherland', of the symbolic architecture of Empire, was offered but not shown to George. By the time he visited those sites they had become tourist emblems, façades hiding a new reality that he knew all too intimately. They had lost the ability they once had to symbolise for him a civilising centre for the modern world.

George's story provides, in snapshot form, a familiar narrative arc that can be seen in countless tales of migration, especially from former colonies to imperial, metropolitan 'centres'. His story echoes with thousands of others. As a mood, it signals a disappointment on a grand scale. But its constellation of feelings is larger than that signalled by 'disappointment' alone. Disappointment marks a point on a narrative arc, a movement from one state to another (from hope to disenchantment). As a cultural feeling, then, it points to an instant of a larger process. George's story articulates a changing situation, a narrative arc, one that is indelibly marked by disappointment but includes other moods and feelings as well. To look at post-war black migration and settlement in England as a pattern of cultural feelings is to ask what shape this pattern takes: What are its contours?[2] Where does it begin and end? What is its geography? What is its duration? It seems to signal an anti-climax, a form of bathos. In Julian Temple's film about London's recent past, called tellingly *London: The Modern Babylon* (BFI 2012), this bathos is telegraphed in a synoptic form by juxtaposing newsreel of the Trinidadian calypso singer Lord Kitchener (Aldwyn Roberts) singing 'London is the Place for Me' and the Jamaican-born dub poet Linton Kwesi Johnson's reggae poem 'Inglan is a Bitch' (written phonetically to express the vocal inflections of Caribbean English). Lord Kitchener's song has the refrain:

> London is the place for me, London that lovely city.
> You can go to France or America, India, Asia, or Australia.
> But you must come back to London city.[3]

It is a joyous, upbeat song of the anticipation of arrival.[4] Linton Kwesi Johnson's poem, on the other hand, speaks of a disenchanted reality. It is a song-poem charting menial jobs, working the least desirable shifts and having your wages taxed by a society that promises much but delivers nothing but insults and indignities. And while it is playing we see newsreel images of black men and women washing dishes and sweeping roads.

But this truncated story of disappointment needs to unfold beyond this moment of disenchantment: it needs to reach back to a time before 'arrival' and it needs to reach forward to the making of a settlement that may be founded on and endlessly marked by disappointment, but also turns that disappointment into something else, something substantial, something sustainable. If disappointment stains this pattern of feeling, its mood is modulated by other feelings too. This is a constellation of feeling animated by the force of 'despite': pride *despite* indignities; exuberance *despite* racism; creation *despite* disappointment. You can see it there in the newsreels, in some of the documentary photographs – a human excess that can't be contained by the desire of a newspaper or a newsreel to mark a group of people as a political or social issue. Carol Tulloch calls it a 'haunted joy' (2016: 171–198); Stuart Hall saw this irrepressibility in the street style and popular culture of a 'black British culture [...] confident beyond measure in its own identity' (Hall 1997: 39). In his 'Minimal Selves' essay from 1987, Hall could mark the distance between his migration from Jamaica in 1951 (or George's at about the same time) and a cultural scene in the late 1980s of music, film and street culture animated by the charismatic presence of people like Jazzy B, Caron Wheeler and Roland Gift, but also there in the everyday life of black Londoners:

> I've been puzzled by the fact that young black people in London today are marginalized, fragmented, unenfranchized, disadvantaged and dispersed. And yet, they look as if they own the territory. Somehow, they too, in spite of everything, are centred, in place: without much material support, it's true, but nevertheless, they occupy a new kind of space at the centre.
>
> *(Hall 1987: 44)*[5]

Is Hall noticing a change in the patterns of feeling from one formative moment (1950s) to another (1980s), from a period of migrant settling to a state of being settled? If we understand cultural feelings as processual then we might also want to see this as part of a narrative arc, as part of a pattern of feeling that is in process, that is constantly becoming, and is constitutionally unfinished. This would be to see the *longue durée* of cultural feelings, and the way that certain patterns of feelings and their attendant moods can stretch across an epoch. Cultural feelings, then, might be particular to specific historical moments, and we should be sensitive to their shifts and changes, but we also need to be able to trace much larger and longer patterns of feelings that stretch across decades and across generations. These are patterns of feelings that come into focus when they are recognised as epic, and when their durations and durability are charted.

The mother country

Where does the arc of this pattern of feeling of black British migration and settlement start? We need to start not at *the* beginning (where could that possibly be?) but just with *a* beginning: in this instance let's start with the school life of George, of Stuart Hall, of Beryl Gilroy and a host of other British subjects who were, in the 1930s and 1940s, being taught about England and Empire in schools in Guyana (which was then British Guiana), Jamaica, Trinidad, Barbados and dozens of other places, where, as Beryl Gilroy puts it, generations of Afro-Caribbeans were 'brought up as we were under a faraway flutter of the Union Jack' (Gilroy 1994 [1976]: 34). They sang 'I vow to thee my country' on Empire Day (where the country being vowed to was England) and 'at the time we West Indians did think of ourselves as English' (Gilroy 1994 [1976]: 34).

For most West Indians[6] in the 1930s and 1940s, schooling taught them all about Britain and its purported values, and precious little about the actual countries that they were living in. For Stuart Hall in Jamaica:

> We took English high school exams, the normal Cambridge School Certificate and A-level examinations [...] The curriculum was not yet indigenized. Only in my last two years did I learn anything about Caribbean history and geography. It was a very 'classical' education; very good, but in very formal academic terms. I learned Latin, English history, English colonial history, European history, English literature, etc.
>
> *(Hall and Chen 1996: 486)*

Hall was politically, as well as academically, precocious and as a school student was already identifying with anti-imperialism and with the Jamaican independence movement. For many others, however, imperialism and its material basis in schooling effectively negated other forms of post-imperialist national identity and imagination.

In their wonderful book *Windrush: The Irresistible Rise of Multi-Racial Britain*, Mike and Trevor Phillips have collected oral testimonies from a generation of West Indians who came to Britain in the late 1940s and after. Some of them had already been in Britain during the Second World War, fighting as Allied troops, precisely because Britain's war was their war too, because they were British emotionally and legally. Ros Hoswell, who came to Britain from Grenada in 1951 remembers:

> We didn't see there was any difference between Grenada and England. 'There'll always be an England and England shall be free' used to be one of our school songs. Empire day was a big day in Grenada. So it was all part and parcel of what we were about, being part of England. So when England went to war, we were at war. There was no 'if' about that.
>
> *(Hoswell, in Phillips and Phillips 1999: 13)*

For some of this generation (as was clear with George) it was the experience of coming to England that was the determining context for identifying as Caribbean say, or as Trinidadian, and collectively as West Indian. In the 1940s and 1950s, for most West Indians with British passports that declared that they were a 'Citizen of the United Kingdom and Colonies', going to England was going to the 'mother country'.

The pattern of feeling that was foundational for the disappointment that would greet a generation of West Indians in Britain was built out of both abstract concepts (for instance, that London was the home of civilised democracies) and out of a cavalcade of small details that become most clearly visible as they are systematically refuted by experience. For instance, this is Norma Sobers arriving from Barbados in 1962:

> I was met at Gatwick Airport by my cousin, and I was quite amazed. I kept looking out for the nice houses and pretty gardens which I thought England would be full of, but all I could see as we travelled was the back of houses and little chimneys on top. I wondered if they were a whole lot of little factories, because in Barbados, the only time you saw a chimney poking up into the sky was on top of a factory which was grinding sugar cane, you know, or engineering work.
>
> *(Sobers and Sobers 1998: 122)*

One of the insistent references for disappointment is aimed at the social and material reality of England. What had been anticipated was an England that had been produced for history books and could be seen in literary renderings, and from the self-publicity that an imperial centre had foisted on its colonial subjects. What had not been anticipated was widespread poverty, the reality of industrial society (an immiserated working class), poor and crowded housing, ignorance, hunger and so on.

The reality that struck them was not at first the deep racism that they would also experience (though that was soon to follow) but the sordid reality of an imperialism based not on lofty ideals but on the sordid actuality of capitalism. Dudley Thompson, who came to Britain from Jamaica in 1940 when he joined the RAF (he returned later in 1947 as a Rhodes Scholar at Oxford), came with an understanding of the world forged from imperialist education, where the highest value is concretised in the residence of the British monarch:

> after Buckingham Palace comes Heaven, that's the order of things, you see what I mean. So, when you leave [Jamaica], you leave with that sort of setting in your mind. And you're used to seeing the white man boss. When you go to England, you find that it is not like that. You get a sudden immediate shake-up when you find an Englishman that can't read and write, you know, it shakes you. And you go and you find a coal heaver, you know, at the place, working, and you don't expect to find that. So you get a psychological change, a change over, that this is the real world.
>
> *(Dudley Thompson, in Phillips and Phillips 1999: 45)*

For Thompson, such a realisation was a psychological event, an event in consciousness that unsettles an entire worldview without replacing it with something else. Thompson's psychical shock in seeing white men labouring is echoed time and again in both oral testimonies and in the various literatures that tell the story of this migration. For the writer George Lamming, this shock was due to the prevalence of a particular image of England that could block out the known reality of class division within white society. In his book *The Pleasure of Exile* (2005 [1960]) he recounts meeting a fellow Trinidadian arriving in England:

> 'But... but,' he said, 'look down there.'
> I looked, and since I had lived six years in England, I failed to see anything of particular significance. I asked him what he had seen; and then I realised what was happening.
> '*They* do that kind of work, *too*?' he asked.
> He meant the white hands and faces on the tug. In spite of films, in spite of reading Dickens – for he would have had to at the school which trained him for the Civil Service – in spite of all this information, this man had never really felt, as a possibility and a fact, the existence of the English worker. This sudden bewilderment had sprung from his *idea* of England; and one element in that *idea* was that he was not used to seeing an Englishman working with his hands in the streets of Port-of-Spain.
> *(Lamming 2005 [1960]: 25–26, emphasis in original)*

But if there was a general shock in seeing white male proletarians, this was just the start of a shock wave that would reverberate further when it was realised that many white women worked in menial positions, and that white porters and attendants would address a black man as 'sir'.

The event of colonial disenchantment that migration time and again reveals is caught up in a hundred little details. This is Jessica Huntley who came to Britain from Guyana in 1958 (and clearly identified with the Guyanese independence struggle):

> So many little things horrified me when I first came here. I couldn't understand how all the houses in a street could almost be the same. There didn't seem to be any individuality [...] And then, what surprised me most of all was the child care, because at home, when we were fighting for self government and independence, we talked about Britain, we said, you know, children are taken care of, provisions are there. And then, of course, you had to take your child to a childminder, surprised me a lot, you know. And, of course, the cold, you didn't realise how intense that cold is, and I knew that there were a couple of people who came with me who went back the first Christmas. We just couldn't take it. And the unfriendliness of the people, that surprised me, 'cos it's like a shock wave you know. I couldn't believe the lack of humanity.
> *(Jessica Huntley, in Phillips and Phillips 1999: 127)*

The shock waves experienced by this migration was the test of social and material reality: poor housing without heating, class inequality, viciously cold winters, unrelenting racism (called 'colour prejudice' at the time), general unfriendliness and a systematic lack of any knowledge among white Englanders of the Caribbean and its material, political and social relations with England.

While forms of racism were constitutive of modern British culture in general, and specifically enacted in many aspects of the colonial project, the post-war Caribbean migration offered a particular target for organised racist groups as well as a more ubiquitous and 'permissible' racism (the first legal act outlawing racial discrimination was only introduced in 1965). Beryl Gilroy remembers the 1950s as a time of 'false accusations by the police, beatings up of innocent people, Black men being offered drinks of urine disguised as beer, and expulsions from clubs and public places were day to day occurrences' (Gilroy 1998: 9). Alongside this was a hostility that took the form of open discrimination regarding housing (for instance, signs saying 'Rooms to Let: No Coloureds'; see Gilroy 2007: 79) and a job market that was openly racist.[7]

One early response to this situation came from academics, often with training in anthropology or sociology, who helped establish the emergent field of 'race relations' and the social policy work that accompanied it. This was a diverse field of positions, including a loose anti-racist leftism (supported by the Fabians, for instance) and state-led initiatives offering booklets for migrants on what to expect in Britain and how to adjust to the new situation (on the discourse of race relations see Waters 1997). A pamphlet published by the Caribbean arm of the BBC, for instance, warned West Indians who were contemplating coming to Britain that the largest 'problem will be getting on with your white neighbours'. Such booklets were designed to be off-putting and painted a grim but quite realistic picture of Britain at the end of the 1950s. As an example of the prejudice that they would face, the pamphlet offered the following evidence from a white employer:

> I was amazed, never having lived with West Indians, that all those we have employed have been honest. One always understood that these uneducated peoples would see something and they would like it and they would take it. This is probably a very ignorant outlook.
> *(from* Going to Britain?, *cited in Glass 1960: 101)*[8]

In her study of West Indians in London at the end of the 1950s, the urban sociologist Ruth Glass (who cited the pamphlet above as part of her analysis) recorded the epistemic shock of the West Indian 'newcomer' in the following way:

> They had thought of Britain as a prosperous, fairly homogenous, middle class society, in terms of their own glimpses of such a society and of textbook instruction […] They can hardly believe their eyes at first when they watch women sweeping the platforms at tube stations or London charladies cleaning the corridors of office buildings. They are surprised to find that so few of

> their neighbours go to church or belong to a religious organisation. They are amazed when English people show their ignorance of the Commonwealth, in general, and of the West Indies, in particular. They are upset not only because they discover that they themselves are ill-informed about Britain, but also because the British know even less about them.
>
> *(Glass 1960: 98–99)*

Such epistemic shock is a vibration that echoes across the decades of this migration; it is the bass line of the songs of disappointment.

One of the most affecting accounts of the racism that this group experienced in the 1950s and 1960s is provided by Beryl Gilroy in her autobiographical account of her teaching life in Britain (she became the first black British head teacher in an English school in 1968). She came to England to continue her studies in primary school teaching, and what interested her were the more progressive pedagogic philosophies that were being developed at the time. Her story tells of numerous frustrations of being overlooked for employment due to the colour of her skin, of having to work in a number of other jobs before someone employed her as a teacher. There is a constant, 'casual' racism that saturates nearly every moment of the book, but what is so shocking is the racial attitudes of the small children that she eventually ends up teaching. Her first teaching job is in 1953 at a Catholic primary school run by nuns. This is Gilroy's account of her first day of teaching:

> But Sister Consuelo, grossly over-worked, had neglected to do one important thing. She hadn't told the class that their new teacher was black.
>
> So when I opened the squeaking door and class came face-to-face with me, there was a gasp of terror, then a sudden silence. A little girl broke into a whimper. Some children visibly shook with fear, and, as I walked across the room, the whole lot – except for two boys – dived under the tables.
>
> *(Gilroy 1994 [1976]: 47)*

While later in the book it will become clear that parents are feeding the children specific racist opinions aimed directly at Gilroy, here in this initial meeting the children (who are between six and eight years old) are reacting to her with the imaginative resources that were available to them. The deep and ambient racism of the children is made up of folk tales of 'black devils' that peppered popular songs, children's stories, advertising and a whole cultural industry based on a fantasy of 'darkest Africa'.[9]

In a reversal of the anticipated colonial situation, Gilroy becomes the 'civilising' mission as she provides a rationalism for debunking atavistic beliefs in folk devils and deeply rooted superstitions (in the children and later the parents). What *Black Teacher* articulates is a racial cosmology that seems to saturate the entire social setting and was ingrained in a plethora of metaphorical articulations of the term 'black'. 'Did I conjure up black deeds,' she asks herself, 'black ingratitude, black-legs or black-hearted villains who ran the Black Market? These thoughts haunted me. How I hated that word "black" and the emotions, concepts and associations it aroused!' (Gilroy 1994 [1976]: 49–50). Later in the book she starts working in multiracial schools and witnesses the way this cosmology of values is internalised by some of the children to the point where they hate the colour of their own skin. And just as the word 'black' is freighted with negative values, so the word 'white' is given almost magical properties of goodness. In one scene, Gilroy is breastfeeding her baby in a local Welfare Clinic while a gawking white mother is commenting on the darkness of her nipple and rhetorically asking the other mothers if they think this is good for the baby. At this point the health visitor intervenes:

> 'You can see that he gets everything that's good for him. Look at his nappies – sparkling white.'
> That did mean something to them. 'Yeh, whiter than white,' the woman whispered hoarsely.
> It was almost a religious concept – whiter than white.
> 'Yeh,' they all breathed devoutly – a sort of suburban Greek chorus – 'whiter than white!'
> *(Gilroy 1994 [1976]: 112–113)*

Where does racism find its resources? The answer is everywhere: in sayings, in stories, in films, in news, in advertising, in songs, in history. We could think of this as an extensive archive made up of official and unofficial materials. At times this is a virtual archive of undocumented (and undocumentable) attitudes, views and opinions; at other times this is a material archive found in libraries, in geography textbooks, in photography collections and so on. It is an unfinished archive, always in progress. By the time Beryl Gilroy was teaching, or George was working at the tannery, that unfinished archive had been added to, often on a daily basis, with news reports of West Indian migration, of photographs of men and women arriving, working and looking for accommodation. Arriving on the *Empire Windrush* in 1948, a group of West Indians, mainly from Jamaica, docked at the port of Tilbury in Essex and entered an archival situation. These archives, in their diversity, are the material supports for the patterns of feeling that I'm looking at in this chapter: how they operate and what we do with them is a crucial aspect of the politics of cultural feelings.

Reconstruction and reclamation

Take, for example, Figure 5.1: a group of men from Jamaica who have saved up the enormous fare for the voyage to find work and lodgings in England. They have clearly been posed for a news item. Several versions of the photograph exist, with very slight adjustments. It was quite obviously a photo opportunity, a solution to the question of how to convey this story of migration. Here the answer is to show half a dozen or so men all sharing one newspaper, supposedly all searching for a job, for a room to let. They are wearing smart clothes. The man on the far right must be having a hard time trying to read the newspaper from there; the man with the beret

FIGURE 5.1 Jamaicans on board the *Empire Windrush*, unattributed photograph in *The Sphere*, 3 July 1948. © Illustrated London News Ltd/Mary Evans.

on the left has stopped following the photographer's instructions and is no longer looking at the paper. Although the photograph was produced with the intention of immediate circulation and fairly immediate obsolescence (the cycle of print news being orchestrated by the idea that there is nothing staler than 'yesterday's papers'), the photograph bears witness to an event. But what sort of an event is it?

In Stuart Hall's important essay 'Reconstruction Work: Images of Postwar Black Settlement', first published in 1984, he is particularly interested in photographs like this for writing the history of black settlement in Britain. 'The past,' he writes 'cannot speak, except through its "archive"' (Hall 1992 [1984]: 106). And its archive will include photographs, newsreels, films and songs, as well as oral history, diaries and other sources. He warns that future historians of black British settlement will need to tread carefully to salvage something of the lives of this generation from the discursive 'fix' that has been placed around them. What does the picture want us to believe? That here are men 'just off the boat' (with all the connotations that that phrase can generate) heading out to an unknown land to secure jobs and somewhere to live? (A good proportion of the men, and it was nearly all men, were returning to England, where they had served during the war, and some were re-joining the military.) Despite the good clothes, does the image want us to see desperation, lack of means, determination, perseverance?

Images do not circulate alone and one way of reading images like the one above is to recognise them as produced for a particular task and belonging to a particular archival force. As Paul Gilroy reminds us in his orchestration of the archival resources of the massive Getty Images Archive, which also holds the Hulton Archive, one of the largest collections of photojournalism including the images created for the British weekly magazine *Picture Post* (a magazine that we have met in previous chapters):

> The pressures that shaped it [the photographic archive] do not correspond to the untidy task of documenting the life of a community in the making. Instead, the archive reproduces the narrower image-world of the popular publications where most of these pictures were first published – not as illustrations but as powerful visual components in larger, urgent arguments about nationality, community, morality, justice, poverty and inclusivity as well as changing patterns of government at home and abroad. Public understanding of the country's racial problems was actually created and transmitted by those pages.
> *(Gilroy 2007: 11–14)*

In other words, this photograph, like other news photographs, had an interest in creating an issue, a news item, a cause for concern. It is an initial move in producing an image-repertoire (which builds on previous image-repertoires) of the black British male as a 'social issue'. These aren't images 'innocently' (and I will come back to this word) registering a group of travelling citizens; these are images engaged in arguments, in debates about race and immigration.

Photojournalist images, like the one above, circulate with written accounts of the event of this ship's arrival. This is how the *Daily Express* reported the docking of the *Empire Windrush*:

> Four hundred and fifty Jamaicans crowded the rails of the *Empire Windrush* as she anchored in the Thames last night. They sailed as refugees from their island's unemployment problem, and have provided a new problem for the Colonial Office and the Ministry of Labour here. Loudspeakers called the 450 work-seekers to a pep talk by Mr Ivor Cummings, a principal officer of the Colonial Office, who welcomed them. They were told: Things will not be easy.
> *(cited in Phillips and Phillips 1999: 81)*

The choice of words matters. The word 'problem' occurs twice, situating these men as an issue, a problem that needs to be 'solved'. 'They' have to be told. Of course the field of journalism is varied and not all newspapers echoed with the irritated paternalism of the *Daily Express*. The *Daily Mirror*, a Labour newspaper, saw the arrival of the ship as a challenge to the imperial sentiments that Britain was, at the time, promoting:

> Is there any meaning in the bond of Empire or is it empty talk? Unwittingly the 450 Jamaicans who inconveniently arrived in the Thames put this matter

to the test. Their assumption that if only they could get to wonderful England all their troubles would vanish may be naïve, but their faith is once a compliment and an obligation. They are entitled to help and sympathy. After all they have only taken our Imperial sentiments seriously.

(Editorial, Daily Mirror, 23 June 1948: 2)

Even here, in what is a left-liberal position in relation to post-war West Indian immigration, the terms by which 'sympathy' is given rids the Jamaicans of agency (they are unwitting), and sees them as naïve in their aspirations. It is only the word 'compliment' that disturbs and challenges an account that renders these voyagers as the pawns of historical forces outside of their jurisdiction. The event that the photograph records, then, isn't the arrival of the *Empire Windrush*. Rather it records the arrival of the ship as it is greeted by a social realm that has already been prepared to treat this group of men as both victims and problems.[10] The 'event' then is *both* the ship docking and the men disembarking, *and* the photographer arranging the group shot and the journalists writing their copy. An archival force has already set out the affective economy, a pattern of feelings, for picturing the lives of West Indians (and others) in their arrival and as they settle in Britain.

Stuart Hall's essay on black British settlement and the photographic archive pivots on the word 'innocence'. As we can see, 'innocence' (as naivety, for instance) plagues the pattern of feeling through which post-war Commonwealth migration has been represented: it moves from the direct racist connotation represented by the racist colloquialism 'fresh off the boat' (meaning ignorant of cultural conventions), to its more liberal sense of the 'innocent victims' of other forces. The book *Windrush*, in contrast, works hard to refute one of the dominant liberal understandings of this migration, namely that the British government actively recruited West Indians to feed the industrial expansion of the post-war years.[11] In other words, the book works to refute a narrative that would paint a group of people as lacking agency and through naivety having been 'tricked' into emigrating. For Hall the first way to inoculate yourself against this perception of innocence is to remember that:

> they have torn themselves up by their roots, saved up what for them (considering the annual average wage), is a colossal sum, paid it over to a steamship company travelling incognito under some assumed Panamanian flag. Half the family is left behind and nobody knows when or whether they will ever be united again. These men and women have just burnt their boats in the determination to carve out a better life.
>
> *(Hall 1992 [1984]: 107)*

But if it is always necessary to refuse the association of innocence in its racist figuration, Hall also wants to recognise another kind of innocence that he hopes to recover from the photographic archive, but without seeing photography itself as somehow innocent.

In an illustrated article in *Picture Post* from June 1956, the journalist Hilde Marchant and the photographer Haywood Magee reported on West Indian migration. The article is titled 'Thirty Thousand Colour Problems', with a strap line that reads 'West Indian immigrants are now arriving in Britain at the rate of 3,000 a month. This year 30,000 are expected. All seek work and homes. Both are becoming difficult to find. Trouble and distress are brewing' (Marchant 1956: 38). The article deploys some of the familiar tropes of this dominant pattern of feeling (most specifically by figuring West Indians in the title as each a problem, but also by describing them as 'bewildered'), but it also delivers another affect-laden set of terms that direct this pattern of feeling towards the opposite of innocence: guilt. For the article, West Indians are innocent and guilty. Most are innocent (bewildered) and some are guilty. These are the black men with nice cars (which in this pattern of feeling is immediately equated with crime) who the writer sees (or imagines) as being involved in prostitution. This is the other side of the 'problem': 'cars owned by immigrants who have only been in this country a year or two, and which invariably pick up the most attractive young girls' (Marchant 1956: 38). Black men, as guilty problems, are positioned as potential criminals, and more specifically as sexually predatory, who might entrap 'the young and pretty', 'coloured or white' into prostitution. Such 'guilt' didn't require criminal activity, it was a feature of being a young black man who could, potentially, couple up with white women and have babies.[12] Time and again the most explosive moments of racist violence against West Indians in the decades following the war are aimed at 'coloured people living with white girlfriends' (*Daily Mirror*, 1 September 1958: 1).

But Hall finds another kind of 'innocence' in the photographic archive, and it is this 'innocence' that is not ignorance which can reveal another pattern of feeling to the dominant emotional economy around innocence-guilt. Another set of feelings

> registers inside the frame – precisely as a kind of 'innocence'. This is another way of referring to that moment of 'waiting' just before you step off the end of the earth into … Britain, the ingrained, embattled nature of whose racism you do not yet know (that is, of which you are still in a way 'innocent') because it hasn't yet hit you between the eyes … A liminal movement, caught between two worlds, hesitating on the brink.
>
> *(Hall 1992 [1984]: 107)*

Hall sees this innocence in the poise of voyagers, in their obvious sense of pride in the way they look, in the way that they are dressed. In these photographs we see people with aspirations, with hope, who have yet to be sullied by the particularly noxious form of racism peddled in Britain.

Again, this isn't an ignorance of racialised thinking. For Stuart Hall, coming to England meant encountering a new form of racial culture, one much less nuanced than the one he grew up with, and one much more easily mobilised as a form of violent populist absolutism (for instance, the Keep Britain White movement of the post-war decades):

> Until I left, though I suppose 98 per cent of the Jamaican population is either Black or coloured in one way or another, I had never ever heard anybody either call themselves, or refer to anybody else as 'Black'. Never. I heard a thousand other words. My grandmother could differentiate about fifteen different shades between light brown and dark brown. When I left Jamaica, there was a beauty contest in which the different shades of women were graded according to different trees, so that there was Miss Mahogany, Miss Walnut, etc.
>
> *(Hall 1997: 53)*

The experience of multiracial, multicultural society was, of course, not new to this generation of citizen migrants. But it had different repercussions and a very different actuality. For instance, when Beryl Gilroy started working in a multiracial school in London, with all of its attendant cross-cultural conflicts, she could compare it with her schooling in Guyana:

> There were five other races in our society – the Chinese, the Portuguese, the American-Indians, the Hindus and the whites.
>   I had particularly enjoyed being at school with the Chinese, who set high standards of neatness and endeavor. There we all were – children of six races – in quite enormous classes of about sixty or seventy children, and yet I can't remember a single day that we ever quarrelled about race. If there was ever any jealousy, it was socio-economic in origin.
>   And so co-operation was possible. I knew it. I'd lived it.
>
> *(Gilroy 1994 [1976]: 150)*[13]

The alternative feelings of 'innocence' that Hall wants to find in the photographic archive is a synecdoche for a whole set of feelings. It is this feeling that is so important for the sort of disappointment that migration brings. We can give it other names: pride, hope, striving. We can hear it, for instance, in the words of some of the passengers on the *Empire Windrush*, and call it optimism. As the *Daily Mirror* records, the passengers on the *Windrush* told its reporter: 'We won't be disappointed in England. Nothing could be as bad as what we have left. We want to help England back on its feet again' (22 June 1948: 1). Disappointment needs this open-hearted and generous optimism to flourish.

The dominant pattern of feeling surrounding West Indian immigration in the 1940s and 1950s establishes a frame for situating the representation of migration and settlement. Its emotional economy is articulated around innocence and guilt, problem and solution, sexual predator and sexual victim. This is a pattern of feeling circulated by a white racist dominant culture. It is therefore necessary to work to reclaim another emotional economy, another pattern of feeling from this dominant form. And this will entail re-mooding the archive, remixing its economy of feelings, foregrounding feelings of pride and optimism in an archival force-field that has foregrounded problems and racial anxiety. What, for instance, can we make of

FIGURE 5.2 A man on the doorstop of a terraced house, Notting Hill, 1961. © Museum of London.

Figure 5.2 that we know was taken in Notting Hill in 1961? On the one hand, we see Victorian terraced housing, initially built for the middle classes. We can see that the area has gone to seed. We can assume that these houses are now owned by landlords and landladies who let out single 'bedsits'.[14] We could read the figure of the man in the doorway as slightly old-fashioned, of keeping up a set of values *despite* the environment, of wearing a hat and a suit because that is how you dress if you are respectable.

And yet it was probably true that this image circulated quite differently at the time that it was made and was already captured by a pattern of feeling syncopated to the beat of 'problem-solution and innocence-guilt'. In 1961 you only had to read the words 'Notting Hill' to bring to mind the racist murder of the Antiguan carpenter Kelso Cochrane two years earlier (see Olden 2011) or three days of civil disturbances or 'race riots' in the area the year before that, riots that involved knives and Molotov cocktails. At this point, the West Indian man either shifts from respectability to potential innocent victim or has 'innocence' forcibly taken away from him by a dominant pattern of feeling that can capture respectability and turn it into something else, something threatening, something sordid. What might at one turn be resilience – a maintaining pride and respectability in the midst of reduced circumstances – can at another be filled with anxious thoughts of white ignorance: is this how 'rude boys' dress? Is this what a pimp could look like?

The work of reclaiming and reworking the archive will not consist of just undertaking the important work of situating the material within particular archival interests, and of reading the images with these interest in mind. It will also require a more imaginative archival procedure whereby the patterns of feeling that are articulated by the archive are refracted and recalibrated by bringing it in contact with other archives. This is done to some extent in a realist manner when the archives of photojournalism are read in relation to oral historical work (as I have been doing to some degree, drawing on the work of Stuart Hall and Paul Gilroy). But there is another, less realist mode that refracts these archival elements by forcefully altering the mood and modulation of their articulation. By re-mooding this archive, another account of it becomes more and more forcefully present, showing us another pattern of feeling. This approach, to my mind, is most engagingly and convincingly seen in the film work of John Akomfrah.

Archival activism

John Akomfrah was one of the founders of the experimental group Black Audio Film Collective (BAFC) (founded in 1982, disbanded in 1998), and directed many of the collective's films. Since 1998 he has been working with some of the same people with the production company Smoking Dogs Films, and seems to have a particularly creative relationship with the sound designer Trevor Mathison. One way of understanding the work of BAFC and Akomfrah is to recognise it as operating quite specifically against and in response to the emotional economy of the 'problem-solution, innocence-guilt' pattern of feeling that we have been tracing and that has been so treacherous in its depiction of black settlement in Britain. What BAFC and Akomfrah have been generating are other patterns of feeling – counter patterns of feeling, so to say – by using, but re-inflecting, the same archive that has supported the 'problem-solution, innocence-guilt' one.[15] This has entailed producing a new aesthetic approach to the archive, one that operates at the level of rhythm, referent and temporality. I am going to look particularly at Akomfrah's film *The Nine Muses* (2010) and suggest that it produces a quilting of the archive, one that takes a set of well-known archival images with their characteristic tempos and durations (the news cycle, predominantly) and throws them into another temporal dimension (the *longue durée* of the voyage and the existential quest). By doing this, the film not only re-moods and re-rhythms these images, but also works analytically to reveal another pattern of feeling at the heart of the experience of migration and settlement. But before turning to *The Nine Muses* it is worth briefly considering BAFC's film *Handsworth Song* (1986) as it provides a valuable context for reading the later film.[16]

Handsworth Song is named after an area of Birmingham where many black and Asian migrants settled in the 1950s and 1960s.[17] The film was a direct response to the so-called

'Handsworth Riots' of 1985. Akomfrah has suggested that 'the questions that animate what we do are not formal but emotional ones' (Akomfrah and Eshun 2007: 133). The emotional question here was, how do you film civil unrest based around racial issues without deploying the dominant pattern of feeling that articulates questions of black settlement and youth, around innocence and guilt, problem and solution? One way that they answered this question was by slowing down the image and inserting it within a new sonic field (one collage sequence was set to a dub reggae version of the English hymn 'Jerusalem'). They 'treated' the image through a number of film processes that included tinting, slowing scenes down, using stills and so on. The group filmed a night of disturbances, including a young black man trying to resist capture by a line of police. Talking about the film and the scene of rioting, Akomfrah has said that they

> had needed to slow it down, open it, stretch it out. Because although you might say this happened in one afternoon, actually what happens in one afternoon has decades in it. We were going to open it up and show you how there are five decades there.
> *(Power and Akomfrah 2011: 61)*

Slowing down the film doesn't, in itself, open up the event of the Handsworth Riots to a different historical temporality, but it does solicit a different responsiveness from the viewer, who is encouraged to quell those internal voices that might want immediate explanations and solutions for the event.

What takes the event into a different temporal dimension is the use of these scenes of civil disturbances, and the archival newsreel images of arrival and settlement, alongside the mementos of personal memory. It results in what Kobena Mercer calls 'disphasure', or what we could see as the stuttering of history:

> *Handsworth Songs* (1986) paid witness to the conflicted relationship between past and present in post-war Britain by revealing an epic disphasure between the private memories of black life contained in family photographs, as documents that testify to diaspora experiences of immigration and the official public records of the archive, as an institution of social memory to be found in yesterday's monumental statues and today's television reportage.
> *(Mercer 2007: 44)*

As history stutters, what is revealed is the lack of a collective national social memory adequate to the history of black settlement in Britain or one that could easily explain the event: 'Instead of a synthesis of memory and history, their films underscore an irreconcilable agonism, for gaps, absences, distortions, fabrications and contradictions arise on all sides' (Mercer 2007: 44).

With its deliberate refusal of synthesis and its insistence on the unfinished, the unreconciled and the inadequacy of representation, the film was attacked by the novelist Salman Rushdie as lacking a language that could register the experience of migration and settlement.[18] What Rushdie failed to see (or simply didn't like) was that BAFC had found a language but that it was something like a 'broken' English that was being spoken by the film. One of the best recent assessments of the film stresses the pattern of feelings and moods that it activated:

> Instead of a declamation of anger or vindication, what is felt is a mourning for abandoned dreams and aspirations, a sense of sorrow for what is lost, for all that was certain. The film takes on the tonality of an allegory, choosing the fragmentary and incomplete over the symbolic and the whole, choosing mournful monody over dramatic discursiveness, the expression of grief over the rhetoric of agon [...] Taken from the annals of postwar newsreels, these images are awakened from their archival slumber and the impending insignificance, opening out onto a secret history of disappointment.
>
> *(Debuysere 2015: 71)*

'A secret history of disappointment' is an acute description of the film. What Akomfrah's more recent films, and particularly *The Nine Muses*, achieve is a refining of this approach and an elaboration of this secret history: disappointment is threaded through with love, with joy, with mourning, with tenacity, and with the anguish of existential homelessness.

The Nine Muses (New Wave Films, 2010) begins with images of snow-covered landscapes, of ships moving across icy waters. We slowly pan across a rugged, mountainous landscape. We are attached to a boat and follow the shoreline. Titles appear telling us the name of the film and the name of the production companies involved. A black frame offers us an intertitle, which reads: 'But the gold fell from very high in the sky, and so when it hit the earth, it went down very, very deep.' We go back to the snowy landscape and the icy water. We see a figure, with his back to us: a witness. He is on the brow of the boat. At the start there is music. It is elegiac, plaintive; it suggests sacred or courtly music from a different era – from the seventeenth or eighteenth century perhaps. But we also gradually start to hear other sonic patterns appearing alongside the music: first there is a low rumble that sounds like thunder, or some sort of celestial grumble, then there are faraway haunting cries and crashes. The camera movement is slow, mostly static, of just very slow pans. Nothing is happening, except the flow of water: the cloudy sky appears motionless (Figure 5.3).

The first piece of archival footage is introduced. The screen shifts from colour to a monochrome that is slightly sepia. The music has gone and we hear some sort of low industrial clatter. We are shown a black man working. It appears to be very hot. It could be the boiler-room of a ship. A voice with a West Indian lilt speaks about coming to England, and how the migrant might take responsibility for what happened, but then goes on to say:

> On the other hand, we think; if they, in the first place, hadn't come to our country and spread false propaganda, we would never have come to theirs. If we had not come, we would be none the wiser and still have a good image of England. Thinking that they are what they are not.

FIGURE 5.3 Still from *The Nine Muses*, dir. John Akomfrah, New Wave Films, 2010.

And then we are back to the ice and snow of Alaska, back to the bleakness of an uninhabited landscape. When we return to the archive of newsreel material we see an England or Britain deep in the midst of a snowstorm, with traffic jams and the usual chaos that follows surprising, but routine, winter weather in Britain: 'ask grandmothers, mothers, and the first thing they'll say about coming here was that it was so cold, and the second thing they'll say is that it was so gray that they felt that they were the only thing with any color in it!' (Power and Akomfrah 2011: 62).

Already (and we are only a few minutes into the film) we get a feel for the sensual resources of this tone poem, which is also a time poem. What sounded like a piece of early modern music for the church or court wasn't: the voice is too extreme, it cracks, a single voice produces two scratchy notes simultaneously. It is from the album *Solitudes* by the avant-garde French singer Tamia Valmont (though she often goes just by the name Tamia) and the Swiss percussionist Pierre Favre. It references a much earlier time, but its odd rhythms and distorted, sometimes anguished voice produces uncanny, unnerving affects. The enigmatic intertitle about gold falling from the sky comes from John Berger and Jean Mohr's 1975 book on the hard lives of impoverished migrants from Turkey, Portugal and Greece working in France and Germany. It comes from a passage that describes an exchange between two migrant workers, one newly arrived the other an 'old hand', both come from the same country of origin:

> They repeated each other's names and the names of their villages. Then, full of the excitement of arrival, he said: 'Here you can find gold on the ground. I am going to start looking for it.' The friend who had been in the city for

more than two years answered him: 'That is true. But the gold fell from very high in the sky, and so when it hit the earth, it went down very, very deep.'
(Berger and Mohr 1982 [1975]: 68)

We get the drift, it's a timeless sentiment: here is the land of opportunity, where opportunities are reserved for those who already have plenty. Time and space is opening out. The time of the timeless is not a place where there is a lack of history: here there is too much history, and it is in a perpetual melancholic mood.

The Nine Muses performs a contact zone of different archival resources. The film is a mosaic, a quilt made out of resources that speak of awkward time, of journeys, of dislocations. There is music from the Australian singer and composer Lisa Gerrard (most famous for her film score for the film *The Gladiator*) which uses 'Eastern' modulations (quarter tones, for instance). The contemporary Estonian composer Arvo Pärt, with his modern sacred music, is included, as well as Franz Schubert's 'Der Leiermann' from the song cycle *Die Winterreise* (from 1828), which tells of an organ grinder (or hurdy-gurdy man) who no one listens to, who stands barefoot in the snow. But this selection of music is also knitted together with the uncanny sonic architecture of Trevor Mathison and a number of songs that are also performed visually by Paul Robeson and Leontyne Price. There is no narrative to the film, instead there are nine chapters dedicated to each of the nine muses of Greek mythology (Dance, Tragedy, Love and so on). Each chapter shows us an endless back and forth between the beautiful, high-definition, stark and icy landscapes of Alaska (often with the silent 'witness' figure looking out into the landscape) and a mass of archival footage from the 1950s, 1960s and 1970s, showing black and Asian British citizens living, settling and getting on with getting on. This back and forth is occasionally interrupted by a black intertitle with an unattributed quotation. Interlacing the whole film is a sequence of passages taken from a range of audio books: we hear from actors reading Milton's *Paradise Lost*, from Emily Dickinson, from Dylan Thomas, from Sophocles and Homer, from Shakespeare and Dante. We hear from Samuel Beckett and from James Joyce. Some of these writers were immigrants, most weren't. But they all talk of voyaging, of the difficulty of arriving, the failure in understanding how they got to where they got to.

This quilting of archives, and especially the quilting of a European literary canon with the Alaskan landscape and the newsreel footage, performs a major recalibration of the archive of black and Asian settlement. It takes it out of one chronotope (a particular genre of space-time orchestration), one that is driven by the false urgency of the news cycle (which is driven by the rhythms of capital), into a chronotope of mythic history, of voyages, that can cross the river Styx or return to childhood. This 'counter-chronotope' is a genre that in this instance is characterised by the temporality of the epic voyage, and by a literary imagination that works to generate new descriptive languages of times, space and consciousness.[19] It takes it out of its temporal rhythms of 'social issue' news, out of its feeling of concern, and throws it into an epic temporality that is recognised in British Sikhs dancing in a community hall, for instance, not a throwaway moment for local news broadcasts, or for a documentary on multiculturalism, but an epic historical event that should be sung as part of a mythic history of courage and tragedy, of overcoming death, of rebirth and survival. It is a recalibration that dignifies the archive of migration and settlement in very particular ways. It is, I think, an analytic procedure, albeit one with a particularly poetic drive. The German sociologist Georg Simmel, at the turn of the nineteenth and twentieth centuries, wrote several essays using the formula 'Momentbilder sub specie aeternitas' (a compound of German and Latin, literally: fleeting images or snapshots seen from the perspective of the eternal). It allowed him to find significance within the disregarded trivia of everyday life (for instance, opening a door becomes a scene for contemplating the phenomenal differences between inside and outside, the public and the private, and so on) (see Rammstedt 1991). Throwing the snapshots of the news industry into the aspect of the eternal (the mythic voyage, the odyssey, scenes of departure) is not to escape history, but to confront it in a different mode.

At times this mode seems to produce particularly affective moments as racist history is thrown into epic dimensions. For instance, there is a passage of archival film where the African-American opera singer Leontyne Price sings the 'Negro spiritual' 'Sometimes I Feel Like a Motherless Child', and intercut with it we see archival shots of a little black girl playing with a white doll (Figure 5.4). The spiritual is from the days of slavery, when slave children were often taken from their mothers and sold at auction. It is a particularly affecting song, especially as sung by Price. Seeing the black child with this white doll produces her as a 'motherless child' (though her mother might well be the woman we see sitting next to her) as children often use dolls as avatars to play out their relationships with adult parents. Such mimesis is blocked in significant ways through the colouring of the doll. But

FIGURE 5.4 Still from *The Nine Muses*, dir. John Akomfrah, New Wave Films, 2010.

the scene is denser even than this, and conjures up another language of motherhood: of the relationship between the colony and the imperium; the colonial subject and the motherland. As we have seen, the voyage of the colonial subject to the imperial motherland effectively kills the 'motherhood' of imperial care.

Throughout the film we see the figure of a black man often wearing a heavy-duty, bright yellow or bright blue cagoule (the figure very infrequently wears a black cagoule). Occasionally we, the viewer, are facing him, but most of the time he has his back to us. This is another archival resource, this time from the German romantic tradition of painting exemplified by Caspar David Friedrich and his painting *Wanderer above the Sea of Fog* from 1818. This is the *Rückenfigur* (back-view figure) who establishes a stand-in for the viewer as a way of emotionally anchoring the picture. At the same time, however, the figure often obscures the very thing that might be the subject of the picture (we can never be sure if we can see what they can see because this figure will also conceal a proportion of the picture plane) (for a discussion of the *Rückenfigur* in relation to painting and film, see Panse 2006). The figure in *The Nine Muses* is a witness: he watches, he testifies. This is also the figure of history – the one who can only watch without interceding. Both witnessing and obscuring, the *Rückenfigur* is a particularly ambiguous figuration. How does this figure judge the material that is brought before him? What political perspective allows judgements to be made?

The ambiguity of the witness is further complicated by the choice of canonical materials that are being used. The literary soundtrack, taken from audio books, finds its resources among a predominantly male and exclusively European tradition of writing (although the figure of George Lamming is a significant presence in the archival film material). In some ways this seems to be a strategic move to allow the migrant images to occupy the Western canon (next time I hear the story of Odysseus being tied to the mast of a ship, my image-bank can now associate this with images of West Indians shivering through their first English winter). On the other hand, it allows the Western literary canon to be seen as significantly preoccupied with themes of leaving, of voyaging and the difficulty of arriving, and it also allows us to recognise that many of the names in this literary canon were also migrants (and James Joyce and Samuel Beckett's migration is tied to a colonial history). But what are we to make of the use of Beckett's work, which is a central resource for the film? We often hear an Irish voice intoning the beginning passages of the 'trilogy' (*Molloy, Malone Dies, The Unnamable*). We often hear the voice reciting:

> I am in my mother's room. It is I who live there now. I don't know how I got there. Perhaps in an ambulance. Certainly a vehicle of some kind. Was she already dead when I came or did she only die later? I mean enough to bury? I don't know.
>
> (Samuel Beckett's Molloy, *as read in* The Nine Muses)

This is another dimension to the quilt that Akomfrah is stitching: a philosophical depth to migration is often offered to the migrating European (for instance, in the novels of Graham Greene) but rarely reserved for the 'mass' migration of blacks and Asians. By the insistent and uncompromising presence of Beckett's words in *The Nine Muses*, the witness of history is cast as an existential aporia: how did I get here? It is, from the perspective of eternity, an impossible question and it is a question that refuses *an* answer (it was for financial reasons, it was because of colonialism, it was for adventure, it was because of fate). The narrator of the trilogy is both unreliable and unanswerable.

The Nine Muses provides a counter-pattern of feeling that is shaped by a space-time orchestration that is both mythic and planetary in scope. Its mood is contemplative, elegiac and celebratory. It reveals new feelings within materials that had already been 'understood' by social historians and documentary television. In its meandering refusal to hit the tempo of most narrative cinema, it enters another time of unfolding and interconnecting spaces: Kingston, Jamaica and Kingston-upon-Thames, of course, but also Notting Hill and Thebes, Handsworth and Dublin, Brixton and Ithaca. It is a space-time haunted by voices: some of those voices are melancholic, some sing redemption songs.

I started this section by claiming that Akomfrah's procedure of re-mooding the archive is an analytical procedure that can reveal and clarify a pattern of feeling that is already there in the archive, but is hidden. Talking about his overarching project Akomfrah talks explicitly about the forms of memory:

> For us, the project was always a kind of investment in memory. The return to the archive was indisputably, in our case, connected with a return to the inventory of black presence in this country. The investment in memory, I would say, took two distinct forms. It seemed to me that, at the time, all projects around the notion of memory had to deal with two things, the question of presence and, obviously, by implication, the question of absence. In the case of the black archive, the question of presence had to do with the fact that official memory denied you a certain kind of intimacy and solitude.
> *(Akomfrah and Eshun 2007: 131–132)*

This is one of the effects of the dominant pattern of feeling: it captures lives neither as collective action nor as singular complexity, but as a 'mass' that requires representing (mass migration). This is the burden of representation. *The Nine Muses* restores intimacy and solitude to the archive and in doing so it reveals a feeling that is at the heart of all migration: we could call it hope; we should recognise it as love. Near the end of the film, the newsreel archive voices its obscured desire. A West Indian man is talking:

> Love, love, love, 'cause I love you. But the majority of you don't love me. Between a black man and a white man community, a black man upset you with all his heart more than how you upset me. But I come pure heart, with my heart pure for you. Love you, would never harm, never do nothing, feel that you were just a man like me.

It was staring us in the face all the time. Of course, the *Daily Mirror* had it in 1948 when it wrote that the passengers on the *Windrush* were paying the mother country an enormous compliment by sailing across oceans to help get England back on its feet after the war. It is there in the welcoming and tired faces. But it was often an unrequited love. The secret history of disappointment is freighted with the unrequited love of migration. The haunted joy that animates this pattern of feeling is testimony to the force of such love.

Nearly 20 years ago, when George was telling me his story, I was acutely aware of feeling white shame and embarrassment while he spoke. But, of course, George wasn't telling me this story to shame me or make me feel guilty. He was telling me an epic story; a story he was proud of. It was often a story of mythic proportions, driven by the melancholy and passions of unrequited love, but that just made it even more epic: here he was, after all, 50 years later. He had never lost faith. That night he was telling me a love story, I just couldn't hear it at the time.

Notes

1. My inconsistent use of the terms Britain and England, and British and English is not to assume that England is synonymous with Britain, but to try and register some of the inconsistency of both the reality and the imaginative world that these terms refer to. Post-war migrations from the Caribbean occurred in Scotland and Wales, and yet in this period it has often been more common to talk about a black British identity and not a black English, Scottish or Welsh one. Clearly 'British' is a much more abstract and vaguer concept than Scottish, for instance, and in relation to mobility it is the name that is embossed on the front of passports. When concerns about migrations from Jamaica were raised in parliament in 1948 the member of parliament representing the ministry of Labour replied that: 'There is no logical ground for treating a British subject who comes of his own accord from Jamaica to Great Britain differently from another who comes to London on his own account from Scotland' (Phillips and Phillips 1999: 69).
2. For the much longer history of a 'black and Asian' presence in Britain see Visram (2002) and Fryer (1984).
3. The second line in this song is often written as 'You can go to France or America, India, Asia, or Africa' (Phillips and Phillips 1999: 66; Proctor 2000: 19). The fact that he switched Australia for Africa when singing to a newsreel journalist at the point of debarkation might be a significant adjustment. The calypso tradition offers lots of room for spontaneous improvisations.
4. Lord Kitchener's other well-known calypso song was written eight years later and has a very different tone. Its title is 'My Landlady's Too Rude' (Proctor 2000: 20). Aldwyn 'Lord Kitchener' Roberts returned to settle back in Trinidad in 1962.
5. Hall's references are predominantly directed towards film, photography and art in general. My references to the music of Soul2Soul (Jazzy B and Caron Wheeler) and the quite different success of the Fine Young Cannibals (Roland Gift) are slightly premature for Hall's talk (Hall's essay is from 1987; Soul2Soul and Fine Young Cannibals were dominating the popular music charts a couple of years later), but they belong to same formation that Hall is interested in.
6. To group a large number of different countries under the name West Indies is to name a colonial reality that existed particularly for the body of people that it named. To refer to this migration in terms of more recent naming practices (say Afro-Caribbean) would be historically anachronistic.

7 In Paul Gilroy's *Black Britain* we are told that 'a survey conducted in 1953 discovered that almost 85 per cent of London landladies would not let rooms to students who were "very dark Africans or West Indians"' (2007: 99). Racism in the workplace was ubiquitous. In Bristol, for instance, the unions and the management of the Bristol Omnibus Company refused work to any non-whites. After a successful boycott of the bus company, the first non-white was employed in 1963.

8 It is interesting to note that a consistent piece of advice offered to Commonwealth immigrants to Britain in the 1950s and 1960s, in the semi-official literature, was to join a trade union as soon as possible. The ubiquity of the white racist employer is shown in this exchange, which is from a newsreel archive used in the film *London: The Modern Babylon*:

Q. Now why is it that there is a prejudice here against coloured men?

A. Oh there's no prejudice Mr Chatterway.

Q. Why is it that they are not taken then?

A. There is this much about the coloured man. The staff feel that they are apt to lose their temper and resort to tactics that the average white man would not resort to.

Q. Have you ever worked with a coloured man?

A. No I haven't.

9 One of the best accounts of this racial cosmology is Anne McClintock's book *Imperial Leather* (1995), which charts this 'image-repertoire' through advertising, adventure literature, travel writing and so on.

10 Weeks before the Windrush arrived, the *Daily Mail* reported: 'Hundreds of West Indians now on their way to Britain will be met at the ship and told how to register at local offices for employment, said Mr. George Isaacs, Minister of Labour, in the Commons yesterday. He gave no assurance of employment, and added that inquiries are being made to discover who is responsible "for this extraordinary thing"' (9 June 1948: 3). The 'extraordinary thing' was that British citizens should travel from the high unemployment of Jamaica, under colonial rule, to try and find better conditions in England.

11 Phillips and Phillips found that this had been significantly exaggerated and that 'the largest block of sponsored workers came from Barbados to work for London Transport and the railways, but between 1955 and 1961 only 4,449 arrived, a relatively insignificant number' (1999: 121).

12 The fear of 'miscegenation' or interracial marriage is foundational to the racist cosmology. In Sheila Patterson's *Dark Strangers*, a section is dedicated to 'inter-group sexual relations and intermarriage' and claims that in 1958 a Gallup Poll 'showed that only 13 per cent of respondents approved of mixed marriages between white and coloured, while 71 per cent disapproved and 16 per cent were undecided' (Patterson 1965: 248).

13 Gilroy's autobiography was written in the 1970s. She uses 'race' to describe what people today usually refer to as ethnicity. 'Race' is a difficult word: it points to a reality (and if it didn't there would be no such thing as racism), but it is also clearly an ideology based on ideas that aren't supported by science. In this sense there is only one race, the human race.

14 The slum landlord Peter Rachman, and his 'enforcers', operated specifically in Notting Hill and Notting Dale at this time and particularly exploited West Indian lodgers. See Sandbrook (2006: 333–335).

15 The idea that re-mooding the archive generates a counter-mood could usefully be compared to Jonathan Flatley's work on black Leninism and 'counter-mood' in Detroit in the 1960s (see Flatley 2012).

16 The film can be viewed on the fantastic ubuweb at www.ubu.com/film under Black Audio Film Collective.

17 'Handsworth', as a name that signalled black British youth, circulated as part of popular culture, for instance, *Handsworth Revolution* was the name of an immensely popular 1978 album by the reggae group Steel Pulse.

18 Rushdie's article and responses by Stuart Hall (supportive of the film) and by that black activist Darcus Howe (critical of the film, and critical of Hall's critique of Rushdie) all originally appeared in *The Guardian* in January 1987; they are collected as 'The Handsworth Songs Letters' in Proctor (2000: 261–265).
19 The classic account of how chronotopes are a fundamental characteristic of genres is the topic of Bakhtin (1981 [1938 and 1973]; the rather odd dating is due to the fact that Bakhtin wrote an important set of concluding remarks that he added in 1973 to a long essay written in 1937–1938).

6

DEEP DOUBTS AND EXORBITANT HOPES

(Something is happening)

> *What did punk feel like as an emotional sensation? Anger or more like a positive, galvanizing energy?*
>
> I had a feeling that the world was changing. I really thought there was a revolution going on and I felt very lucky to be alive and at the epicentre of it. I can't remember whether it was anger or not, but it was this kind of wild, unfocused energy.
>
> *(Gina Birch, in Reynolds 2009: 196)*

What happens when a pattern of feeling isn't stretched out across a period of time, when it doesn't describe a narrative arc, when it isn't linked to a particular geography? What happens when, instead, it names an evanescent force, when it describes a complex simultaneity of energies and forms? Something happens. In an eruption of gestures, of sounds, of rhythms, something takes place, and that something is felt. Not by everybody. A marshalling of feelings requires supplicants who can capture, if only momentarily, those feelings, and can, in turn, be captured by them. Something is happening in that loose pattern of feelings that gets called post-punk. I want to follow some of the contours of these feelings not by analysing lyrics or by paying close attention to the movement's intentions, but by trying to apprehend the sensuous particularity of its musical forms. Some patterns of feelings seem to require explanations or argument, or some lucid historical narration. But other objects of feeling seem to demand a different, less academic form of attention. Here I work in short bursts, bursts that don't run in a linear fashion (one section doesn't prepare the way for the next). What I want to describe in this fractured chapter is a sensuous form and the energies and moods it set in play.

Something is happening

A roiling, surge of feelings. Something is bubbling up around us. It finds its sonorous forms in raggedy voices, in clattering drums, in looping bass lines, in stuttering and frenetic guitar breaks. It finds its gait in skanking dance and feverish gestures. In the beginning, there was rhythm. In the end, a shape was found for frustration, an architecture of anxiety, a poetics of fury. And something else, always something else. A cosmic echo reverberating through sound systems. A wild laughter. A negation so sensuously complete that it blossoms with promise. It was joyous, rambunctious and alarming; at its best it flirted with disintegration.

The great music critic Greil Marcus describes it as it surges through the live performance of the punk (and post-punk) group the Slits during a live performance in 1977:

> Nothing could keep up with it. Shouting and shrieking, out of guitar flailings the group finds a beat, makes a rhythm, begins to shape it; the rhythm gets away and they chase it down, overtake it, and keep going. Squeaks, squeals, snarls, and whines – unmediated female noises never before heard as pop music – course through the air as the Slits march hand in hand through a storm they themselves have created. It's a performance of joy and revenge, an armed playground chant.
>
> *(Marcus 1997: 39)*

The description makes it sound like a battering of energy, a small siege of sonic conflicts, little bursts of emotional shards and sparks. Gone is a critical language that might refer to influences or harmonies, that might recognise virtuosity or musical genres. Just as the music is running to catch up with itself, so too is the description. And what is the 'it' that Marcus is describing? Is 'it' music, a performance, an outpouring? Or is 'it' an atmosphere, an orchestration of energy, a mood, a concatenation of feelings?

The post in post-punk

Like most posts (post-impressionism, post-modernism), the post in post-punk doesn't really do any descriptive work. It signals an afterwards, an aftershock, an afterburn. It comes in the wake of punk, but is not itself punk, but something else. How would you tell the difference between punk and post-punk, and how would you know if something was 'post-punk', rather than simply 'not punk'? You can get a feel for this difference through comparing the sonic orchestration of the Sex Pistols and the initial version of Public Image Limited (PiL); both bands were fronted by the same singer, the former under the name Johnny Rotten, the latter under his birth name John Lydon.[1] The Sex Pistols, for all their attitude and pared-down rock, are essentially a conventional rock and roll group but with a singer who has a uniquely venomous delivery and expertise in sarcasm.[2] Both groups share the same instrumentation: drums, bass guitar, guitar and singer. And yet the sonic landscapes that are produced couldn't be more different. The Sex Pistols' sound is a garage rock, where the guitarist plays a riff of chords that gives the song its structural hook, supported by a driving bass line and urgent drumming, over which the singer provides some kind of tune laid out in a verse-chorus arrangement. PiL turns this instrumentation into a set of sonic textures, rhythms and melodies that effect a very different outcome. To start with, the guitar, rather than providing a riff, establishes an aural grain built out of a sequence of arpeggios (chords played one note at a time) channelled through various distortions and reverbs that return it as something distinctive and new. If you had to describe the sound, you could say that at times it sounds like a churning sea of iron filings on a windy day. It is the bass line that provides the melodic heart and structural identity of a PiL song. The drums, rather than providing muscular clout, widen the sonic ground of the song: splashy cymbals don't punctuate the sound, they provide an inverse drone, a crashing froth riding on the top of the sound.

We mean it, man

Punk was not so much a style or a genre as a style-bomb, an anti-style. It was an emetic, purging the bloated body of rock of its self-aggrandising pomposity. It was a caustic poultice, drawing out the fetid poisons of bombast made from big hair and even bigger egos. It was an enema used to flush out a rancid concoction of '*luuuurve* songs' and a petrified imagination conjuring up sub-Tolkien goblins in sword and sorcery landscapes. Punk was, for all its excesses, puritanical about rock. It was a scorched earth policy. Rockism was the enemy. And Rockism was anything and everything that a bunch of young people with fire in their belly would see as self-indulgent, established, faux-rebellious, tired, pompous, expensive. Rockism was the folk culture of rock in its most alienated form: a form that could only be played by 'proper' musicians, with expensive instruments (and usually a lot of them) and a stage craft that favoured dry ice. Punk's ethos was back to basics, music stripped back to reveal rock in its 'proper' folk form: something that anyone could play, something that wasn't concerned with skill but with energy, with anger, humour, with recklessness, with irritation and sarcasm, with silliness, with sheer bravado. The sarcasm of Johnny Rotten snarling 'we mean it, man' was an invective aimed at the authenticity of Rockism's sincerity. Being sarcastic about Rockism's sincerity was neither cynical or insincere. It was a new order of sincerity: Day-Glo authenticity.

As a zero-degree of rock, punk could open the way for something else, for a way of returning to complexity, to ambitious music, but differently. It meant that the values and personnel of Rockism could be rejected and in its place other traditions, other musical forms could come to the fore: instead of Eric Clapton's cushy guitar gymnastics you could have John Cale's viola playing in the Velvet Underground; instead of the dippy theatrics of groups like Genesis, Yes, and Emerson, Lake & Palmer (ELP) you could have the raw power of Iggy Pop and the Stooges and the queer aesthetics of the New York Dolls; instead of Rockism's maudlin ballad singing you could have the cracked honesty of a Billie Holiday.[3] And just as Rockism could be negated, so too could a Popism made of insipid disco pop, easy-listening reggae and increasingly daft glam rock. Punk opened a space for returning to versions of those musical forms that hadn't been mediated by a rock industry that made money by peddling diluted versions of musical genres. Now you could go back and search out the roots of roots reggae, become a connoisseur of heavy dub, discover the pioneering funk of Betty Davis, now you could return to your first loves of glam: David Bowie and Roxy Music.

Openings

Punk opened a door or a window through which all sorts of things could pass. It was a permission slip to reinvent yourself. It was a permission slip for the young to supersede their parent culture. It created an opening that, for a while at least, seemed to allow lots of people who were normally excluded from the citadels of rock to enter. Kids who hadn't been brought up with piano lessons and choir practice were newly emboldened to see that as a positive advantage:

> Punk's impact as a transfigurative force was instant and extremely powerful. Overnight, hair was cut, clothes were torn and a newly empowered noise started exploring individual, anarchic freedoms. One of the most tangible aftershocks of punk, both in its immediate aftermath and in its wider impact on pop culture, was its urgency to prompt individuals into action. Document your reality: do it yourself.
>
> (King 2012: xxi)

And doing it yourself meant being yourself, refusing the set of roles that had been laid out for you, and in the world of pop and rock that meant that women should be sexy and alluring, or meek and mild, and pander to a heterosexual male image-repertoire. What punk did, for many, was to allow space for women to be part of pop and rock without having to follow the script: 'there was that window open that let girls be who they wanted to be' (Ari Up, in Howe 2009: 21). For Chrissie Hynde, who was in England working part-time as a journalist for the *New Musical Express* but was determined to form a band: 'The great thing about punk was that the fact that I was a girl was no longer any kind of a feature. There was a six-month window where you could sneak in there and see if you could get away with it' (Hynde in 'Girls will be Girls', BBC 2 *Culture Show* 2014).[4]

The great emetic of punk was fundamentally an act of critical analysis: it acted as a provocation, against which the familiar poses, gestures and performances, which rock had decreed as impressive, important, and convincing, were punctured at source. Now the preening and posing of golden-haired men suggestively twirling microphones or ecstatically jiggling their guitars was rendered as the empty rhetoric of 'cock rock'. Punk pulled the masks off self-serious 'rock gods' and showed them as equivalent to overcompensating balding, pot-bellied, middle-aged men with sports cars. Punk punctured and deflated the rhetorical masculinity of Rockism. At the same time, Rockism offered the women in punk and post-punk an image of femininity (as adoring fan or sexy singer) to systematically derail and derange. Ana da Silva, from the group the Raincoats, explains:

> Being a woman is both feeling female, expressing female and also (for the time being at least) reacting against what a woman is told she 'should' be like. This contradiction creates chaos in our lives and if we want to be real, we have to neglect what has been imposed on us, we have to create our lives in a new way. It is important to try and avoid as much as possible playing the games constantly proposed to you.
>
> *(Ana da Silva, cited in Reynolds 2005: 214)*

Creating new ways of life might have to start out by finding your resources in the deliberate negation or reversal of the old dominant script. The contradiction of fashioning a world out of the ruins of ideological femininity was lived out by punk and post-punk in a number of ways. Some deliberately performed it through clothing and attitude. Look at any interviews with the Slits or the Raincoats, or with any other female punk and post-punk musicians, and what you see is a concentrated refusal of the demure or the alluring, unless it is a sarcastic parodying of such styles. What you also see is the witty sabotaging of femininity, most vividly demonstrated by figures like Viv Albertine (from the Slits) combining ballet tutus with heavy boots (or 'bovver boots' as they were often called at the time). This sabotaged femininity isn't just a negation; it also provides the material for building the new.

What punk revealed, by implication, was that the various formal elements of Rockism, as music, were also gendered. Thus the 'power chord' and the fast runs of the frenetic guitar solo were (and still are) part of Rockism's performance of masculinity, just as much as the strutting that accompanied it. But certain aspects of punk didn't just reveal this, they also, at times, embodied and amplified it. Punk wasn't a misogyny-free zone. Thus the swaggering bravado of the punk guitar riff (for instance in the Clash's 'London Calling') was part of a peacock-preening masculinity that differed from Rockism only by being slightly more self-conscious, more self-reflexive. It took female punk and post-punk groups to find the musical forms for the 'sabotaged femininity' that was the basis for both new life and new music. Groups like the Raincoats and the Slits introduced new subject matter through their lyrics, but just as importantly they fashioned new musical forms as well. In many ways this was through a different relationship to rhythm: while the Slits developed reggae lilts to animate a punky dance music, the Raincoats had a more idiosyncratic relationship to rhythm – songs slowed down and speeded up in unexpected ways. They also used a form of amateurism (which for their classically trained violin player necessarily had to be learnt, or at least unlearnt) to dismantle and re-mantle forms of pop music. Greil Marcus offers this description of watching the Raincoats play:

> They leaped into their first number, Aspinall getting a hard, abrasive sound out of her violin, the beat stuttering, three high voices harmonizing with an off-stage realism across the sharp edges of the melody, and within a minute or so the Raincoats seemed to have trashed every female stereotype in rock 'n' roll. It was a matter of demeanor, backed up by a new sound; without gestures, without a trace of rhetoric, the Raincoats got it across that they had no interest in whatever images of the-woman-in-rock one might have brought to their show, and no interest in providing any.
>
> *(Marcus 1994: 112)*

If punk and post-punk could, at times, be macho and sanctimonious, it could also be joyful, jubilant, and create the sorts of utopian sounds demonstrated by the Raincoats, where 'feminine' music is found as a ferocious love, as a fierce fragility made up of tumbling, stumbling rhythms and wild calls to the future.

A concatenation of feelings, sensations, moods

Not just one thing. In a very different context, the art historian T.J. Clark wrote about the various strategies of the modernist avant-gardes of the late nineteenth century onwards as performing 'practices of negation'. He was finding a way of grouping together a plethora of very different painterly practices and visual performances to be found in such different movements as Impressionism, Fauvism, Art Brut, Dada and Surrealism, and so on. What Clark named as 'practices of negation' could include all sorts of different approaches: deliberately awkward and naïve ways of painting (for instance, in the paintings of Paula Modersohn-Becker); use of discarded and degraded materials (Kurt Schwitters, for example); lack of conscious control (the various aleatory techniques developed and deployed by the surrealists) and so on (see Clark 1985: 55). Visual art, of course, is not music. Clark was showing how you could group together a range of performances that were primarily united by what they opposed. You can see something like this happening in a much more concentrated form in post-punk. If Rockism favoured the melodic line, whether in the tunefulness of a song or in the melodic flight of an instrumental break, then post-punk might favour the drone as a particular practice of negation. If Rockism favoured a complex depth of sound, where the bass supplements and thickens out the chord sequence, then post-punk often seemed to enjoy a thin, scratchy sounding treble guitar sound that was counterpoised to the bass guitar.

If punk rock acted as an emetic, emptying beat music of its bombastic pretensions and muscular masculinity, then the job that was left to do was to rebuild. Post-punk was that rebuilding, and clearly if it was going to emerge out of the ground zero of punk, while keeping something of the flavour of punk, then it was going to have to rebuild using a different blueprint from Rockism. The aesthetic forms that emerged in the name of post-punk could be said to perform a number of sensorial reversals. If Rockism was smooth and warm, then post-punk would be jagged and icy: if Rockism was hierarchical, with everything supporting the voice and guitar, then post-punk would be radically democratic, treating the bass and the drums as individual 'voices'. Rockism's love of virtuosity (soaring vocals, shredding guitar work) would be replaced by a love of amateurism and awkward playing.

Post-punk's redistribution of rock orchestrations is fundamentally informed by its love of reggae in all its forms and its love of dub reggae in particular. The soundtrack to punk wasn't punk or similar thrash rock, but reggae. When you were at a punk or post-punk gig, you would usually be hearing reggae playing on the sound system as you waited for the band to come on. Don Letts, a reggae DJ (and filmmaker), was the house DJ at the punk venue the Roxy in 1977. He started out by playing a mix of punk and reggae but 'in the end, people wanted me to just play reggae, and not bother with punk rock. There wasn't that many good tunes in punk, you could play all the best ones in about twenty minutes' (Don Letts, in Savage 2009: 613). Reggae provided post-punk with a different way of working. If Rockism's hierarchy meant that drums, bass and rhythm guitar were less important than vocals and lead guitar, reggae was distinctly anti-hierarchical, with bands working as ensembles where each instrument has its part to play. This also opened up the spatiality of the song. As Gina Birch, the bass player of the Raincoats, remembers:

> The first bassline I ever learned was 'Funky Kingston' by Toots and the Maytals. I thought that was the most brilliant thing I'd ever heard. The reason I liked reggae was because the bass did hold a melody and a rhythm at once. And it was clear. It kind of sat up in a space. I like to hear space between the notes. I really like that kind of emptiness.
>
> *(Gina Birch, in Reynolds 2009: 197)*

This new spatiality was crucial. Even if post-punk and reggae seemed to be operating at different speeds, with different atmospheres, what they shared was more important: it was a way of organising sound, a way of layering it so that the effect produced was wide and airy rather than condensed and thick. Both forms also shared a strong sense of being rebel music.[5] As Greil Marcus described it at the time, many of the most intense post-punk groups – and Marcus has a distinct fondness for bands like Gang of Four and the Au Pairs, bands that combine a sort of stuttering funk with politicised lyrics (often politicised by feminism and a critique of commodity culture) – favoured the orchestrations of reggae. Marcus' favourite post-punk outfits:

> all work from a fundamentally Jamaican aesthetic, in which musical (and, in a band that includes both women and men, sexual) hierarchy is bypassed: the bass states and shifts the theme; lead guitar is mostly omitted; rhythm guitar

supports or pulls against the theme by jumping off and back onto the main pulse. All are attuned to dub, the reggae form in which instruments and voices continually drop out of a song and then reappear in slightly different shape.

(Marcus 1994: 189)

Classic reggae tracks became the main songs worth covering in punk and post-punk: Junior Murvin's 'Police and Thieves', for instance, or Dennis Brown's 'Man Next Door' (which was itself a cover of a 1960s song).

Deep doubts and exorbitant hopes

What is the tonality of post-punk? Is there a common feeling lurking and lurching across its brittle and brooding soundscapes? Is there a set of feelings that we can associate with the quite different rhythms and sounds that pepper the genre, a genre that can include the repetitious chugging of the Fall's 'Country and Northern' music, alongside the frenetic funk of groups like 23 Skidoo, A Certain Ratio and Maximum Joy? In conversation with Simon Reynolds, Scritti Politti's singer Green Gartside describes the first incarnation of his group (before they adopted and adapted the sounds of smooth soul) as a 'kind of scratching, collapsing, irritated, dissatisfied music' (Gartside, in Reynolds 2009: 186). Reynolds' response extrapolates from Gartside's insight:

with so much of the music of that period, but especially Scritti, there's precisely what you're talking about: a feeling of precariousness. A real sense of anxious struggle, people grappling with these deep doubts and exorbitant hopes: where do we go next after punk?

(Reynolds 2009: 186)

Would precariousness and frustration describe the overarching mood of post-punk? There is, I think, a set of musical idioms within post-punk that seem to suggest feelings of uncertainty, frustration and anxiety. The leap from the sensuous actuality of the music (jerky, say) to the pattern of feeling that it both produces and connects to (an agitated mood, for instance) seems unforced. If at times the bridge between aesthetic form and social experience can seem precarious, in post-punk it often seems relatively secure. For instance, when Simon Reynolds describes the idiom of 'brittle' guitar-playing of many post-punk bands he is also describing 'a nervous twitchy style' (Reynolds 2005: xix).[6] Rather than being smooth and flowing, such twitchy guitar sounded jerky, made up of sudden explosions and disconcerting twangs. The Leeds-based group Gang of Four played a funk grove that was constantly punctuated by Andy Gill's spasmodic guitar licks. Gill relates his playing to a negation of the guitar solos heard in Rockism: 'instead of guitar solos, we had anti-solos, where you stopped playing and just left a hole' (Andy Gill, cited in Reynolds 2005: 113). The aesthetic forms of post-punk could, at their best, sabotage Rockism at the same time as providing the new forms that urgently seemed to connect to a social reality.

The mix of democratic orchestrations taken from reggae coupled with distinctive ways of directing the instruments as angular and agitated works very well as a description of Gang of Four. This is Greil Marcus witnessing a Gang of Four gig in 1980:

> The band took the stage and threw out an instantaneous, doomstruck, forbidding tension. The high volume and the syncopated metallic grate of the sound produced a direct attack, but behind that attack was its contradiction, and before long one heard the contradiction as the attack. Rhythms shifted, stopped, re-formed; violent pauses broke the songs into pieces [...] As Gill aimed clipped notes against the groove and the rhythm seemed to retreat under his assault, the band made that distance [from Rockism] almost physical, and without ever losing the backbeat.
>
> If the band had a centre, it was Allen's bass: rough and taut in tone, each note standing out, it hung over the music like some final synthesis of Motown finesse and reggae weight.
>
> *(Marcus 1994: 113–4)*

But this mix of anti-hierarchical orchestration alongside forms of musicianship that often appear agitated (working in furious fits and starts) or have an aggressive dimension wouldn't necessarily help in drawing connections to other motifs, and other post-punk forms, which are shared to a greater or lesser extent.

Perhaps there is another clue to a collective tonality in the timbre of the voices of post-punk. There does seem to be a grain of voice that appears in post-punk that seems unusual in music (popular or classical). It is, like all the other musical idioms in post-punk, directed in opposition to Rockism, but in that opposition something else also appears. Perhaps we could say that the tones of post-punk's vocals belong more to the world of ordinary life rather than what was usually associated with music. If most music is happy with a tone of voice that can express love, anger or loss, or perhaps even bitterness, it seems less obviously at ease with tones such as sarcasm, petulance, irritation and annoyance. Alongside these tones of dissatisfaction there are also much flatter tones of a general boredom, or simply unemphatic feelings. And alongside these there are also joyful tones, but rather than these being filled with warmth and empathy, they are often the elated tones that are about to explode in laughter or dissolve into a fit of giggles. Post-punk, I think, takes the vocal tonalities of voices more often heard in day-to-day life.

Greil Marcus, for instance, describes the voice of Lesley Woods, singer for the group the Au Pairs as acrid: 'It's *acrid* – it may be the most acrid voice ever to stake a claim on pop music, and it's precisely the sound pop music has not prepared us to hear from a woman' (Marcus 1994: 191, emphasis in original). And it is this acrid tonality that, for Marcus, draws on the energies of feminism as 'a first principle that continually forces the questioning of the obvious, and it produces a never-ending argument: nothing can ever be settled, but nothing can be assumed, either' (1994: 191). Ordinary voices with their range of tones allow rock to convincingly move past songs of love and loss, to move towards another world that is both utterly mundane and, I think, utopian.

The voice of the 'singer' Mark E. Smith might, on the face of it, seem an unlikely example of the sort of post-punk that I've been describing. The Fall's music is garage rock infused with the durational procedures that can be found in the so-called 'Krautrock' of 1970s experimental band Can. On top of this, Mark E. Smith delivers vocals whose tone is distinctly unmusical, but neither is it ordinary speech. It is sometimes paranoid, sometimes sarcastic, often flat and descriptive, as if recounting a series of incidents to sceptical listener, or reporting the incidents of a particularly peculiar crime scene. Occasionally it snarls. What it does mostly is narrate. In this, the voice is the perfect vehicle for a set of stories about life in northern industrial towns and cities that seem to be in the throes of malevolent forces. This isn't social realism. As Smith proclaims: 'we [the Fall] are the white crap that talks back', which seems to promise protest music, but instead offers something altogether stranger. For music journalist Barney Hoskyns, the music that the Fall were producing around 1980 with albums like *Grotesque* and *Slates* constituted:

> wastelands of sound without themes, messages, or politics. These records *were* politics, living conjurations of the crass and the grotesque in Northern prole life... What [the Fall's music] implied was that the whole bastion of comfortable working-class traditions – the institutions of barbiturates, boozing, and bingo – could be transformed, could even transform themselves, into a deep cultural revolution.
>
> *(Hoskyns, cited in Reynolds 2005: 194)*

Smith's lyrics conjured a world that seemed both recognisable and totally alien, a world of drab streets, pubs and arguments, with Bowie look-a-likes standing around in car parks, where the person sitting next to you on the bus is probably some spy from an obscure government agency, and where goblins have taken up residency in the unemployment benefits offices. If this is utopian, it isn't because it pictures a perfect world but because it throws a portal into this world and allows you to glimpse this world differently even in its most mundane state. That is a utopia as a method, not for imaging the future, but for excavating the present so as to turn enervating forms into energising culture.

Post-punk has a utopian strain in its tones, in its moods. It doesn't weave a world of Elysian fields and liberation. And it certainly doesn't trade in the sort of nostalgic renderings of Rockism's love of the bucolic. Post-punk generates utopian energies in its orchestrations of sonic worlds, in the various tones it deploys in its vocals. It is utopia as a method, because it finds something new, something generative, something that points to the future, and it finds this in the ruins of the present, in the sabotaging of Rockism, in the shards left over from trashed identities.[7] It uses these resources to punch a hole in what passes for stable reality and opens up the world to what José Esteban Muñoz sees as a 'crashing wave of potentiality' (2009: 185) that he finds in the queer culture that he was captivated and captured by.

Broken flows

There is no argument here. No gradual building of a coherent narrative. Gaps. Bursts. Silence. Noise.

TV surprises

Watching TV at a time when there were only three channels meant that you saw an awful lot of dross (not that things have necessarily improved with the availability of hundreds of channels), but it also meant that TV could at times shock you in a way that seems rare today. I remember being about 15 and seeing a film about the Norwegian painter Edvard Munch on television (later I discovered it was by Peter Watkins). I had never seen anything so slow *and* compelling, something that could dwell, interminably, on dying. It opened up a hole in the world of television through which crawled all sorts of feelings and possibilities, including the idea that it might be possible to have a different relationship to death than the endless denial and disavowal that seemed to characterise the culture of death as I knew it.

But what surprised me more than anything was seeing Patti Smith on television. I don't trust my memory. I have no idea when it was, I'm not entirely convinced that I haven't misremembered it. I have seen, on YouTube, her performance on British TV (on *The Old Grey Whistle Test*, in 1976, which was the 'serious' rock TV show at the time) where she performs 'Horses' and 'Hey Joe'. It is a mesmerising performance but it isn't quite the one I remember. I remember her playing her guitar in a way that broke all the strings, and left just one. Perhaps it happened, perhaps it didn't. When I watch her writhing on the floor of the stage, on the 1976 *The Old Grey Whistle Test* clip, as she mimes the guitar playing of Jimi Hendrix, but reduced to an insistent wailing noise, I don't think it matters much. Here is I think the ur-scene of punk and post-punk, in the way that it is both a systematic refusal of Rockism (and in this she reveals Hendrix as a shaman and not a leader of Rockism) while generating a utopian scene from the ruins.

The energy of punk and post-punk seems to have found its antecedent form in the performance of Patti Smith. This is Ana da Silva from the Raincoats remembering seeing Smith playing in London in early 1976:

> It was really inspirational, she [Patti] was doing something I wasn't used to, being really feisty with this band, all guys, but she was in the front and just giving everything – both a physical presence and an 'I'm not taking shit from anybody' kind of attitude. She came onstage with a flower, she put it in her mouth and she spat it, it was like the end of flower power, spitting it out. I will never forget that until I die.
>
> *(Ana da Silva, in Howe 2009: 14)*

The gig coincided with Smith promoting her debut album *Horses*, an album which was clearly an animating force in the world of punk and post-punk. In the oral testimonies that are collected by the commentators on the subject, *Horses* is a referent for all sorts of people.[8] Viv Albertine who has yet to form the Slits bumps into her friend Mick Jones (who will go on to form the Clash) in the record shop just after the album has been released in the United Kingdom. This is Albertine's appraisal of that album:

> It hurls through stream of consciousness, careers into poetry and dissolves into sex. The structure of the songs is unique to her, not copies of old song structures, they're a mixture of improvisation, landscapes, grooves, verses and choruses. She's a private person who dares to let go in front of everyone, puts herself out there and risks falling flat on her face. Up until now girls have been so controlled and restrained. Patti Smith is abandoned.
>
> *(Albertine 2014: 79–80)*

Abandoned, yes, in the meaning of liberated, lost, unconscious. But also the systematic abandonment of a set of forms, of a set of norms.

Meanwhile in 1981

It was a particular time, a time when social contradictions were being lived out on the surface of the news. Between the announcement of Prince Charles and Lady Diana Spencer's engagement in February and their wedding in July, a number of momentous civil disturbances erupted in areas with the largest concentrations of black British citizens. Babylon was burning. In April, Brixton, in South London, was in flames during a weekend of rioting. In early July, in the Toxteth area of Liverpool, rioting occurred over three days and was only quelled when the police used CS gas (or 'tear gas') grenades, which had previously only been used in Northern Ireland (this then was the first time the British police had used them on the mainland). Both disturbances can be seen as partly a reaction to the Sus laws, a form of 'stop and search' that allowed the police to stop anyone that they perceived as suspicious. This law was used particularly to target young black men to such an extent that it was evident that merely being black and young was 'criminally suspicious' for a constitutionally racist police force.

In 1981 I was living in a shared co-op house in London, jobless (to be honest, I wasn't looking), and going to gigs when I could afford to (they tended to be relatively cheap, compared with today's prices, and there were always other ways of getting into gigs beside paying for a ticket).[9] I remember going to the 100 Club on Oxford Street and one week seeing Prince Far I, supported by the Roots Radics Band (mixed by Adrian Sherwood), producing a ganja-fuelled dub reggae that was simultaneously densely material *and* spacey and ethereal, and that we seemed to perceive through our spines as much as through our ears. Another week it was the poet and saxophonist Ted Milton and his band Blurt, who had a fantastic single titled 'My Mother is a Friend of the Enemy of the People'. Blurt only had about three other songs, so they played all their songs several times.

That was a dense wall of sound, a frontal attack, with psychotic vocals and abrasive saxophone playing. Milton's honking, barking sax playing was a world away from the sweet swooshes of Deadly Headley's playing (Deadly Headley was the sax player in the Roots Radics) and yet they both seemed to belong to the same world of feeling, seemed to take part in the same sonic brew that occasionally erupted into something that seemed to poke a hole in the here and now and give you a glimpse of other worlds.

To say that these sonic brews shared a world of feeling with what was going on around us seemed to us at once obvious and yet something that would be hard to pinpoint beyond the vaguely gestural. It was the soundtrack of a time, experienced by a particular disposition. Was it working on the level of analogy? My housemates and I heard about the Brixton riots on the radio on the Sunday morning of that weekend in April, and we walked over to see what was going on (it was about a mile from where we lived in South London). We were held back by the police lines, of course, but the mood and energy was palpable: a solid air of energy, anxiety and something else, something that also seemed to be erupting and making holes in reality. The author Mike Phillips had been there the previous day: 'there was an intense throbbing vibe in the air, like feeling the bass on some incredible sound system pounding into action, but the vibe was more like excitement than anger' (Phillips and Phillips 1999: 359).

That August my favourite band, the Slits, were playing at the Notting Hill Carnival. The Carnival fed on a sonic world of immense and often dissonant sounds, most noticeably with the sound systems that were set up on the streets around Ladbroke Grove and Portobello Road. Each sound system was a huge tower of speakers with enormous bass bins, pounding out reggae grooves at a window rattling volume. As you walked along the street you were often walking between two sound systems, in a zone where the dissonance between two slightly different rhythms and two different keys often produced sonic disturbances of a particularly physical sense (sound quakes). That year the Slits were playing with a number of reggae acts on a stage near the Meanwhile Gardens and under the Westway, an elevated dual carriageway that feeds traffic in and out of the west of London.[10]

The Slits, by 1981, were creating wildly infectious and ferocious punky reggae with a high degree of improvisation that seemed to respond to the instance of its creation, and the world it was being made in. I don't think I've ever felt so 'in-the-moment' as I have just at that point while dancing to the Slits. Their performance was driven by Ari Up whose singing and dancing drew out an idiom of rhythmic intensity (reggae 'stepping', mixed with a bodily abandonment to some primal force of nature) and sonic intonation that felt like a contagion. It sent our legs skanking, our voices soaring, our bodies grooving. All at once, and in a way that seemed both in the moment and completely out of it, I had an awake dream, I imagined the traffic up above, no longer able to keep to the straight and narrow. At first the cars, buses and lorries would start swaying, then dancing to the syncopated rhythms…[11]

Post-punk feelings

Viv Albertine's autobiography begins with a primal scene for the love of rock and pop. She is describing the first time she listens to a record of a musical idiom that completely grabs her:

> Kristina opens the lid of the record player and takes a shiny liquorice-black disc out of one of the wrappers, puts it onto the central spindle and carefully lowers a plastic arm onto the grooves. There's a scratching sound. I have no idea what's going to happen next.
> Boys' voices leap out of the little speaker – 'Can't buy me love!' No warning. No introduction. Straight into the room. It's the Beatles.
> I don't move a muscle whilst the song plays. I don't want to miss one second of it. I listen with every fibre of my being. The voices are so alive. I love that they don't finish the word *love* – they give up on it halfway through and turn it into a grunt. The song careens along, only stopping once for a scream. I know what that scream means: *Wake up! We've arrived! We're changing the world!* I feel as if I've jammed my fingers into an electricity socket, every part of me is fizzing.
>
> *(Albertine 2014: 16, emphasis in original)*

What Albertine is describing is a sort of aural equivalent to an epidural injection, a sense of music bypassing the worlds of discussion, of liking and disliking as a form of consideration, and instead being something that affects the nervous system. Excitement and hunger: a noise, a sound appears that talks to you somehow more immediately than anything you have encountered previously. You want to devour it, to feast on it.

But that frontal attack of music, that crashing, crunching kerr-plang of an electrified chord being struck with conviction ('we mean it, man') is hard to maintain. Conventions become sclerotic, over-fed, pompous. All pose, all going through the motions. The other side is to fill those conventions with details and guardrails, build cathedrals on the basis of honky-tonk pianos. (At its worst, the world of progressive rock produced a window-less baroque architecture.) You search out those moments when you can recapture that electricity, that initial kerr-plang that made your heart skip a beat, and filled your body with potentiality. Punk and post-punk was an attempt to renew that love with the form. But if certain elements of punk required a strict return to basics, other elements were prepared to be promiscuous in searching out the sites where such electricity could be found. This is Albertine discussing the early days of the Slits:

> We play each other our records and point out backing vocals, string sections or guitar riffs we like. We especially love *Dionne Warwick sings Burt Bacharach* and *Low* by David Bowie. We also listen to *The Sound of Music*, the Beatles, the Ramones, MC5 and Iggy and the Stooges.
>
> *(Albertine 2014: 159)*

The search for some vital energy can't afford to be dogmatic or puritanical. If what you wanted were sounds that could energise and affect the nerves, then why not find them in the minimalist orchestrations of strings and choppy guitar licks that accompany the unfussy delivery of Dionne Warwick singing 'Walk on By'? Or in the alien burble of Bowie and colleagues on *Low*?

In 1980 or 1981 I saw the Raincoats supported by the group Furious Pig at the London Institute of Contemporary Arts, which became a venue for some of the more experimental elements of post-punk. Furious Pig had taken the do-it-yourself aesthetic of punk and post-punk to extremes and produced a sound entirely made up of the human voice and various found objects (cardboard tubes and such like). It was striving to reconnect to the vital source. When the Raincoats came on, that striving seemed to take on a new form, not the immodest arrogant posing that often marked punk as an adolescent form, but something sliding in from the side, an oblique strategy and a purposefully minor form. The bass guitar sounded like it was playing itself, not as a virtuoso performance of all that is possible from a bass but as if the bass wanted to tell you what its bass-ness was at some basic level. You could feel the fat worm strings thrum and produce a sloppy, gloopy, dollop of sound. The violin grating across the room seemed to produce a new sonic furniture that you couldn't lie back in, but you could somehow live in anew. A thousand school assemblies, with mass violin playing, condensed into something else, something fungible. The drums neither accompanying or leading, but vying, answering, demanding. And voices, sometimes together sometimes alone, singing 'the void', not because there was despair in the air, but because they (and you) knew that you had to embrace that negation to find the future, you had to open up that hole to creep into the utopian gamble of something else, that could all too easily get dismissed as pretentious, as nonsense. But there in the ICA, it seemed to call across the void, to embrace future feelings, made up of something that anyone might take part in.

Against the status quo

Explainers of culture, including those who were most active in producing that culture, often refer to punk's emergence as taking place within a social scene of extreme disaffection, social unrest, economic and national decline. This, for instance, is how Zoë Street Howe begins her account of the group the Slits: 'It is 1976, and England is bristling with discontent. The nation is crippled by strikes and blackouts, and the air reeks as decaying rubbish piles up on street corners. Prejudice, chauvinism and boredom rule, dole queues snake round the block' (Howe 2009: 1). This is conventional wisdom, a dystopian setting for a music with 'nothing to lose'. You can hear it repeated by any number of punk musicians for whom punk changed their lives in 1976. Yet this image of the streets piled high with rubbish is not from 1976; most likely it is from the January and February of 1979 during the so-called Winter of Discontent, where the refuse collectors' strike in late January – coinciding with a bitterly cold winter – provided the press with endless images of a shivering country sinking under mounds of rubbish. And it is an image, again from 1979, produced by the advertising agency Saatchi & Saatchi of a snaking queue of people we assume to be unemployed, under the banner 'Labour Isn't Working', in the run up to Thatcher's first electoral victory.

The historian Andy Beckett writes: 'I have lost track of how many times I have read or heard that the punk revolt of 1976–7 was a "reaction" to the Winter of Discontent of 1978–9' (Beckett 2009: 6).[12] Conjuring up an image of causality where the caused form precedes the causal force suggests that we need to change how we look at the cultural formation of punk and post-punk. One way of shifting our gaze is by refusing to explain punk and post-punk and instead treat it as something that is doing the explaining. This, perhaps, is the advantage of looking at the work of contemporary criticism, rather than the world of rock and pop history. The best critics are trying to draw out the way a particular form, a particular sound resonates in the wider world. Greil Marcus, who in some ways has been my spirit guide to the pattern of post-punk feeling that I've been exploring in this chapter, was working as a critic in California, mainly for the magazine *Rolling Stone* and *New West*. In an article for *New West* about the group the Au Pairs titled 'The Au Pairs in Their Time', Marcus begins with two 'news items'. The first is from 4 July 1981 and gives an account of a riot in Southall, London started by racist skinheads who favoured a form of punk called 'Oi' and supported the National Front, a violent racist political organisation. The second news item is from 9 July, five days later, and describes a wave of civil disturbances in cities across the country and is centred on issues of racism. The third item isn't a news bulletin but a letter from his friend, the music critic and sociologist Simon Frith. Frith is telling Marcus about the rise in attacks on Asians, on West Indians, on leftists, gays, women. He ends his letter by writing:

> more and more I feel I live in a society that bears no relationship whatsoever to the way it is perceived/conceptualized by Thatcher, Foot, the BBC, etc. Rock (the Au Pairs' l. p., for example) is the *only* medium that makes any sense of life – aesthetically or politically – at all.
>
> (Simon Frith, cited in Marcus 1994: 188, emphasis in original)

It's an important epistemological shift, and a crucial way of attending to culture if what you want to do is to pay attention to the emotional currents that cultural forms parlay and often analyse, amplify and respond to. In lots of ways, this has been my method in this book, and it is, I think, crucial for work on cultural feelings.

At the end of 1980 Marcus is providing *New West* with his round-up of post-punk music for the year. He is telling his readers about records by the Clash and Blondie as well as music by the ludicrously talented Prince. He is looking, as he usually does, across the Atlantic, to what is happening there and producing the music he loves. He is looking at the various 'players', the various actors at work and pinpoints a crucial actor:

> Most valuable player: Prime Minister Margaret Thatcher of the United Kingdom. Raising unemployment and inflation with her right hand, while

slashing social services and pressing if-you're-white-you're-right immigration policies with her other right hand, she fostered an upsurge of music made in a critical spirit. From PiL's 'Death Disco' to the Beat's wary bop, it was music in which the critical energy was directed not only at the powers that be, but also at the seductive conservatism of pop itself: a symbolically crucial institution based on passive audiences, sexist role models, racist categories, banal ambitions, the hegemony of the charts. For some, no-future is turning out to mean take nothing for granted.

(Marcus 1994: 175)

This isn't a model of explanation. In this Thatcher doesn't explain PiL or the Beat (whose song about Thatcher, 'Stand Down Margaret', from 1980, was always a guaranteed floor-filler) but it certainly suggests that Thatcher was a force to be reckoned with, and that post-punk was either implicitly or explicitly going to be doing that reckoning. A music with nothing to lose becomes a music that takes nothing for granted. Rather than seeing Thatcher as the explanation for post-punk, we can take post-punk as a form for trying to describe what Thatcherism felt like for those who hated everything she stood for.

Notes

1 I'm thinking, particularly, of PiL's second album which was originally called *Metal Box* (Virgin, 1979) because it was issued in what looked like a metal film canister with three 12-inch singles (which ran at 45rpm rather than 33rpm, which was the usual speed for an album). It was reissued the following year as *Second Edition*.
2 Of course, music was only part of what punk was about. As a social and cultural form, it would often be the clothing and behaviour that would get reported in the papers. Thus *The Daily Mail* could claim that: 'The Rolling Stones were rebels. The Who smashed everything in sight. Alice Cooper chopped up dolls with an axe. But the latest pop phenomenon called Punk Rock makes all the rest look like nursery rhymes. It is the sickest, seediest step in a rock world that thought it had seen it all' (*Daily Mail*, 2 December 1976: 2), and refer to haircuts, body decoration, slogans on T-shirts and so on.
3 An extended investigation of the relationship between punk, post-punk and progressive rock would, I think, reveal a more complex situation. What is clear is that for the generation of punk/post-punk, progressive rock was the culture of a parent generation. To some degree, this was almost literally true. For instance, the singer of Yes, Jon Anderson, was the godfather of Ari Up, the singer of the Slits, while Yes guitarist Steve Howe taught Keith Levene, the PiL guitarist (and one of the original members of the Clash) to play guitar. I can't imagine the sound of PiL without Howe's input. Eric Clapton had shown himself to be deeply racist in the summer of 1976 when he vocally supported Enoch Powell and the repatriation (deportation, in other words) of black and Asian British citizens (though he used more racially inflammatory language) (see Gilroy 2015).
4 Hynde doesn't elaborate on her choice of this time frame (six months) here, but she seems to be alluding to the way that a good deal of punk rebellion was quickly absorbed within the music industry who then wanted to re-inscribe the dominant script. Of course such rebellion and absorption is never a once-and-for-all affair, as, of course, Hynde is aware.
5 Accounts of what was called (by Bob Marley) a 'punky reggae party' can be found in Letts (2008), Sullivan (2014) and Bradley (2013). For a history of reggae and its diasporic performance see Bradley (2001) and Henry (2012).

6 In the same paragraph he describes post-punk guitar as follows: 'Rather than rama-lama riffing or bluesy chords, the post-punk pantheon of guitar innovators favoured angularity, a clean and brittle spikiness'.
7 The idea of utopia as method is a central argument in the work of the social scientist Ruth Levitas (see Levitas 2013).
8 Don Letts argues that the birth of punky reggae was the moment that Patti Smith invited him onto the stage of her gig and he started reggae 'toasting' with her band in 1976 (Don Letts on *Front Row*, BBC Radio 4, 12 August 2016).
9 Cooperative housing consisted of registered groups of people, in need of housing, who would officially borrow a house owned by the council or by a housing association. The house would be empty and would be waiting for refurbishment, normally at some point at the start of another financial year. The houses would be on loan for anything between six months and six years. We all paid a small rent to the co-op for the materials for rudimentary repairs and to connect the water and the electrics, etc., which we did ourselves. The legal way of getting into a gig for free would be to try and blag your way onto a guest list. The less legal way was by copying the simple 'stamp' that venues would ink the back of your hand with. It was quite easy to fake this with some felt-tip pens.
10 The Westway was a controversial piece of urban planning, cutting through large residential areas. The Meanwhile Gardens was so named because it was a piece of land that was left uninhabited after the building of the Westway (local authorities are deciding what to do with it, meanwhile it is a garden). Local communities have used it and turned it into a lively area, particularly for children. For a short introduction to the geopolitics of the Westway see McCreery (1996).
11 I think I had recently seen the film of Günter Grass' *The Tin Drum* (directed by Volker Schlöndorff, 1979) in which the protagonist, the diminutive Oskar, hides beneath a bandstand during a Nazi rally. The band is playing military marching music, and Oskar starts playing his drum in such a way as it alters the rhythm of the music, turning it into a waltz. The marchers start to sway and dance…
12 Beckett's useful account of the politics of 1970s Britain shows that the term 'Winter of Discontent' was first tried out in 1973–1974 as an assessment by a predominantly right-wing press on the power of the unions at the time. Their real success with the term was in the winter months of 1978–1979 where the term achieved much greater social traction and leverage, and could be seen as an important ingredient in ushering in a conservative government led by Margaret Thatcher, who was determined to weaken the power of the unions.

7
MOOD, GENERATION, NATION
(Feelings and cultural politics)

In this final substantive chapter, I want to start by briefly remapping the trajectory of this book in its pursuit of cultural feelings. The case study chapters (from Chapter 3 onwards) have looked at cultural feelings in relation to a variety of registers. In Chapter 3 I looked at the feelings that circulated at a very specific historical moment (the period of the Second World War) and how they shaped and were shaped by the work of morale-building. In Chapter 4 the theme of destruction continued but this time the focus was directed at the way that cultural feelings and energies can become embedded in a certain form of landscape, a specific kind of space (in this case 'waste-ground'). Chapter 5 explored a specific situation: the experience of migration in the second half of the twentieth century in Britain as 'Commonwealth' populations set out on a voyage to start a new life in Britain. The heroic dimension of this story was hidden in the folds of narratives that would seek to paint this epic story as 'social problem'. In Chapter 6 I looked at more momentary feelings that can flare up as an evanescent effervescence (so to say). We could say that the four registers of cultural feelings have been time, space, narration and moments.

If we step back from these particular scenes and take a moment to reflect, we could agree, I think, that cultural feelings never simply *belong* to any of these particular registers. Using our own experiences, it would not be hard to see how these registers bleed into each other, or how feelings are threaded through and across specific spaces, while being shaped by the nature of social relations and their narrative forms, conditioned by a historical moment, and animated by moments of intense overflowings of energy. What is a 'whole way of life' if it is not something like a life made up of places (a local church, a factory, a home, a pub, say), played out over time (recessions, the rise of far-right nationalism, periods of stability), structured by power and social relations (ubiquitous racism, the support of a specific community), and punctuated and given sustenance by the blossoming of fierce and caring passions (music, celebrations, shared joys)?

The world is nothing if not elaborate. To overcome the extraordinary complexity of the world, forms of analyses edit the world, choosing to explore a specific space or a particular time while purposefully ignoring a clamouring barrage of forms and phenomena that are intent on complicating and undermining the very possibility of venturing an analysis. Analysis knows it can only ever offer provisional, partial renderings of the world; just a partial glimpse of a 'whole way of life'. At the same time, however, we measure the value of analysis on its ability to capture something of the complexity of the world. We could say, then, that we need to find a way of bringing together these various registrations of feeling and mood into more complex orchestrations of the patterns of feeling that characterise experience. In this it is worth returning to Raymond Williams and his discussion of 'structures of feeling'.

In the dialogues between Williams and the editors of *New Left Review*, the concept of 'structures of feeling' is scrupulously explored. Reading the discussions, you get a feeling that Williams' interlocutors are highly sceptical about the theoretical exactitude of the concept. Is Williams claiming that there is a single 'structure of feeling' that characterises a period? How would this accommodate the sorts of social differences that we name as class, race, gender, or sexual orientation? Do we all experience a structure of feeling in the same way? What is the scope and scale of the concept: is it nationally specific; does it refer to a milieu, a generation, a population? These are the same questions that trouble me, and have been troubling this book. Is the analysis of cultural feelings always working with approximations, generalisations that always assume a particular cultural position? How can structures of feeling be analysed so that they can attend to the real bite of social experience?

The *New Left Review* editors recognise that for Williams: '*The essential point of reference for the notion of structure of feeling here appears to be not so much a class, or a society, as a generation*' (Williams 1981: 157).[1] To this insight Williams readily agrees:

> The way in which I have tended to apply the term [structures of feeling] in analysis is to the generation that is doing the new cultural work, which normally means a group which would have a median age of around thirty, when it is beginning to articulate its structure of feeling.
>
> *(Williams 1981: 157)*

It is clear that as a literary historian Williams is referring specifically to the age of the authors whose work he is using to extract patterns of feeling in a particular epoch or period. We could say that this is the age when a writer emerges as a public figure. But even given this qualification, it still poses significant problems for analysis, as the *New Left Review* editors point out:

> *Another problem posed by your unit of analysis, so to speak, is how one delimits a particular generation in any given society. For it is a delicate methodological question*

where you actually draw the lines between age-groups. To take your criterion, at any one moment there are those with a median age of thirty: but what about those with a median age of twenty-five or forty? Where do they fit?

(Williams 1981: 161)

My concern is not the same as that of Williams: I'm not concerned with identifying a generation of writers and mining their work for a shared set of expressive values and social themes. I'm more interested in what this discussion offers for thinking about the complexity of cultural feelings more generally. In other words, what happens when we add 'generation' to our catalogue of time, space, relation and moment?

To see generation as a category that could be useful for registering patterns of feeling seems to correspond to an increasing focus on generation in popular culture. Today, people belong to 'Generation X' or they are 'Baby Boomers' or 'Millennials' or 'Generation Y' and so on. In post-traditional society, where extreme technological and social change is often a fundamental aspect of life, generational experience marks a particular set of cultural resources. Were you, for instance, born before or after the internet? Was your childhood marked by the possibility of global annihilation through nuclear war or does the vision of chronic global warming shape your nightmares? Was your university education free or did it saddle you with enormous debt? Or was university simply not a choice when you were 18 as it was reserved for a tiny minority? What films did you grow up with, what was TV like when you were young? Life is lived across changing possibilities; its forward movement sees dreams being dashed or realised or turning into nightmares. Life is the expansion and diminution of love and fear, of hope and despair. We would be naïve to assume that these patterns of energy are an individual affair. We can often give social and political names to these felt forms: names like 'recession' or 'Welfare State' or 'permissive society'.

But the editors of *New Left Review* raise a question: if at any single point a number of generations are active in shaping and being shaped by cultural feelings then should we think of a historical moment as including multiple structures of feeling that could include a number of generations, but might also include patterns of feeling that link to other social differences such as race, class, gender and sexuality. In terms of historical work, does 'structure of feeling' name a discrete set of moods, responses and feelings that are particular to a specific group or does it name something much larger; does it name the orchestration of these different feelings? In some sense this is a technical question and not one that can be usefully answered with any finality. It is also an abstract question that is more concerned with an epistemology of analysis than it is with actual lived experience. A more fruitful response is instead to treat it technically, to treat it as something that is constantly the topic of representation.

In what follows I want to look closely at two drama serials. Both of them look at the progress of a generation or a generational milieu over a specific period of time. In other words, they are looking precisely at the interconnections between generation and social history and its effects and affects. Each of the two drama series takes a set of close friends and follows them across a period of time. In *Our Friends in the North* (BBC 1996) we follow the path of four friends from 1964 to 1995. In the film *This is England* (dir. Shane Meadows, 2006), and in the various TV miniseries that followed it (*This is England '86, '88* and *'90* [Channel 4 2010–2015]) we see a large group of friends over a much shorter period, from 1983 to 1990. Both dramas are extraordinarily powerful and ambitious film cycles and work to weave together an orchestration of mood and affects felt by a small milieu that connect them to the larger world of historical events (the miners' strike, the Falklands War). But the complexity of these drama cycles also shows a world of changing social and cultural moods and values (the rise of a particularly virulent form of racism, for instance), which is registered both from social action and cultural performances, and through individual worlds of love, sex, illness, abuse and ambition, which are also, of course, social phenomena.[2]

Both series offer a complex articulation of cultural feelings seen through the prism of a generation. They also register a generation (or more particularly a class-specific generational milieu) as a collective subject for whom patterns of mood are determined by an inheritance from a parent culture (including reactions against this parent culture) and a repertoire of hopes and fears for the future. Cultural feelings are partly registered as the rise and fall of optimism, of hope, of anxiety. Cultural feelings are animated by memories and the cultural resources that we carry with us as historical subjects. Such feelings can register as a sclerotic sense of having 'no future', or that 'things never change', but, as we have seen in the previous chapter, they can also take shape in other ways, carrying recalcitrant energies with wild affects that are future-oriented. Before I go on to discuss these series in detail I want to momentarily consider the role of dramatic narrative for figuring cultural feelings, and for describing the role of mood in cultural life.

Drama, cultural feelings and historical forms

We are used to seeing feelings as internal states that somehow belong to us on an individual level: we grieve a loss, we take pride in a success, and this pride and grief we feel to be ours, and we feel it at some level to be unshareable. But, as I've been arguing throughout this book, feelings are also shared; cultural conventions around grief and pride, for instance, give form to how we can respond to loss and success, which means that we share emotional forms with those who are similarly reliant on the same cultural resources. The idea that we share what feels unshareable might seem counterintuitive, but it merely registers the connection between people whose emotional turmoil, for instance, makes them feel that they have dropped out of the world of shared sense and shared sensibility. We could also say that the cultural forms for 'deep feeling' change over time, such that grief and pride, fear and anxiety are historically specific, even if that specificity seems quite loose and the historical dimension quite broad.[3] Thus 'personal' feelings are social precisely because they are historically specific even if they don't feel like it at the time. It is trite but true to assume that the loss of a loved one during wartime would probably be felt slightly differently than during peacetime, and trite but true to say that each occasion of loss would have its own singularity.

But if we can talk about gradual historical changes in our sensibilities, are we any nearer to understanding the relationship between socio-economic cycles, cultural forms and lived experience? How, in other words, do we calculate and calibrate the world of individual feelings and the larger social world we all inhabit? To put it crassly: is there a strong enough correlation between a depressed economy, for instance, and feeling 'down'? Clearly, in as much as an economic recession produces its own forms of misery, we would be foolish not to see a link between individual feelings of anxiety and vulnerability and larger cycles of affluence and recession. And yet for some these financial cycles appear as golden opportunities for making money. For others whose lives remain unchanged across these cycles (either through extreme poverty or extreme wealth) a recession might hardly be 'felt' at all. And for those whom recessions impact on there may well be a range of feelings to occupy: anger, for some, but for others a sense of inevitability, a feeling that the hand of fate is at work.

The question of feeling, at the level of culture, is unresolved, and this I think is part of its nature. Did I feel a particular anxiety about the possibility of nuclear war in the early 1980s, when I was entering my twenties, due to having a nervous disposition? Or was that anxiety part of an assessment of a situation that was shared by millions who felt the terrible absurdity of that chronic build-up of planet-annihilating weaponry? And perhaps there were determining conditions acting on that experience of anxiety that I wasn't particularly aware of; namely that my anxiety about nuclear war was at one level a luxury. Perhaps I had space for that anxiety because I wasn't anxious about finding the money to feed a child or to pay the rent. I think if the study of cultural feelings is going to develop, then the question of the collective nature of feelings needs to be examined alongside the way that particular feelings might be specific to certain groups, or indeed specific to certain individuals and their life stories.

To this end we could say that this is precisely what dramatic narrations have been doing for eons. What narrative drama often gives us is an exploration of a historical moment or period as it is refracted through the particularities and peculiarities of specific characters. The very notion of 'character' suggests characteristics and capacities that will mean that an event will not be experienced in precisely the same way by different characters. One is endlessly hopeful and will find the resources to overcome a defeat, while another will be floored by exactly the same event. We could say, then, that drama, instead of showing how a situation (political, social, cultural) is reflected in the lives of protagonists, takes a much more heuristic approach to that situation by showing us how the situation is refracted in the characters' lives. Refraction rather than reflection acknowledges uneven capacities, differences in cultural and social resources, different life trajectories that impinge on how social moods are registered and responded to. The challenge that drama lays down (and this was why Williams was so endlessly fascinated by it, I think) is: is there a level of feeling 'in general' that can be seen and captured precisely because it is experienced so differently by different people? Is there a pattern of feeling, in its complexity, that drama reveals through its exploration of the different ways people react and live their lives?

Because narrative dramas are often concerned with exploring the lives of characters facing particular events (both personal and social) within specific contexts (epochal, geographic, historical and so on), we could say that they often deploy a form of feminist epistemology known as 'situated knowledge' (Haraway 1988). For Donna Haraway, the idea of an overarching 'objective' view of the world is a masculinist 'god trick'; there are only ever partial perspectives and situated knowledges. But rather than seeing such a state of affairs as a limitation on knowing the world, Haraway reverses its productivity: because the world is complex, because it is organised to produce differences and inequalities, those perspectives that can recognise their partiality and the 'subjective-ness' of their responses are necessarily *more* sensitive to complexity and social forces and better able to describe the world than those that fail to see their own partiality. Drama, unlike the sciences (whether natural or human), has never found much benefit in the 'god trick' and has pursued a line of inquiry that purposefully pursed the epistemology of partial perspectives. This understanding of drama as a partial perspective designed to extrapolate tones and moods from across the particular feelings of a set of characters is how I will approach the two TV serials under discussion.

Negotiating inheritance and hope: Our Friends in the North

The TV series *Our Friends in the North* follows four working-class characters from the north-east of England (from the same region as that inhabited by the 'likely lads' that we met at the end of Chapter 4). It follows them from young adulthood (or adolescence) in 1964, when they are in their late teens, through 30 years of historical events and political and social change in Britain. We last see the foursome in 1995 at the funeral of Nicky Hutchinson's mother (Florrie Hutchinson, played by Freda Dowie), as they now symbolically take the mantle of the 'older generation' (two of the characters are now grandparents). The drama is ambitious, not just in terms of the amount of time it covers but also in the complex of themes and topics it pursues. Themes of class, gender, generation and politics are threaded through issues of corruption, housing and changing social mores and manners. Generation is explored, not just in terms of a generation gap, but in terms of the difficulty of escaping the inheritance from one generation to the next. Generational differences are signalled by phenomena such as the growing opportunity of a younger generation for social mobility: at the start, Nicky (Christopher Eccleston), the son of a shipbuilder who marched as part of the 1936 Jarrow Crusade (a protest march about hunger and unemployment) has just got back from the United States to begin an undergraduate degree at a university. But generational continuity is demonstrated by the way patterns of parenting, gender roles and addiction seem to be passed like a baton across generations.

The theme of politics and progressive social change, and the lack of it, is the most insistent topic across the series. Of the four protagonists, two are (or become) significantly involved with left-wing politics, and two seem, at first, to be non-political and only interested in having a good time. Nicky and Mary (Mary Soulsby, played by Gina McKee) develop political careers: Nicky moving through local government, into extra-parliamentary armed struggle and finally into journalism; Mary starts her professional career as a lawyer after a period of being a housewife and carer, and ends up as a Labour Member of Parliament. Mary's husband, Tosker (Terry 'Tosker' Cox, played by Mark Strong), another of the protagonists, starts out by wanting to be a pop singer but then develops a successful career as a small business man (grocery shops and then pubs); his initial 'apolitical' stance finds its expression within the Conservative Party, the local chapter of the Masons and his endless optimism about the free market. The fourth and final protagonist is Geordie (George 'Geordie' Peacock, played by Daniel Craig), who leaves the north-east to escape his abusive and alcoholic father, and becomes caught up in a crime organisation that sells pornography in London's Soho. He is sent to prison, and ends up (after his release) homeless and an alcoholic.

The relationship between politics and feelings is fundamental to how the series progresses. On one level, this sense of feeling is located at the level of empathy: Nicky and Mary witness poverty and misogyny and strive to do something about it, while Tosker doesn't seem to be capable of such 'fellow feelings'. And yet it becomes clear that progressive politics can be as narcissistic and egotistical as its less altruistic opposite. But what drives the relationship to politics are feelings about possibilities for change. Geordie, for instance, feels deeply that change isn't possible: at one point he says to Nicky, 'You're wasting your time trying to change things. Things are this way because that's the way things are.' And Geordie seems to embody this feeling of fate and endless repetition as he spirals downwards into homelessness and mental instability, repeating the life of his father. On the other hand, Tosker, who is conservative both politically and culturally, is the character who is most insistently hopeful, even if his hope is limited to his undying belief in his ability to succeed through hard work.

It is Nicky's political trajectory and his relationship with his father that is most complexly tied up with changing feeling of hope versus defeatism, of optimism about progressive social change and feelings that nothing can alter the basic unfairness of society. Partly these feelings are driven by Nicky's relationship with his father (Felix Hutchinson, played by Peter Vaughan) and his understanding of Felix's politics. For Nicky Hutchinson, his father's politics is defeatist, and it is true that Felix has turned his back on the Labour Party and what he sees as the betrayals of his comrades. Yet Nicky's sense of hope and defeat is constantly fluctuating: at times he is convinced that life can change for the better; at other times he has no faith in parliamentary democracy and feels that any change will have to come through violent struggle; and sometimes he takes the same defeatist position as his dad.[4] Feelings change, and changes aren't always what they seem. And corruption always promises the continuation of the *ancien régime*.

One way of understanding *Our Friends in the North* as an exploration of cultural feelings is to see it as studying the rising and falling 'quota' of hope or defeat that is circulating among a milieu across 30 years, years that saw the might of the state directed at smashing the National Union of Mineworkers (NUM) in the mid-1980s.[5] Across the series we see an orchestration of cultural feelings, we see the falling and rising pulse of feelings of hope and opportunity, and we see this rising and falling activated by and acted on the various characters in the drama. At times these are political pulses in the most immediate sense, but at other times they are the longer pulses of a social politics that includes the structural sexism that leaves Mary imprisoned in her flat with two small children while her husband Tosker pursues his dream of music stardom. An understanding of *Our Friends in the North* as an investigation of cultural feelings requires seeing patterns of feeling in relation to character (and their particular characteristics and potential capacities), it requires seeing patterns of feeling in relation to social and political events (for instance, the rise of Thatcherism in the 1980s), it requires seeing patterns of feeling in relation to much smaller and more intimate relations of friendship and love (both sexual and filial) and the smaller opportunities for flourishing. And lastly it requires seeing patterns of feeling being produced by the investigation of patterns of feeling in the drama itself. In other words, a crucial aspect of the investigation of cultural feelings in *Our Friends in the North* is that produced by the drama. We can see how this works if we follow one thematic more thoroughly.

Building with steel, glass and sunlight

One of the central motifs in *Our Friends in the North* is the role of housing in the pulsing rise and diminution of hope for progress. Slum housing (Figure 7.1) is what first encourages Nicky to become actively involved in local left-wing politics. It will later be a major subject of his photojournalism as he photographs homeless men and women (which is when he meets Geordie again in the 1980s). Renting houses to people on social benefits adds to the wealth of Tosker in the 1980s. The loss of his flat while he is prison is what drives Geordie onto the street. Changes in Mary's housing situation register her changing fortunes. Housing is also one aspect of the drama that draws on a real-life case of substantial corruption in 1960s and 1970s political life.

In an early scene from the series, Nicky is out 'on the knocker' canvasing for the local elections on behalf of the Labour Party candidate, and is shown into a house so damp and squalid that the wallpaper is simply sliding off the wall. There is a woman who is clearly dying. It seems that the dereliction of the houses has infected her: she is dying in this deathly housing. It is during this election campaign that Nicky meets the charismatic Austin Donahue (played by Alun Armstrong) who will become the labour leader of Newcastle Council. Donahue is a visionary and talks with great passion about changing the nature of housing in the north-east. His visionary talk is compelling; he talks of building 'high-quality, high-rise apartment blocks, made from steel, glass and sunlight' and claims that 'together we can build a

FIGURE 7.1 Slum housing, *Our Friends in the North*.

bonfire for decay, dereliction and despair'. It is of course a rhetorical display of how cultural feelings can be deployed.

To build these blocks made from 'steel, glass and sunlight', Donahue establishes a business relationship with John Edwards (Geoffrey Hutchings) who holds the licence for a Scandinavian system of housing, which he calls Edwards' System Building (Figure 7.2). *Our Friends in the North* stays fairly close to the real case of 'Mr Newcastle' – T. Dan Smith – who was leader of Newcastle City Council in the 1960s and sought to regenerate Newcastle through mass housing and civic building. The figure of John Edwards is based on the architect John Poulson. Both T. Dan Smith and John Poulson were eventually sent to prison in the 1970 on fraud and bribery charges. What we see in *Our Friends in the North* is the way that corruption takes root and takes over. Edwards and Smith offer 'incentive' trips abroad to persuade other officials to vote in favour of their housing projects. 'Bribery and corruption', rather than 'glass and sunlight' turn out to be the foundations for their housing projects.[6] And it is sustained corruption, both in politics and the police, that leads to feelings that nothing will ever change.

While Nicky is working for Donahue he becomes disenchanted with the political process of local government and with the corruption he sees around him. But this isn't a moral quandary where 'the greater good' (good housing for impoverished citizens) could excuse the odd bribe: what is revealed is something more monstrous. The show-house block that is initially built is the Willow Lane Flats, which will become an insistent landmark within the series and at various times will be the home to all four 'friends'. We first see the inside of this block in a promotional film

FIGURE 7.2 Edwards' System Building, *Our Friends in the North*.

that is made for Edwards' System Building and that will be used to sell the system to other councils and, eventually, to other countries. The promotional film features Nicky's first love Mary (heavily pregnant) and her husband Tosker (Figure 7.3). It shows the flats as a model of modernity: spacious, light and airy with all mod cons.

The flat is initially just like the promotional film: an image of a thriving modernity; an image of high-rise living as a rational and humane solution to a housing crisis. Compared to the terraces of back-to-back slums we saw earlier in the series, Edwards' System Building is clearly a hugely improved way of living. And yet it quickly changes. On the one hand, it changes symbolically: it takes on the image of a prison-like space where Mary is incarcerated. But this symbolic change is nothing compared to the material degradation that the flat undergoes. Within a few years of their arrival, Mary and Tosker's flat looks exactly like the rooms in the slums that they were set to replace in the name of progress (Figure 7.4).

It is here where you can see another pattern that is being used to give form to the investigation of patterns of feeling. We could see this as the meta-pattern, the pattern that organises the changing orchestration of feelings for these characters during their 30 years of adulthood. The imposition of feelings is an inevitable aspect of studying cultural feelings (and the book you are reading now is similarly involved in the production of feeling alongside the mapping of feeling). But we need to investigate this meta-pattern of feeling. In *Our Friends in the North*, it follows the logic of the cyclical: sons repeat the sins of the fathers; what starts out as a cure for an illness becomes the new illness. It is in the end a defeatist set of feelings that saturate the dramatic investigation of feelings of hope as well as defeat. It is a

FIGURE 7.3 Promotional film for Edwards' Systems Building, *Our Friends in the North*.

FIGURE 7.4 'New' slum housing, *Our Friends in the North*.

cyclical repetition where corruption seems to be part of the system (perhaps the only durable part), where nothing can counter structural inequality, and where the only hope that is possible is in romantic relations (Nicky finally decides to seize the moment and asks Mary to go out with him) or in the self-serving political sentiments that Stuart Hall called the 'authoritarian populism' of Thatcherism (Hall 1988: 122–160). While we constantly see the devastating effects of Thatcherism (lawless estates, lack of 'fellow feeling'), we are left with feelings of hopelessness and the sort of unregulated self-interest of emerging neoliberalism, represented by the speech of the Conservative politician who states that:

> The heart of politics is people, and how they want to live their lives. The recovery of the country from these bitter Labour years will not be based on dogma, but common sense […] the common sense that would say hard work should pay and common sense rewarded.

'Common sense' declares 'every man and woman for themselves'. And the 'failed' dream of Welfare Socialism symbolically and materially disintegrates as the Willow Lane Flats are razed to the ground.

Fatherland: this is England

Our Friends in the North, produced and broadcast in the mid-1990s, looks at the emergence and consolidation of what we now call neoliberalism from the perspective of the failure of the left. That neoliberalism has turned out to be the name of a seemingly durable form of unregulated capitalism (its durability vouchsafed by being the 'only game in town'), while its cultural form has been amorphous. Neoliberal culture is, in some sense, unformed. In neoliberal society, culture simply has to pay its way, which might mean creating the cheap populism of 'game show', reality TV (as its most vivid exemplification), but should also include a variety of other cultural idioms that often have the suffix 'porn' attached to them: property-porn, ruin-porn, poverty-porn and so on. At its meanest, neoliberal culture names the spiritual vacuity of the culture of capitalism.[7] But cultural forms are never simply a reflection of economic determinants, and include an active critical response to the social forms that capitalism generates. *This is England* is part of that response.

This is England is the name of a film made by Shane Meadows in 2006, but it also names a number of drama series made for television, always including the same actors, that have been titled *This is England '86*, *This is England '88* and *This is England '90*. The initial film was set in 1983. In what follows I will use the title *This is England* to refer to both the film and the three TV series; in other words, to name the narrative drama that follows a small milieu of young people across seven years from 1983 to 1990. Already the similarities and differences between *Our Friends in the North* and *This is England* are beginning to be evident: both follow a close-knit group across a period of time, but while *Our Friends in the North* covers 30 years *This is England* only covers seven years. But other similarities and differences are more profound: both are 'state of the nation' dramas; both are concerned with working-class life, culture and inheritance; both investigate a world of feelings and moods where the personal and the social constantly overlap. But if *Our Friends in the North* revolves around social and geographical mobility, *This is England* remains tied to a specific location (everyone lives in a small, down-at-heel, seaside town), and the only signs of social mobility are either downward (the character Woody is from a lower middle-class background but chooses loyalty to his gang of friends over the life his aspirational parents want for him) or only tentatively upward (both the characters Shaun and 'Smell' attend the local further education college to study photography and fashion). *This is England* differs from *Our Friends in the North* in thematic ways as well: rather than exploring the failure of the left, *This is England* explores the attractions of the ultra-right, the place of racism in English culture and the effects of parental abuse, particularly sexual abuse.

At several points in *This is England* (in the film and in *'88* and *'90*) we are presented with a title sequence that is an extended montage of archival TV materials from the year shown in the title of the particular series or from the very recent past (for instance, the film includes material from the 1982 Falklands War, which is also included in a montage sequence in *This is England '90*). These TV sequences offer us a context for the dramas that both precede and follow the montages. But they do much more than provide historical 'colour' for the drama; or rather that colour is both complex and is a series of synecdoches for cultural feelings. The sequences, then, provide a constellation of moods and feelings that establish a setting for the drama, but also provide a set of material forms that can be used to measure and place the world of *This is England*. These sequences include the sorts of materials that might be included in the nostalgia programmes with such titles as *We Love the 70s*, and juxtapose children's TV and toys, the 'must-have' commodities of the time, period clothing, sporting highlights and various news events. *This is England* both follows this format and also undercuts it by including the sorts of materials that such programmes deliberately delete: war, violence, poverty, death.

The sequence that starts the film is accompanied by the song '54-46 Was My Number' by the ska reggae band Toots and the Maytals. The montage includes: the children's TV presenter Roland Rat; Margaret Thatcher driving a bulldozer; the TV series *Knight Rider* (starring David Hasselhoff and a futuristic, magical talking car); desolate and derelict housing with boarded up windows and graffiti; the ultra-right and racist National Front marching (Figure 7.5); the pop group Duran Duran; a Jane Fonda-style workout; the Royal Wedding between Prince Charles and Lady Diana Spencer (Figure 7.6); high-rise flats being blown up; CND and anti-nuclear feminists demonstrating at the US base Greenham Common; BMX bikes; Thatcher using a computer; the Battle of Orgreave during the miners' strike; incidents of racist abuse; street violence; soldiers marching with the Union Jack flag during the Falklands War; dead bodies being removed from the 'theatre of war'.

These sequences hang together in the manner of existing in a simultaneity that invites comparisons, connections and correspondences: what, for instance, links the National Front, the Royal Wedding and the Falklands War? What meaning are we

150 Mood, generation, nation

FIGURE 7.5 National Front supporters and Union Jack flags in *This is England*.

FIGURE 7.6 A royal wedding (Prince Charles and Lady Diana Spencer) in *This is England*.

to draw from the juxtaposition of Roland Rat and Margaret Thatcher? What we are presented with, however, isn't a riddle, but a deeply conflictual world that doesn't 'add up' to a unified whole, but instead articulates a world of uneven developments and unequal distributions. When we leave the TV montage and we meet the actual protagonists of the drama we are presented with a world of semi-urban life, of 'out-of-town' council housing, with poor public transport and little or no local amenities beyond a corner shop and a 'flat roof pub'.[8] In this world, the local pub is a lively community centre where people come together for karaoke nights, to watch football matches and to celebrate a wedding. Here there is unemployment, drugs, sexual abuse and racism; but there is also humour, shared parenting, fierce loyalties and dancing. It is a world that we can measure, to some extent, against the montage sequences of political, social and cultural events.

In the sequence that starts *This is England '88*, we see the Ethiopian famine, we see Margaret Thatcher and Ronald Reagan together, we see the huge mobile phones that were becoming available for the very wealthy, we see football and snooker, and we see the comedian Harry Enfield's character called 'Loadsamoney'. Loadsamoney was a character that Enfield invented to satirise working-class Conservative voters, some of whom were relatively affluent during a time of the 'right to buy' council housing, booming house prices and attractive share options from the government as it sold off state utilities.[9] In the dramatic world of *This is England*, there is little sign of this larger world: affluence is absent, technology is never cutting-edge, the Loadsamoney character would have little meaning. But there isn't chronic starvation either. The larger world impacts implicitly, but the only time it is explicitly invited in is via sport and music. The world that is painted is on one level parochial but on another level it is the actual material existence of kinship relations, friendship networks, local financial transactions and so on. The montages, rather than anchoring the dramatic world in a specific time and place, often show us precisely how far the world of *This is England* is left behind and left out of the self-image of a nation that is presented in newspapers and on TV programmes.

As in *Our Friends in the North*, housing plays an important role in *This is England*. Most of the characters live in suburban council estates or in semi-ruined housing blocks (Figure 7.7). These houses and flats are the consistent scenography of the drama. Unlike *Our Friends in the North* there is nothing outside of this housing stock and unlike *Our Friends in the North* there is no aesthetic or moral opprobrium

FIGURE 7.7 *This is England '88*.

that is aimed at such housing. It is clear however that much of the 'block' housing (and there are no 'towers' in *This is England*) belongs to a previous epoch. In some respect, the very fact that such housing is remaindered makes it available for the improvised households that are such a crucial part of *This is England*. For instance, Gadget (played by Andrew Ellis), Harvey (Michael Socha) and Kelly (Chanel Cresswell) share a maisonette within a large housing complex, where most of the other housing is boarded up. They seem to spend their days smoking weed (marijuana), playing video games or watching daytime TV. Harvey also sells weed. It is Harvey's flat but he lets the others stay, until he discovers that Kelly is using heroin, at which point he kicks her out.

This is housing where people get by, look out for each other and look after one another. There is morality here too: weed and ecstasy are fine, but heroin is definitely not OK. If this world lacks aspiration it doesn't lack empathy, or laughter. Much of *This is England* is hilarious, ridiculous and ribald. At its heart, the world of *This is England* is filled with a love based on childhood friendships and shared lives. These are local lives: everyone knows everybody else. Friendships find their expression through occasional drunken declarations of love, by heart-to-heart conversations and by the ubiquitous, affectionate humour of 'taking the piss' out of each other (constantly, inventively).

The flat where Harvey and Gadget (and for a time, Kelly) live is in a famous housing estate near the centre of Sheffield. The Park Hill estate was built at the end of the 1950s to replace the slum housing of Sheffield's notorious back-to-backs. It was opened in 1961 and was generally seen as a phenomenal success combining good quality maisonette housing (with some single-storey dwellings), superb amenities (schools and shops), lots of play areas and wide 'sky decks' that joined the blocks together and gave you access to your maisonette. Within a decade or so, Park Hill suffered from serious dis-investment: shops closed down, amenities such as communal laundry rooms were left to disintegrate, and the general upkeep of the buildings simply didn't happen.[10] By the 1980s, the ribbons of housing were becoming places where families didn't want to live. The Park Hill estate is often used in films as a place of alienation and violence.[11] But in *This is England* it is simply a home for Harvey and Gadget and far better than the home where Harvey grew up where his father would regularly beat him. There is freedom here, autonomy.

Park Hill has one final role to play in the series. As I have mentioned above, the one sign of upward social mobility is in the figure of Shaun (who is clearly an autobiographical cipher for the director and writer Shane Meadows). College is where Shaun makes friends outside the class milieu of his 'gang'. We see him being introduced to an intellectual world of photographic history, learning about Henri Cartier-Bresson and 'the decisive moment'. The students are sent out to take photographs, and Shaun is approached by a young woman who is clearly not from Park Hill or from anywhere like it. She wants to go out and take photographs with him. For her Park Hill is an exotic location, somewhere where you might do a fashion shoot. For Shaun it is somewhere he knows, but also somewhere that, for him at

FIGURE 7.8 *This is England '90*, Park Hill Flats, a suitable case for photographic treatment.

least, is becoming less of a place to live and more of an object of aesthetic contemplation. Social mobility has its own feelings and changes in perception.

Trauma, love and living

While the tone of *This is England* is often comedic and light-hearted (the haircuts and clothes are frequently ludicrous exaggerations of period style), the overarching narrative of *This is England* is driven by a number of appalling and traumatic events. These catastrophically violent events affect all the characters in the series, but particularly the character Milky (played by Andrew Shim), Lol (played by Vicky McClure) and Combo (played by Stephen Graham). Describing these events synoptically does little to show the intensity of them and the sensitivity of the series' depiction of them. These traumas include the brutal, murderous racist violence inflicted on Milky by Combo after Combo is rejected by Lol (which occurs at the end of the initial film). It includes Lol killing her father with a hammer as he tries to rape her, an event which is set in motion when Lol's father rapes Trev (a member of the gang and Lol's best friend), but was also the outcome of years of sexual abuse that Lol suffered from her father. And it includes the moment when Milky has Combo taken away by his family, presumably to be killed as retribution for Combo's racist violence.

Described like this, it is hard to get a sense of the emotional complexity of these events. There is throughout *This is England* a religious sensitivity at work. Or rather religion, specifically Christianity, is a cultural resource that is used to try and register how these traumas are lived by those involved, and by the larger group of friends and family. *This is England* negotiates the relationship between love and hate through a series of religious motifs of sacrifice and forgiveness. Combo's racism is at the heart of the story: it is catastrophic, unforgiveable. And the systematic sexual abuse that Lol has suffered is also central: it is corrosive, cancerous. The series never excuses Combo, though it does provide a context for his actions. The National Front is seen as provoking feelings of lost national pride and actual loss for Shaun (whose father was killed in a neocolonial war). The final trigger for Combo's violence is his rejection by Lol and by his jealousy of Milky's large, close and loving family (like other characters, Combo suffered loveless, abusive parenting). Combo is sent to prison for grievous bodily harm. He is released at roughly the same time that Trev gets raped. Combo knows nothing about this, and goes around to see Lol, only to find her traumatised in her mother's house sitting next to the dead body of her father. Combo immediately takes responsibility for the murder ('let me do a good thing, let me do a good thing', he pleads), planting evidence on himself and setting up the crime scene, so that Lol doesn't have to be tried. Combo is sent away to prison again. When he is finally released from this prison sentence (and by this point he has become a practising Christian) he is determined not to recidivate again (though his last 'criminal action' was sacrificial). He goes to live with Lol and Woody (Milky is the father of Lol's first child, so the child moves out to be with her dad). Milky meets up with Combo and drives him to an out-of-town café. There Combo tells Milky how sorry he is and how he has changed. Some of Milky's family arrives and take Combo out to a van. They drive him away and deliver him into the hands of some people who look as if they will dispatch him from this world. Milky is left crying in the café. The entire series ends at the reception of Lol and Woody's wedding. Everyone is having a good time, apart from Milky who is still clearly devastated by his actions (which had already been set in motion many years ago when Milky's brothers swore retribution).

My first viewing of the world of *This is England* was on a laptop in a small hotel room. I don't think that I've seen anything more affecting: I cried, I laughed, and often did both together. I didn't know what to do when it finished (I just had the DVD of *This is England '88* at the time, which I had borrowed from my daughter), so I just sat and watched it all again. It had the same affect again. There were sublimely comic moments, but the scenes of Lol's depression, as she is haunted by the awful apparition of her dead father were simply harrowing, devastating. I loved the way that at times the background instrumental music intervened in a scene and simply silenced everything else. But what I ended up loving most about this series was the range of feelings it puts in circulation, and the way it simply refuses to let any particular feelings dominate, or to submerge the others.

I think it is the particular orchestration of feelings that allow the series to refuse the amnesia that can be a product of narrative forms. Here we weren't allowed to forget the racist attack on Milky, but nor could we put to one side Combo's sacrifice for Lol. In the final scenes we see people dancing (including the joyously daft figures of Woody's lower middle-class parents throwing themselves into the fun) while Milky's sadness echoes in the room next door. I have never come across something with quite so much unrelenting awfulness that was at the same time so madly joyous, so genuinely uplifting. As a study of cultural feelings as they are refracted through particular people with their different capacities, with their different histories, *This is England* refuses to stamp an overarching mood or tone across its world. At times melancholy rightly saturates a scene, but it is never left to reign supreme, it is always undercut with joyous, boisterous LIFE. What *This is England* offers is a study of the felt process of world-making, of life-building, within the particular social histories of a country that has allowed racism to fester, that has allowed sexual abuse to remain an open secret and that has turned its back on the communities it can no longer extract surplus value from. And despite all this, people are making lives for themselves out of the scant resources that are available: living in the remaindered ruins of the Welfare State; finding new familial groupings, different ways of loving; making a livelihood out of the few spaces that are available to them (Lol runs a team of 'dinner ladies' who run the kitchens in the school they all attended). As an amalgam of different moods and feelings *This is England* offers a mood-world that refuses to hide the hurt that this society produces and refuses to let that hurt define the lives that are being made.

Generational feelings and cultural politics

'Generation' is always a partial perspective, and it is an important one, primarily because it is rarely a single perspective. Generation always suggests multiple perspectives, as one generation defines itself in respect to the older and younger generations that frame it and give it a sense of identity. And long-form generational drama adds another complexity to this as we see one generation moving from being a younger generation to being an older generation. Such multiple perspectives are important for complexly refracting the cultural feelings of a period. Today some of the most significant cultural feelings are posed as cross-generational feelings, as a younger generation not only inherit astronomic debt from previous generations, but are charged with having to work to pay for the care of that previous generation while they are excluded from what a previous generation took for granted: homeownership, stable employment and such like.

Cross-generational feelings are the feelings that shape a time, just as cross-cultural (multiracial, multiethnic) feelings also shape that time. And here we can again see some differences in the trajectories of the two series. The much longer historical scope of *Our Friends in the North* makes it much more attentive to the gaps and continuities between generations. But this isn't really the result of the temporal scope of the drama so much as a feature of the social mobility it registers. What causes intergenerational conflict in *Our Friends in the North* is a form of class conflict: Nicky has been to the United States, he has education, he feels he knows things that his father doesn't; Mary's son is a local policeman and perceives his mother as deeply patronising because she is a Member of Parliament, so he thinks that she thinks she knows better. But because the drama takes place over 30 years, intergenerational conflict and class conflict synchronise because we see the changing nature of social mobility over this period, and we see this not just as social opportunity and the lack of it, but as a set of feelings to do with moods of hope and hopelessness, of feeling opportunity as an energy that could enervate, even if it only enervates anger or envy.

This is England doesn't feature cross-generational conflict. In this, the lack of social mobility unifies generations in the name of class: in the local pub all ages sing and dance together. Where conflict exists, it is racist conflict and this is proposed as historically specific. In this drama it is a historical moment due to the rise of the National Front in the 1980s, a period that coincided with a rise of nationalism and the morbid resurrection of Victorian values and other strange symptoms. While racism continues, it isn't a feature of the world of *This is England* after the terrible events that end the initial film. Indeed, the racism that is aimed at the local Asian shopkeeper in the film disappears and he becomes Shaun's new stepdad. If Shaun can't initially cope with his mother sleeping with him, this has less to do with racism and more to do with Shaun's feeling that his mum is cheating on his dead father. Where there is cross-generational tension again, as in *Our Friends in the North*, it turns out to be class-based. Between Lol and Woody and Woody's parents lies a certain amount of anxiety, but this is precisely based on Woody's refusal to return to the middle classes, and it finds its most peculiar expression in Lol's mother's fight with Woody's mother, and with Woody's parents informal 'adoption' of Woody's previous girlfriend.

As I mentioned at the start of this book, Karl Marx once proclaimed that people make their own history but that

> they do not make it as they please; they do not make it under self-selected circumstances, but under circumstances existing already, given and transmitted from the past. The tradition of all dead generations weighs like a nightmare on the brains of the living.
>
> (Marx 1852: 96)

We could also say the same about the world of cultural feelings: the world of feeling that is generated by a generation is produced within circumstances that are inherited from the past. We make our own mood-worlds but out of moods and feelings that we inherited, that through class, race, generation and gender pull at us and saturate our worlds. But out of these sometimes meagre and sometimes generous resources, we don't just repeat the tones of the past. Or at least we don't have to. We generate feelings complexly, sometimes incoherently, as we wrestle our lives into shapes that allow us to keep on keeping on.

Notes

1. In this book the editors' words are written in italics to differentiate them from those of Williams, which are written in roman.
2. In using these drama cycles I'm enlisting them as resources that are involved in articulating patterns of feeling within recent history. This to a large degree was their brief.

I'm not going to try and reveal something that might be hidden with following recent work within literary studies that seeks to promote reading'. In their discussion of 'surface reading' Stephen Best and Sharc 'we take surface to mean what is evident, perceptible, apprehensible i neither hidden nor hiding; what, in the geometrical sense, has length a no thickness, and therefore covers no depth. A surface is what insists on b rather what we must train ourselves to see *through*' (Best and Marcus 2009:   ......s in original). See also Felski (2015).

3 The literature on the history of feelings and emotions is now too vast to try to itemise it here, but for those who are new to this area a good place to start would be Rosenwein (2016) and Reddy (2001). From there it might be necessary to historically explore various formations of feeling around, say, love (Kern 1992; Langhamer 2013; Collins 2003; Høystad 2007), and then move on to look at fear, boredom, anxiety, melancholia and so on.

4 The mood of defeat within European history is the topic of Schivelbusch (2001). McCracken (2014) provides a wonderful riposte to Schivelbusch.

5 Sigmund Freud used the term 'quota of affect' (*Affektbetrag*) to describe emotional energy as both a quality and importantly a quantity (see Laplanche and Pontalis 1985: 374–375). Such an economic model of affect could be extended to think about cultural feelings as not simply describing states, but describing 'amounts' as well. To move from a position of describing a set of feelings as 'hopeful' to actually auditing the amount of hope that was available at a particular moment seems to me to be in line with Raymond Williams' dedication to adding to the 'resources of hope'.

6 A short account of the Smith-Poulson scandal is given in Sandbrook (2011: 506–515) and is part of the critical discussion of the series in Eaton (2005).

7 The literature on neoliberalism is vast. The special issue of *New Formations* on neoliberal culture offers a good overview of the issues (Gilbert 2013) as does Harvey (2007) and Hall (2011). McCarthy (2007) is particularly good on reading reality TV as a morbid symptom of neoliberalism.

8 The best guide to this world of suburban social housing is provided by Hanley (2012).

9 Enfield's character was hugely popular, but it became clear that his popularity was often due to people treating it as a celebration of wealth rather than a critique of the values associated with it. Enfield 'retired' the character after a short time. For historical overviews of Britain in the 1980s see Turner (2010) and McSmith (2011).

10 I have written about Park Hill in a general discussion of 'streets in the air' housing; see Highmore (2010). For a series of accounts of Welfare State Housing see the collection by Swenarton et al. (2015).

11 For instance, in the film '71, about a young English soldier who is sent to Northern Ireland in 1971, Park Hill is the setting for a harrowing search by members of the IRA and by the 'intelligence' arm of the British army who are both interested in killing the young soldier.

8

POST-REFERENDUM BLUES

(Postscript)

This book was written about cultural feelings within a specific national context. That national context, however, is not easy to specify in any clear and concise fashion. Some of what I've been writing about has been focused either explicitly or implicitly on London (although Newcastle has made its presence felt). When I type 'London' into my search engine, Wikipedia tells me that it is the capital city of England, Great Britain and the United Kingdom. Confusingly, it is not the only capital city in Great Britain and the United Kingdom (Cardiff, Edinburgh and Belfast are also capital cities). Today London is one of the most cosmopolitan cities on the planet: you don't expect to hear the person next to you speaking English. The Mayor of London, Sadiq Khan, is a native Londoner, a Sunni Muslim and the son of working-class British Pakistanis (his father was a bus driver, his mother a seamstress). In his particularity, Khan articulates a condition shared by many: identity, belonging and nation is a complex assemblage of different components. Raymond Williams, whose spirit hangs over this book, often described himself as a Welsh European.

In the final stages of writing this book, a national referendum (or plebiscite) took place to decide whether the United Kingdom should remain (Vote Remain) within the European Union or leave it (Vote Leave or Brexit, as it came to be known). On Thursday 23 June 2016 votes were cast and early on Friday 24 June, it became clear that the Brexit campaign had won by a slim majority (51.9 per cent voted Leave, 48.1 per cent voted Remain). A week before that vote, the Labour MP Jo Cox was murdered by a far-right terrorist who supported the racist group Britain First. Cox, who had been a Member of Parliament for just over a year, represented a constituency in West Yorkshire, and in her 'maiden' speech in Parliament (given just two weeks before she was murdered) she had spoken a sentiment that was clearly in a different 'emotional universe'[1] to her killer:

It is a joy to represent such a diverse community. Batley and Spen [her constituency] is a gathering of typically independent, no-nonsense and proud Yorkshire towns and villages. Our communities have been deeply enhanced by immigration, be it of Irish Catholics across the constituency or of Muslims from Gujarat in India or from Pakistan, principally from Kashmir. While we celebrate our diversity, what surprises me time and time again as I travel around the constituency is that we are far more united and have far more in common with each other than things that divide us.

(Cox 2016)

The belief that our common humanity was more significant and noble than our differences was echoed by Cox's grieving husband and seemed to resonate across the country. And yet the evidence was also clear that fundamental differences not only existed but were actively dividing 'us' as a national population. If Jo Cox's murder by a white supremacist fuelled a wave of empathetic reflection, the referendum result seemed to offer a permission slip to those who seethed with xenophobic resentments and racist indignation at Britain's multiculturalism.

In the immediate aftermath of the Brexit win, the number of hate crimes rose exponentially: on the first couple of days the police were talking about a rise of about 50 per cent; by the end of the first week they were talking about a rise of 500 per cent (Payton 2016). Various neo-fascist groups were clearly emboldened by what they perceived as a 'win' for their racist and xenophobic views. Reports were coming in of racist abuse being aimed at anyone not speaking English. The reports registered a huge rise in the number of non-whites being threatened and abused. Clearly the violent racism erupting wasn't limited to a specific European situation as much of it was aimed at the grandchildren of Commonwealth migrants coming from the Caribbean and the Subcontinent in the decades following the end of the war. In Glasgow, Manchester and parts of London it seemed that organised racist groups were making their presence felt on the street.[2]

One of the most depressing phrases that emerged in that week was 'celebratory racism', describing the outpouring of virulent racist feelings as a symptom of a euphoric victory by a small minority of those that voted 'Leave'. On Sunday 26 June 2016, the Polish Social and Cultural Association (POSK) in London's Hammersmith had been daubed with graffiti demanding that Polish people in the UK should 'go home'. The next day POSK was inundated with bunches of flowers, with telephone calls, with cards. They all said roughly the same things:

Dear Poles, I am so sorry to hear about what happened yesterday. We the Brits are grateful to you for fighting alongside us in the war and now for the enormous contribution you make to our society. We love you.

> *Dear Polish friends, we wanted to let you know how very sorry we are to hear about the abusive messages graffitied on to your building. It's depressing enough that the UK (or part of it) will be leaving the EU. That the result of the referendum seems to have been interpreted by some as a licence to express their racism and xenophobia is truly horrifying.*
>
> (Khomami 2016)

On the day of the referendum vote I worked as a volunteer for the Labour party (part of the Vote Remain campaign) in the electoral ward of Easton in Bristol. It is probably the most diverse and impoverished ward in Bristol. It was also a solidly 'Vote Remain' ward. This was a neighbourhood where the inhabitants might be descendants of grandparents who were born in Barbados or Bangladesh, homeowners with citizenship in Poland or Portugal, they might come from a long lineage of inhabitants of Bristol and its environs. This was not, however, a neighbourhood of 'immigrants', it was a neighbourhood of neighbours. In the streets of Easton, the feeling echoed Paul Gilroy's assertion 'It ain't where you're from, it's where you're at…' (Gilroy 1991). But this feeling clearly wasn't shared in other places, places where there were often much less 'actually existing' multiculturalism.

In the months leading up to the referendum and the weeks following the Brexit vote, a varied range of feelings and moods seemed to be in circulation. The whole campaign, both for Remain and Leave, had been pursued by factions of the Conservative Party as a set of intense feelings and emotions. The 'Remain' campaign had been dubbed 'Project Fear' and had stressed how a Brexit victory would result in the economy spiralling down into a prolonged recession that might take a decade to overcome. The Leave camp played on nostalgia and nationalism, and stirred up hatred with a poster campaign showing thousands of dark-skinned men, who were 'stretching' Britain to 'breaking point', or so the posters proclaimed. Within a political culture and a news media whose stock in trade was inflated emotions of fear and hate, such positioning was in many ways depressingly familiar. But the referendum vote seemed to 'fix' those feelings that usually circulated on radio, TV and newspapers and ground them into a more concrete sphere of daily life. Or at least this is what it felt like. I remember taking the dog for a walk the day after the referendum result. Usually I'm a very friendly dog walker, and say hello to anyone I pass, and I always enjoy it when my slightly shy dog is keen to say hello to other dogs. But in the immediate aftermath of that vote I felt a sense of anxious trepidation when I came upon my fellow dog walkers: had they voted Leave or Remain? Were they part of a xenophobic wave of feeling that seemed to have found a newly material expression? Yesterday's neighbours might become today's enemies. At the same time there was an almost spontaneous eruption of marches and events that sought to foster camaraderie and support for migrants and refugees and for Europe. These events couldn't help but be emotional: people were anxious about the fate of our communities; they were filled with love and empathy for those whose lives were being made newly precarious; they were mournful of what was happening to Britain in relation to Europe; and they were intensely fearful about what new legislation could be imposed once the safety net of European law was lost.

Politics conducted at this level of emotional intensity seemed to be a thoroughly bad way of doing politics; something to be avoided at all costs. In the wake of this pell-mell of conflicting passions it might seem that the answer would be to insist on a discourse of cold rationality. Yet what kind of cultural feelings were being deployed by the referendum campaigns? On the one hand, these dominant modes of fear and hate are clearly not the only cultural feelings that could have been deployed. For Jacqueline Rose one of the overarching experiences of the referendum was the way it was almost entirely orchestrated by men, and that the permissible feelings encouraged sentiments of 'control' and 'certainty' while outlawing feelings of 'care' and 'vulnerability'. For Rose, then, the referendum's pattern of feeling was ultimately masculinist:

> What vision of hearts and minds, as well as of nation states, are we being asked to buy into? It is the curse of masculinity that men are expected to shed any sign of vulnerability, to hold themselves erect as they strut across the world's stage, above all behave as if they have always, with no flicker of doubt, believed in themselves.
>
> (Rose 2016)

Threaded through this pattern of feeling, and in many ways providing its dominant impetus, was a feeling that needs to be described as cynical. In the field of cultural feelings, the sorts of contradictions that could include a will to control, alongside a sense of general cynicism, is not unusual.

Cynicism is a pattern of feeling that is premised on anti-collectivist feelings. We have already seen the groundwork for this explored in the TV series *Our Friends in the North*, discussed in the previous chapter. It is a historical sentiment often experienced by those whose dreams were dashed on the optimistic feelings that circulated in the immediate post-war years or in some of the hopes emerging in the 1960s and 1970s. But within the era of neoliberalism it became a more dominant form that didn't require an experience of disappointed dreams to take root. In a world where corruption (in its 'polite' old-boy network form, as well as in more modern forms) is often thought of as both endemic and natural, cynicism could be seen as a rational form. Yet cynicism is a more general form that is evident in music, in drama and perhaps especially in humour. It is often a form of satire that has quite an intimate feeling alongside it. It suggests that 'they' have all been duped by some specious nonsense, but 'you and I' (and keep this under your hat) know the truth, we know that this is all charlatanism.[3] Cynicism is deeply attractive, and as Kieran Curran (2015) shows, it is the sentiment that drives some of the most compelling post-war culture in Britain.[4]

Perhaps one of the most vivid examples of cynicism during the referendum campaigns was when Michael Gove (who was at the time Justice Secretary and had previously been Minister of Education) was asked to name any economist who was prepared to back Britain's exit from the European Union. His reply was simple: 'people in this country', he said, 'have had enough of experts' (Mance 2016). To assume that you know something that is a superior form of knowledge to experts in the field is the *sine qua non* of the cynical feeling. We feel it all the time, especially when we feel hard done by. Students feel it when they feel that their work is far superior to the mark they have been given. What is more unusual is the idea of a political leader simply declaring all expertise as specious, and declaring the untried, intuitive sense that people have as being far superior. This from someone who has power to steer education and justice.[5] And yet there was a cynicism on behalf of the Remain campaign when they simply assumed that the only way people would vote Remain was in the name of individual self-interest and financial gain. Cynicism is the cultural form that is most suited to a culture that seeks to refute our collective condition and promote a form of alienated individualism.

Cynicism, as part of a pattern of feeling that also includes fear and hate, is not always expressed in the intense forms that it took during the referendum campaigns. Cynicism also exists as a low-intensity feeling that is spread across a whole variety of cultural forms. You can see it throughout most daily newspapers as a general cultural tone. It is part of a cultural atmosphere where enthusiasm and commitments are hard to sustain (unless they are for football or other sports, or something similar) in an ethos that finds such positioning naïve. In a culture where it is much 'cooler' to look askance at someone's belief in socially progressive ideas, cynicism is something that can unite wealthy bankers and people who have had years and years of social degradation. As a low-level form it is the individualised way that 'belief' becomes 'lifestyle' rather than something that might need to be struggled for.

In this book I've not only tried to present a non-cynical version of the kinds of analyses that cultural studies can do, I've also tried to analyse patterns of feeling where the collective nature of cultural feeling is a crucial aspect of its character (as opposed to a characteristic that is hidden within the ideological folds of 'mass' individualism). And in this I'm building on cultural studies work that has been undertaken by a milieu of scholars who have managed to inoculate themselves against some of the seductive effects of cynicism. The cultural forms I've been looking at here have mostly been forms that have presented a collective subject (for instance in the films *Listen to Britain* and *The Nine Muses*) and solicited collective responses. Not all cultural forms that conjure up a collective identity or maintain a collective reception are progressive. Far from it. Some of the most repugnant cultural forms are precisely premised on such a collective form. National Socialism in Germany is one example, but so too is the sort of racist nationalism of the National Front, and the sort of 'posh' version of such forms that are peddled by the right in the form of UKIP. In this light, cynicism can sometimes seem the 'least bad' option. Yet if this is the cultural field we are faced with then it is more and more important to find cultural forms that can *both* offer collective sociality *and* are progressive in the social future they try to imagine and feel.

The cultural feelings that I have been keen to foster here, I hope, give some idea of the sustainable forms that have produced non-cynical patterns of feeling that are collective and at times utopian. They are clearly not a unified body of cultural forms. The works of Jennings and Akomfrah suggest a very different film poetics than we normally associate with narrative film. We need to add to these examples. Reggae provides, to my mind, one of the least cynical musical forms I know, and so too does the exorbitant evanescence of the Raincoats and the Slits. In their different ways the defiant, melancholic optimism of Rose Macaulay and Marie Paneth are to me examples of the complex, contradictory patterns of feeling that need to be rekindled. We don't need to rekindle the Rabelaisian spirit of television serials such as *This is England*: it is still very much alight. But we can champion it. And in championing such forms I will try to remind myself to be uncool, to be embarrassingly hopeful in the face of what often seems like an unfolding tragedy.

Notes

1 'Emotional universe' is a phrase that Bertrand Russell uses in a letter to the fascist leader Oswald Mosley. Russell, an ardent peace campaigner, was responding to Mosley's invitation to share a political platform with him: 'I feel obliged to say that the emotional universes we inhabit are so distinct, and in deepest ways opposed, that nothing fruitful or sincere could ever emerge from association between us' (Russell 1962).
2 No doubt elsewhere as well, these were just the most widely reported incidents.
3 At times, this cynical pattern of feeling is demonstrated by intellectual disciplines. At its worst cultural studies promotes this feeling. In this book and in others I have written I have been trying to steer cultural studies away from promoting such patterns of feeling.
4 The most extensive account of cynicism as a pattern of feeling (one that can be redeemed, to some degree) is offered in Sloterdijk (1988), but Bewes (1997) is also particularly useful.
5 Expertise should of course be greeted with a certain degree of scepticism, otherwise we would be hostages to all sorts of ideologies paraded before us as knowledge. Yet the wholesale refusal of expertise (of climate scientists, of teachers and educational researchers, of economists looking for sustainable approaches to the economy, etc.) is less a new 'flat earth mentality' and more a cynical instrumentalism that is looking to sell off the future for financial gains and small-minded victories.

BIBLIOGRAPHY

Addison, Paul and Jeremy A. Crang, eds. (2010) *Listening to Britain: Home Intelligence Reports on Britain's Finest Hour – May to September 1940*, London: Bodley Head.
Ahmed, Sara (2004) *The Cultural Politics of Emotion*, Edinburgh: Edinburgh University Press.
——— (2010) *The Promise of Happiness*, Durham, NC and London: Duke University Press.
Akomfrah, John and Kodwo Eshun (2007) 'An Absence of Ruins: John Akomfrah in Conversation with Kodwo Eshun' in Kodwo Eshun and Anjalika Sagar, eds., *The Ghosts of Songs: The Film Art of the Black Audio Film Collective 1982–1998*, Liverpool: Liverpool University Press, pp. 130–137.
Albertine, Viv (2014) *Clothes, Clothes, Clothes, Music, Music, Music, Boys, Boys, Boys*, London: Faber and Faber.
Aldgate, Anthony and Jeffrey Richards (2007) *Britain Can Take It: British Cinema in the Second World War*, London: I.B. Tauris.
Allen, Marjory and Mary Nicholson (1975) *Memoirs of an Uneducated Lady: Lady Allen of Hurtwood*, London: Thames & Hudson.
Allen of Hurtwood, Lady (1946) 'Why Not Use Our Bombsites Like This?' *Picture Post*, 16 November, pp. 26–29.
Altieri, Charles (2003) *The Particulars of Rapture: An Aesthetics of the Affects*, Ithaca, NY: Cornell University Press.
——— (2012) 'Affect, Intentionality, and Cognition: A Response to Ruth Leys', *Critical Inquiry*, vol. 38, no. 4, pp. 878–881.
Anderson, Ben (2009) 'Affective Atmospheres', *Emotion, Space and Society*, vol. 2, no. 2, pp. 77–81.
——— (2014) *Encountering Affect: Capacities, Apparatuses, Conditions*, Abingdon: Routledge.
Anonymous (1940) 'Should We Feel Fear?', *Picture Post*, 5 October, pp. 35–37.
Auslander, Leora (1996) *Taste and Power: Furnishing Modern France*, Berkeley, CA: University of California Press.
Bakhtin, M.M. (1981 [1938 and 1973]) 'Forms of Time and of the Chronotope in the Novel', *The Dialogic Imagination: Four Essays*, edited by Michael Holquist, Austin, TX: University of Texas Press, pp. 84–258.
Banton, Michael (1955) *The Coloured Quarter: Negro Immigrants in an English City*, London: Jonathan Cape.

Barthes, Roland (1979) *A Lover's Discourse: Fragments*, translated by Richard Howard, London: Jonathan Cape.
Bateson, Gregory (1935) 'Culture, Contact and Schismogenesis', *Man*, December, item 199, pp. 178–183.
—— (1958 [1936]) *Naven*, 2nd edn, Stanford, CA: Stanford University Press.
—— (1972 [1941]) 'Experiments in Thinking about Observed Ethnological Material', in *Steps to an Ecology of Mind*, Chicago, IL: University of Chicago Press, pp. 73–87.
—— (1972) *Steps to an Ecology of Mind*, Chicago, IL: University of Chicago Press.
Beckett, Andy (2009) *When the Lights Went Out: What Really Happened to Britain in the Seventies*, London: Faber and Faber.
Bell, Amy Helen (2011) *London Was Ours: Diaries and Memoirs of the London Blitz*, London: I.B. Tauris.
Benedict, Ruth (1932) 'Configurations of Culture in North America', *American Anthropologist*, vol. 34, no. 1, pp. 1–27.
—— (1934) *Patterns of Culture*, Boston, MA: Houghton Mifflin Company.
Benjamin, Walter (2003) *Walter Benjamin Selected Writings, Volume 4, 1938–1940*, edited by Michael W. Jennings, Cambridge, MA: Belknap/Harvard University Press.
Berg, Leila (1972) *Look at Kids*, Harmondsworth: Penguin.
Berger, John and Jean Mohr (1982 [1975]) *A Seventh Man: A Book of Images and Words about the Experience of Migrant Workers in Europe*, London: Writers and Readers.
Berlant, Lauren (2008a) *The Female Complaint: The Unfinished Business of Sentimentality in American Culture*, Durham, NC and London: Duke University Press.
—— (2008b) 'Thinking about Feeling Historical', *Emotion, Space and Society*, vol. 1, no. 1, pp. 4–9.
—— (2011) *Cruel Optimism*, Durham, NC and London: Duke University Press.
—— (2015) 'Structures of Unfeeling: *Mysterious Skin*', *International Journal of Politics, Culture and Society*, vol. 28, no. 3, pp. 191–213.
Best, Beverley (2012) 'Raymond Williams and the Structure of Feeling of Reality TV', *International Journal of Humanities and Social Science*, vol. 2, no. 7, pp. 192–201.
Best, Stephen and Sharon Marcus (2009) 'Surface Reading: An Introduction', *Representations*, no. 108, pp. 1–21.
Bewes, Timothy (1997) *Cynicism and Post Modernity*, London: Verso.
Bloch, Ernst (1935) 'Nonsynchronism and the Obligation to its Dialectics', translated by Mark Ritter, *New German Critique*, no. 11 (1977), pp. 22–38.
Böhme, Gernot (1993) 'Atmosphere as the Fundamental Concept of a New Aesthetics', *Thesis Eleven*, no. 36, pp. 113–126.
—— (2014) 'Urban Atmospheres: Charting New Directions for Architecture and Urban Planning', in Christian Borch, ed., *Architectural Atmospheres: On the Experience and Politics of Architecture*, Basel: Birkhäuser, pp. 43–59.
Bourke, Joanna (2005) *Fear: A Cultural History*, London: Virago.
Boym, Svetlana (2001) *The Future of Nostalgia*, New York: Basic Books.
Bradley, Lloyd (2001) *Bass Culture: When Reggae Was King*, London: Penguin.
—— (2013) *Sounds Like London: 100 Years of Black Music in the Capital*, London: Serpent's Tail
Brinkema, Eugenie (2014) *The Forms of the Affects*, Durham, NC: Duke University Press.
Burlingham, Dorothy and Anna Freud (1942) *Young Children in War-Time: A Year's Work in a Residential War Nursery*, London: George Allen & Unwin.
Calder, Angus (1971) *The People's War: Britain 1939–1945*, London: Panther Books.
—— (1992) *The Myth of the Blitz*, London: Pimlico.
Centre for Contemporary Cultural Studies (1982) *The Empire Strikes Back: Race and Racism in 70s Britain*, London: Hutchinson.

Certeau, Michel de (1984) *The Practice of Everyday Life*, translated by Steven Rendall, Berkeley, CA: University of California Press.
Chapman, James (1998) *The British at War: Cinema, State and Propaganda, 1939–1945*, London: I.B. Tauris.
Civil Defence Handbook (1963) *Advising the Householder on Protection against Nuclear Attack*, London: Her Majesty's Stationery Office.
Clark, T.J. (1985) 'Clement Greenberg's Theory of Art', in Francis Frascina, ed., *Pollock and After: The Critical Debate*, London: Harper & Row, pp. 47–63.
——— (2012) 'For a Left with No Future', *New Left Review*, no. 74, pp. 53–75.
Clough, Patricia T., ed. (2007) *The Affective Turn: Theorizing the Social*, Durham, NC and London: Duke University Press.
Collins, Marcus (2003) *Modern Love: An Intimate History of Men and Women in Twentieth-Century Britain*, London: Atlantic Books.
Connolly, William E. (2011) 'The Complexity of Intention', *Critical Inquiry*, vol. 37, no. 4, pp. 791–798.
Coole, Diana and Samantha Frost, eds. (2010) *New Materialisms: Ontology, Agency, and Politics*, Durham, NC: Duke University Press.
Cox, Jo (2016) 'Maiden speech in the House of Commons', given 3 June 2016, accessed online at www.parliament.uk/business/news/2016/june/jo-cox-maiden-speech-in-the-house-of-commons (accessed 2 July 2016).
Curran, Kieran (2015) *Cynicism in British Post-War Culture: Ignorance, Dust and Disease*, Houndmills: Palgrave Macmillan.
Cvetkovich, Ann (1992) *Mixed Feelings: Feminism, Mass Culture, and Victorian Sensationalism*, New Brunswick: Rutgers University Press.
——— (2003) *An Archive of Feelings: Trauma, Sexuality, and Lesbian Public Cultures*, Durham, NC and London: Duke University Press.
Damasio, Antonio (2000) *The Feeling of What Happens: Body, Emotion and the Making of Consciousness*, London: Vintage.
——— (2004) *Looking for Spinoza*, London: Vintage.
Debuysere, Stoffel (2015) 'Close-Up: John Akomfrah and the Black Audio Film Collective: Signs of Struggle, Songs of Sorrow: Notes on the Politics of Uncertainty in the Films of John Akomfrah', *Black Camera: An International Film Journal*, vol. 6 no. 2, pp. 61–78.
Demos, E. Virginia, ed. (1995) *Exploring Affect: The Selected Writings of Silvan S. Tomkins*, Cambridge: Cambridge University Press.
Deville, Joe and Gregory J. Seigworth (2015) 'Everyday Debt and Credit', *Cultural Studies*, vol. 29, no. 5–6, pp. 615–629.
Di Michele, Laura (1993) 'Autobiography and the "Structure of Feeling" in *Border Country*' in Dennis Dworkin and Leslie Roman, eds., *Views Beyond the Border Country: Raymond Williams and Cultural Politics*, New York and London: Routledge, pp. 21–37.
Dreyfus, Hubert L (1991) *Being-in-the-World: A Commentary on Heidegger's Being and Time, Division 1*, Cambridge, MA: MIT Press.
Eagleton, Terry (1988) 'Resources for a Journey of Hope: The Significance of Raymond Williams', *New Left Review*, no. 168, pp. 3–11.
Eaton, Michael (2005) *Our Friends in the North*, London: BFI.
Edensor, Tim (2005) *Industrial Ruins: Space, Aesthetics and Materiality*, Oxford: Berg.
——— (2012) 'Illuminated Atmospheres: Anticipating and Reproducing the Flow of Affective Experience in Blackpool', *Environment and Planning D: Society and Space*, vol. 30, no. 6, pp. 1103–1122.

Eshun, Kodwo (2007) 'Drawing the Forms of Things Unknown', in Kodwo Eshun and Anjalika Sagar, eds., *The Ghosts of Songs: The Film Art of the Black Audio Film Collective 1982–1998*, Liverpool: Liverpool University Press, pp. 86–99.
Eshun, Kodwo and Anjalika Sagar, eds. (2007) *The Ghosts of Songs: The Film Art of the Black Audio Film Collective 1982–1998*, Liverpool: Liverpool University Press.
Farley, Paul and Michael Symmons Roberts (2011) *Edgelands: Journeys into England's True Wilderness*, London: Jonathon Cape.
Feigel, Lara (2013) *The Love-Charm of Bombs: Restless Lives in the Second World War*, London: Bloomsbury.
Felski, Rita (2015) *The Limits of Critique*, Chicago, IL: University of Chicago Press.
Field, Geoffrey (2002) 'Nights Underground in Darkest London: The Blitz, 1940–1941', *International Labor and Working-Class History*, vol. 62, pp. 11–49.
Filmer, Paul (2003) 'Structures of Feeling and Socio-Cultural Formations: The Significance of Literature and Experience to Raymond Williams's Sociology of Culture', *British Journal of Sociology*, vol. 54, pp. 199–219.
Fisher, Jean (2007) 'In Living Memory… Archive and Testimony in the Films of the Black Audio Film Collective', in Kodwo Eshun and Anjalika Sagar, eds., *The Ghosts of Songs: The Film Art of the Black Audio Film Collective 1982–1998*, Liverpool: Liverpool University Press, pp. 16–30.
Flatley, Jonathan (2008) *Affective Mapping: Melancholia and the Politics of Modernism*, Cambridge, MA: Harvard University Press.
——— (2012) 'How a Revolutionary Counter-Mood is Made', *New Literary History*, vol. 43, pp. 503–525.
Fryer, Peter (1984) *Staying Power: The History of Black People in Britain*, London: Pluto.
Gardiner, J. (2011). *The Blitz: The British under Attack*. London, HarperCollins.
Gates, Henry Louis (1995) *Colored People*, Harmondsworth: Penguin.
——— (2000) 'A Reporter at Large: Black London', in Kwesi Owusu, ed., *Black British Culture & Society: A Text Reader*, London: Routledge, pp. 169–180 (originally published in *The New Yorker* in April and May 1997).
Gilbert, Jeremy, ed. (2013) 'Neoliberal Culture', *New Formations*, nos. 80–81.
Gilroy, Beryl (1994 [1976]) *Black Teacher*, London: Bogle-L'Ouverture Press.
——— (1998) *Leaves in the Wind: Collected Writings*, edited by Joan Anim-Addo, London: Mango Publishing.
Gilroy, Paul (1991) 'It Ain't Where You're From, it's Where You're At…', *Third Text*, vol. 5, no. 13, pp. 3–16.
——— (1993) *The Black Atlantic: Modernity and Double Consciousness*, London and New York: Verso.
——— (2002 [1987]) *There Ain't No Black in the Union Jack*, London: Routledge.
——— (2005) *Postcolonial Melancholia*, New York: Colombia University Press.
——— (2007) *Black Britain: A Photographic History*, London: Saqi Books.
——— (2010) *Darker than Blue: On the Moral Economies of Black Atlantic Culture*, Cambridge, MA: Harvard University Press.
——— (2015) 'Rebel Souls: Dancefloor Justice and the Temporary Undoing of Britain's Babylon', in Syd Shelton, ed., *Rock Against Racism*, London: Autograph, pp. 23–26.
Glass, Ruth (1960) *Newcomers: The West Indians in London*, London: Centre for Urban Studies and George Allen & Unwin.
Grass, Günter (2010 [1959]) *The Tin Drum*, London: Vintage.
Green, André (1999 [1973]) *The Fabric of Affect in the Psychoanalytic Discourse*, translated by Alan Sheridan, London and New York: Routledge.

Gregg, Melissa and Gregory J. Seigworth, eds. (2010) *The Affect Theory Reader*, Durham, NC: Duke University Press.
Grossberg, Lawrence (2010) 'Affect's Future: Rediscovering the Virtual in the Actual', in Melissa Gregg and Gregory J. Seigworth, eds., *The Affect Theory Reader*, Durham, NC: Duke University Press, pp. 309–338.
Guignon, Charles (1984) 'Moods in Heidegger's *Being and Time*', in Cheshire Calhoun and Robert C. Solomon, eds., *What is an Emotion? Classic Reading in Philosophical Psychology*, New York: Oxford University Press, pp. 230–243.
Hall, Stuart (1972) 'The Social Eye of *Picture Post*', in *Working Papers in Cultural Studies*, Birmingham: University of Birmingham, pp. 71–120.
—— (1987) 'Minimal Selves', in Lisa Appignanesi, ed., *Identity: the Real Me (ICA Documents 6)*, London: Institute of Contemporary Arts, pp. 44–46.
—— (1988) *The Hard Road to Renewal: Thatcherism and the Crisis of the Left*, London: Verso.
—— (1992 [1984]) 'Reconstruction Work: Images of Postwar Black Settlement', *Ten: 8*, vol. 2, no. 3, pp. 106–113.
—— (1993) 'Aspiration and Attitude... Reflections on Black Britain in the Nineties', *New Formations*, no. 33, pp. 38–46.
—— (1997) 'Old and New Identities, Old and New Ethnicities' in Anthony D. King, ed., *Culture, Globalization and the World-System: Contemporary Conditions for the Representation of Identity*, Minneapolis, MN: University of Minnesota Press, pp. 41–68.
—— (2001) 'Constituting an Archive', *Third Text*, vol. 15, no. 54, pp. 89–92.
—— (2011) 'The Neo-Liberal Revolution', *Cultural Studies*, vol. 25, no. 6, pp. 705–728.
Hall, Stuart and Les Back (2009) 'At Home and Not at Home: In Conversation', *Cultural Studies*, vol. 23, no. 4, pp. 658–687.
Hall, Stuart and Kuan-Hsing Chen (1996) 'The Formation of a Diasporic Intellectual: An Interview with Stuart Hall', in David Morley and Kuan-Hsing Chen, eds., *Stuart Hall: Critical Dialogues in Cultural Studies*, London: Routledge, pp. 484–503.
Hall, Stuart, Chris Cricher, Tony Jefferson, John Clarke and Brian Roberts (1978) *Policing the Crisis: Mugging, the State, and Law and Order*, Houndmills: Palgrave Macmillan.
Hanley, Lynsey (2012) *Estates: An Intimate History*, London: Granta.
Haraway, Donna (1988) 'Situated Knowledges: The Science Question in Feminism and the Privilege of Partial Perspective', *Feminist Studies*, vol. 14, no. 3, pp. 575–599.
Hardt, Michael (1999) 'Affective Labor', *Boundary 2*, vol. 26, no. 2, pp. 89–100.
Harrison, Tom (1976) *Living Through the Blitz*, London: Collins.
Harvey, David (2007) *A Brief History of Neoliberalism*, Oxford: Oxford University Press.
Hatherley, Owen (2011) *A Guide to the New Ruins of Great Britain*, London: Verso.
Heide, Morten and Kjell Grønhaug (2009) 'Key Factors in Guests' Perception of Hotel Atmosphere', *Cornell Hospitality Quarterly*, vol. 50, no. 1, pp. 29–43.
Heidegger, Martin (1995 [1929–1930]) *The Fundamental Concepts of Metaphysics: World, Finitude, Solitude*, translated by William McNeill and Nicholas Walker, Bloomington and Indianapolis, IN: Indiana University Press.
—— (2008 [1927]) *Being and Time*, translated by John Macquarrie and Edward Robinson, New York: Harper Perennial.
Hemmings, Clare (2005) 'Invoking Affect: Cultural Theory and the Ontological Turn', *Cultural Studies*, vol. 19, no. 5, pp. 548–567.
Henry, William 'Lez' (2012) 'Reggae, Rasta and the Role of the Deejay in the Black British Experience', *Contemporary British History*, vol. 26, no. 3, pp. 355–373.
Hersey, John (1946) *Hiroshima*, Harmondsworth: Penguin.
Highmore, Ben (2010) 'Streets in the Air', in Clare Zimmerman and Mark Crinson, eds., *Neo-avant-garde and Postmodern: Postwar Architecture in Britain and Beyond (Studies in British Art 21)*, New Haven, CT and London: Yale University Press, pp. 79–100.

―― (2011) *Ordinary Lives: Studies in the Everyday*, Abingdon: Routledge.
Hinton, James (2010) *Nine Wartime Lives*, Oxford: Oxford University Press.
―― (2013) *The Mass Observers: A History, 1937–1949*, Oxford: Oxford Universi.
Hochschild, Arlie Russell (1983) *The Managed Heart: Commercialization of Human F*, Berkeley, CA: University of California Press.
Hodgkinson, Anthony W. and Rodney E. Sheratsky (1982) *Humphrey Jennings: More than* ι *Maker of Film*, Hanover, NH: University Press of New England.
Hoggart, Richard and Raymond Williams (1960) 'Working Class Attitudes', *New Left Review*, no. 1, pp. 26–30.
Howe, Zoe Street (2009) *Typical Girls? The Story of the Slits*, London: Omnibus Press.
Høystad, Ole M. (2007) *A History of the Heart*, London: Reaktion.
Hume, David (1985 [1739–1740]) *A Treatise of Human Nature*, London: Penguin.
Humphry, Derek and Gus John (1972) *Because They're Black*, Harmondsworth: Pelican Books.
Inglis, Fred (1995) *Raymond Williams*, London: Routledge.
―― (2014) *Richard Hoggart: Virtue and Reward*, Cambridge: Polity.
Jackson, Kevin, ed. (1993) *The Humphrey Jennings Film Reader*, Manchester: Carcanet Press.
―― (2004) *Humphrey Jennings*, London: Picador.
James, William (1962 [1899]) *Talks to Teachers on Psychology and to Students on Some of Life's Ideals*, New York: Dover.
Jennings, Mary-Lou (1982) *Humphrey Jennings: Film-maker, Painter, Poet*, London: BFI.
Johnstone, William (1980) *Points in Time: An Autobiography*, London: Barrie and Jenkins.
Jones, Edgar, Robin Woolven, Bill Durodié and Simon Wessely (2004) 'Civilian Morale During the Second World War: Responses to Air Raids Re-examined', *Social History of Medicine*, vol. 17, no. 3, pp. 463–479.
Kern, Stephen (1992) *The Culture of Love: Victorians to Moderns*, Cambridge, MA: Harvard University Press.
Khomami, Nadia (2016) '"The Vote Made People Just Explode": Polish Centre Reeling After Graffiti Attack', *The Guardian*, 27 June, accessed online at www.theguardian.com/uk-news/2016/jun/27/brexit-polish-centre-london-reeling-after-graffiti-attack (accessed 2 July 2016).
King, Richard (2012) *How Soon is Now? The Madmen and Mavericks Who Made Independent Music 1975–2005*, London: Faber and Faber.
Kluge, Alexander (2014 [2008]) *Air Raid*, translated by Martin Chalmers, London: Seagull Books.
Konings, Martijn (2015) *The Emotional Logic of Capitalism: What Progressives Have Missed*, Stanford, CA: Stanford University Press.
Kozlovsky, Roy (2008) 'Adventure Playgrounds and Postwar Reconstruction', in Marta Gutman and Ning de Coninck-Smith, eds., *Designing Modern Childhoods: History, Space, and the Material Culture of Children*, New Brunswick: Rutgers University Press, pp. 171–190.
Kynaston, David (2007) *Austerity Britain, 1945–51*, London: Bloomsbury.
―― (2009) *Family Britain, 1951–57*, London: Bloomsbury.
Lamming, George (2005 [1960]) *The Pleasure of Exile*, London: Pluto.
Langhamer, Claire (2013) *The English in Love: The Intimate Story of an Emotional Revolution*, Oxford: Oxford University Press.
Laplanche, Jean and Jean-Bertrand Pontalis (1985) *The Language of Psychoanalysis*, London: Hogarth Press.
Lazzarato, Maurizio (1996) 'Immaterial Labor', in Paolo Virno and Michael Hardt, eds., *Radical Thought in Italy: A Potential Politics*, Minneapolis, MN: University of Minnesota Press, pp. 133–147.
Leavis, F.R. (1972 [1932]) *New Bearings in English Poetry: A Study of the Contemporary Situation*, Harmondsworth: Pelican.

Bibliography

Leavis, Q.D. (1968 [1943]) 'Academic Case-History', in *A Selection from Scrutiny: Volume 1*, compiled by F.R. Leavis, Cambridge: Cambridge University Press, pp. 1–7.

Lefebvre, Henri (1991) *Critique of Everyday Life: Volume 1*, translated by John Moore, London: Verso. This edition was first published in France in 1958.

Letts, Don (2008) *Culture Clash: Dread Meets Punk Rockers*, London: SAF.

Levin, Joshua (2016) *The Secret History of the Blitz*, London: Simon & Schuster.

Levine, Caroline (2015) *Forms: Whole, Rhythm, Hierarchy, Network*, Princeton, NJ: Princeton University Press.

Levitas, Ruth (2013) *Utopia as Method: The Imaginary Reconstitution of Society*, Houndmills: Palgrave Macmillan.

Leys, Ruth (2011a) 'The Turn to Affect: A Critique', *Critical Inquiry*, vol. 37, no. 3, pp. 434–472.

—— (2011b) 'Critical Response II: Affect and Intention: A Reply to William E. Connolly', *Critical Inquiry*, vol. 37, no. 4, pp. 799–805.

Lindqvist, Sven (2012 [2001]) *A History of Bombing*, translated by Linda Haverty Rugg, London: Granta.

Lipset, David (1982) *Gregory Bateson: The Legacy of a Scientist*, Boston, MA: Beacon Press.

Love, Heather (2009) *Feeling Backward: Loss and the Politics of Queer History*, Cambridge, MA: Harvard University Press.

Lynd, Robert and Helen Lynd (1929) *Middletown: A Study in Modern American Culture*, Orlando, FL: Harcourt Brace & Company.

Macaulay, Rose (1958 [1950]) *The World My Wilderness*, Harmondsworth: Penguin.

MacCurdy, J.T. (1943) *The Structure of Morale*, Cambridge: Cambridge University Press.

Mackay, Robert (2002) *Half the Battle: Civilian Morale in Britain During the Second World War*, Manchester: Manchester University Press.

Mance, Henry (2016) 'Britain Has Had Enough of Experts, says Gove', *Financial Times*, 3 June, accessed online at www.ft.com/cms/s/0/3be49734-29cb-11e6-83e4-abc22d5d108c.html (accessed 11 September 2016).

Marchant, Hilde (1956) 'Thirty Thousand Colour Problems', *Picture Post*, 9 June, pp. 27–28, 38.

Marcus, Greil (1994) *In the Fascist Bathroom: Writings on Punk, 1977–1992*, Harmondsworth: Penguin.

—— (1997) *Lipstick Traces: A Secret History of the Twentieth Century*, London: Picador.

Marwick, Arthur (1976) *The Home Front: The British and the Second World War*, London: Thames & Hudson.

Marx, Karl (1852) *The Eighteenth Brumaire of Louis Bonaparte*, in Karl Marx and Frederick Engels, *Selected Works*, London: Lawrence and Wishart, 1967.

Marx, Karl and Frederick Engels (1968 [1872]) *Manifesto of the Communist Party*, in *Marx/Engels: Selected Works in One Volume*, London: Lawrence and Wishart, pp. 31–63.

Mass-Observation (1937) *Mass Observation*, introduction by Julian Huxley, London: Fredrick Muller.

—— (2009 [1940]) *War Begins at Home*, London: Faber and Faber.

—— (2009 [1949]) *Report on Juvenile Delinquency*, London: Faber and Faber.

Massumi, Brian (1995) 'The Autonomy of Affect', *Cultural Critique*, vol. 31, pp. 83–109.

—— (2002) *Parables for the Virtual: Movement, Affect, Sensation*, Durham, NC and London: Duke University Press.

—— (2005) 'Fear (The Spectrum Said)', *Positions*, vol. 13, no. 1, pp. 31–48.

—— (2015) *The Politics of Affect*, Cambridge: Polity Press.

Maxwell, Brigid (1948) 'Junk Playground', *Housewife*, November, pp. 24–27, 97.

McCarthy, Anna (2007) 'Reality Television: A Neoliberal Theatre of Suffering', *Social Text*, vol. 25, no. 4, pp. 17–41.

McClintock, Anne (1995) *Imperial Leather: Race, Gender and Sexuality in the Colonial Contest*, London and New York: Routledge.
McCracken, Scott (2014) 'The Mood of Defeat', *New Formations*, no. 82, pp. 64–81.
McCreery, Sandy (1996) 'Westway: Caught in the Speed Trap', in Iain Borden, Joe Kerr, Alicia Pivaro and Jane Rendell, eds., *Strangely Familiar: Narratives of Architecture in the City*, London: Routledge, pp. 37–41.
McLaine, Ian (1979) *Ministry of Morale: Home Front Morale and the Ministry of Information in World War II*, London: George Allen & Unwin.
McSmith, Andy (2011) *No Such Thing as Society: A History of Britain in the 1980s*, London: Constable.
Mellor, Leo (2011) *Reading the Ruins: Modernism, Bombsites and British Culture*, Cambridge: Cambridge University Press.
Mercer, Kobena (2007) 'Post-Colonial Trauerspiel', in Kodwo Eshun and Anjalika Sagar, eds., *The Ghosts of Songs: The Film Art of the Black Audio Film Collective 1982–1998*, Liverpool: Liverpool University Press, pp. 43–59.
——— (2015) 'Close-Up: John Akomfrah and the Black Audio Film Collective: Becoming Black Audio: An Interview with John Akomfrah and Trevor Mathison', *Black Camera: An International Film Journal*, vol. 6, no. 2, pp. 79–93.
——— (2016) *Travel & See: Black Diaspora Art Practices since the 1980s*, Durham, NC and London: Duke University Press.
Middleton, Stuart (2016) 'The Concept of "Experience" and the Making of the English Working Class, 1924–1963', *Modern Intellectual History*, vol. 13, no. 1, pp. 179–208.
Milner, Andrew (1994) 'Cultural Materialism, Culturalism and Post-Culturalism: The Legacy of Raymond Williams', *Theory, Culture & Society*, vol. 11, pp. 43–73.
Ministry of Home Security (1942) *Front Line 1940–41: The Official Story of the Civil Defence of Britain*, London: His Majesty's Stationery Office.
Mulhern, Francis (1979) *The Moment of 'Scrutiny'*, London: New Left Books.
Muñoz, José Esteban (2009) *Cruising Utopia: The Then and There of Queer Futurity*, New York: New York University Press.
Ngai, Sianne (2005) *Ugly Feelings*, Cambridge, MA: Harvard University Press.
——— (2010) 'Our Aesthetic Categories', *PMLA*, vol. 125, pp. 948–958.
——— (2012) *Our Aesthetic Categories*, Cambridge, MA: Harvard University Press.
Nietzsche, Friedrich (1968 [1901]) *The Will to Power*, translated by Walter Kaufmann and R.J. Hollingdale, New York: Vintage Books.
Olden, Mark (2011) *Murder in Notting Hill*, Winchester: Zero Books.
Orwell, George (1970a) *The Collected Essays, Journalism and Letters of George Orwell, Volume 2: My Country Right or Left, 1940–1943*, Harmondsworth: Penguin.
——— (1970b) *The Collected Essays, Journalism and Letters of George Orwell, Volume 3: My Country Right or Left, 1943–1945*, Harmondsworth: Penguin.
Paneth, Marie (1944) *Branch Street: A Sociological Study*, London: George Allen & Unwin.
Panse, Silke (2006) 'The Film-maker as *Rückenfigur*: Documentary as Painting in Alexandr Sokurov's *Elegy of a Voyage*', *Third Text*, vol. 20, no. 1, pp. 9–25.
Patterson, Sheila (1965) *Dark Strangers: A Study of West Indians in London*, Harmondsworth: Pelican Books.
Payton, Matt (2016) 'Racist Hate Crimes Increase Five-Fold in Week After Brexit Vote', *The Independent*, 1 July, accessed online at www.independent.co.uk/news/uk/crime/racism-hate-crimes-increase-brexit-eu-referendum-a7113091.html (accessed 2 July 2016).
Phillips, Mike and Trevor Phillips (1999) *Windrush: The Irresistible Rise of Multi-Racial Britain*, London: HarperCollins.

Bibliography

Power, Nina and John Akomfrah (2011) 'Counter-Media, Migration, Poetry: Interview with John Akomfrah', *Film Quarterly*, vol. 65, no. 2, pp. 59–63.
Probyn, Elspeth (2005) *Blush: Faces of Shame*, Minneapolis, MN: University of Minnesota Press.
Proctor, James, ed. (2000) *Writing Black Britain 1948–1998: An Interdisciplinary Anthology*, Manchester: Manchester University Press.
Protevi, John (2009) *Political Affect: Connecting the Social and the Somatic*, Minneapolis, MN: University of Minnesota Press.
Rammstedt, Otthein (1991) 'On Simmel's Aesthetics: Argumentation in the Journal *Jugend* 1897–1906', *Theory, Culture & Society*, vol. 8, no. 3, pp. 125–144.
Reddy, William M. (2001) *The Navigation of Feeling: A Framework for the History of Emotions*, Cambridge: Cambridge University Press.
Reynolds, Simon (2005) *Rip it Up and Start Again: Postpunk 1978–1984*, London: Faber and Faber.
—— (2009) *Totally Wired: Post-Punk Interviews and Overviews*, London: Faber and Faber.
Richards, I.A. (1976 [1929]) *Practical Criticism*, London: Routledge & Kegan Paul.
Riley, Denise (1983) *War in the Nursery: Theories of the Child and Mother*, London: Virago.
Rose, Jacqueline (2016) 'The Twin Curse of Masculinity and Male-Dominated Politics Helped Create Brexit', *The Guardian*, 2 July, accessed online at www.theguardian.com/commentisfree/2016/jul/02/twin-curse-masculinity-male-dominated-politics-brexit (accessed 2 July 2016).
Rose, Nikolas (1989) *Governing the Soul: The Shaping of the Private Self*, London: Routledge.
Rosenwein, Barbara H. (2016) *Generations of Feeling: A History of Emotions, 600–1700*, Cambridge: Cambridge University Press.
Russell, Bertrand (1962) 'Letter to Oswald Mosley', accessed online at www.lettersofnote.com/2016/02/every-ounce-of-my-energy.html (accessed 3 July 2016).
Samuel, Raphael (1994) *Theatres of Memory: Past and Present in Contemporary Culture*, London: Verso.
Sandbrook, Dominic (2006) *Never Had It So Good: A History of Britain from Suez to the Beatles*, London: Abacus.
—— (2007) *White Heat: A History of Britain in the Swinging Sixties*, London: Abacus.
—— (2011) *State of Emergency – the Way we Were: Britain 1970–1974*, London: Penguin Books.
Sansom, William (2010 [1947]) *The Blitz: Westminster at War*, London: Faber and Faber.
Savage, Jon (2009) *The England's Dreaming Tapes*, London: Faber and Faber.
Scandura, Jani (2008) *Down in the Dumps: Place, Modernity, American Depression*, Durham, NC: Duke University Press.
Schivelbusch, Wolfgang (2001) *The Culture of Defeat: On National Trauma, Mourning and Recovery*, translated by Jefferson Chase, London: Granta Books.
Sebald, W.G. (2004) *On the Natural History of Destruction*, translated by Anthea Bell, New York: Modern Library.
Sedgwick, Eve Kosofsky (2003) *Touching Feeling: Affect, Pedagogy, Performativity*, Durham, NC and London: Duke University Press.
Seigworth, Gregory J. (2012) 'Reading Lauren Berlant Writing', *Communication and Critical/Cultural Studies*, vol. 9, no. 4, pp. 346–352.
Shapira, Michal (2013) 'The Psychological Study of Anxiety in the Era of the Second World War', *Twentieth Century British History*, vol. 24, no. 1, pp. 31–57.
Shouse, Eric (2005) 'Feeling, Emotion, Affect', *M/C Journal*, accessed online at http://journal.media-culture.org.au/0512/03-shouse.php (accessed 8 October 2015).
Simpson, David (1992) 'Raymond Williams: Feeling for Structures, Voicing "History"' *Social Text*, no. 30, pp. 9–26.

Sinfield, Alan (2000) 'Culture, Consensus and Difference: Angus Wilson to Alan Hollinghurst', in Alan Sinfield and Alistair Davies, eds., *British Culture of the Postwar: An Introduction to Literature and Society 1945–1999*, London: Routledge, pp. 83–102.

Singh, Greg (2014) *Feeling Film: Affect and Authenticity in Popular Cinema*, Abingdon: Routledge.

Sloterdijk, Peter (1988) *Critique of Cynical Reason*, London: Verso.

────── (2009) *Terror from the Air*, translated by Amy Patton and Steve Corcoran, Los Angeles, CA: Semiotext(e).

Smith, Dai (2008) *Raymond Williams: A Warrior's Tale*, Cardigan: Parthian.

Sobers, Norma and Theo Sobers (1998) 'Deep Freeze, New Family', in *Origins: Personal Stories of Crossing the Seas to Settle in Britain*, coordinated by Geraldine Edwards, Bristol: The Kuumba Project, pp. 122–126.

Spender, Stephen (1945) *Citizens in War and After*, London: George E. Harrap & Co.

Stewart, Kathleen (2007) *Ordinary Affects*, Durham, NC and London: Duke University Press.

Sullivan, Paul (2014) *Remixology: Tracing the Dub Diaspora*, London: Reaktion.

Swenarton, Mark, Tom Avermaete and Dirk van den Heuvel, eds. (2015) *Architecture and the Welfare State*, London: Routledge.

Symons, Stéphane and Matthias De Groof (2015) 'Close-Up: John Akomfrah and the Black Audio Film Collective: Memory and Creative Forgetfulness in The Nine Muses', *Black Camera: An International Film Journal*, vol. 6, no. 2, pp. 147–153.

Thien, Deborah (2005) 'After or Beyond Feeling? A Consideration of Affect and Emotion in Geography', *Arena*, vol. 37, no. 4, pp. 450–456.

Thomas, James (2007) '"Bound in by History": The Winter of Discontent in British Politics, 1979–2004', *Media, Culture and Society*, vol. 29, no. 2, pp. 263–283.

Thompson, E.P. and Dan Smith, eds. (1980) *Protest and Survive*, Harmondsworth: Penguin.

Titmuss, Richard (1971 [1950]) *Problems of Social Policy*, Westport: Greenwood Press.

Tubbs, Ralph (1942) *Living in Cities*, Harmondsworth: Penguin.

Tulloch, Carol (2016) *The Birth of Cool: Style Narratives of the African Diaspora*, London: Bloomsbury.

Turner, Alwyn W. (2009) *Crisis? What Crisis? Britain in the 1970s*, London: Aurum Press.

────── (2010) *Rejoice! Rejoice! Britain in the 1980s*, London: Aurum Press.

────── (2014) *A Classless Society: Britain in the 1990s*, London: Aurum Press.

Vidler, Anthony (2010) 'Air War and Architecture', in Julia Hell and Andreas Schönle, eds., *Ruins of Modernity*, Durham, NC: Duke University Press, pp. 29–40.

Virno, Paolo (1996) 'The Ambivalence of Disenchantment', in Paolo Virno and Michael Hardt, eds., *Radical Thought in Italy: A Potential Politics*, Minneapolis, MN: University of Minnesota Press, pp. 13–34.

Visram, Rozina (2002) *Asians in Britain: 400 Years of History*, London: Pluto Press.

Vonnegut, Kurt (2000 [1969]) *Slaughterhouse Five*, London: Vintage.

Ward, Colin (1978) *The Child in the City*, London: Architectural Press.

Waters, Chris (1997) '"Dark Strangers" in Our Midst: Discourses of Race and Nation in Britain, 1947–1963', *Journal of British Studies*, vol. 36, pp. 207–238.

Weart, Spencer R. (2012) *The Rise of Nuclear Fear*, Cambridge, MA: Harvard University Press.

Wetherell, Margaret (2012) *Affect and Emotion: A New Social Science Understanding*, London: Sage.

Wiener, Norbert (1954 [1950]) *The Human Use of Human Beings: Cybernetics and Society*, New York: Da Capo.

Williams, Raymond (1964 [1952]) *Drama from Ibsen to Eliot*, Harmondsworth: Penguin.

────── (1977) *Marxism and Literature*, Oxford: Oxford University Press.

────── (1980) *Problems in Materialism and Culture*, London: Verso.

―――― (1981) *Politics and Letters: Interviews with New Left Review*, London: Verso.
―――― (1983 [1976]) *Keywords: A Vocabulary of Culture and Society*, London: Fontana.
―――― (1989 [1958]) 'Culture is Ordinary', in *Resources of Hope*, London: Verso, pp. 3–18.
―――― (1989a) *What I Came to Say*, London: Hutchinson Radius.
―――― (1989b) *Resources of Hope*, London: Verso.
―――― (1990 [1975]) *Television: Technology and Cultural Form*, edited by Ederyn Williams, London: Routledge.
―――― (1992 [1961]) *The Long Revolution*, London: Hogarth Press.
―――― (1993 [1950]) 'Books for Teaching "Culture and Environment"', in John McIlroy and Sallie Westwood, eds., *Border Country: Raymond Williams in Adult Education*, Leicester: National Institute of Adult Continuing Education, pp. 174–180.
―――― (1993 [1973]) *The Country and the City*, London: Hogarth Press.
―――― (2006 [1960]) *Border Country*, Cardigan: Library of Wales.
Williams, Raymond and Michael Orrom (1954) *Preface to Film*, London: Film Drama.
Winder, Robert (2004) *Bloody Foreigners: The Story of Immigration to Britain*, London: Little, Brown.
Winston, Brian (1999) *Fires Were Started*, London: BFI.
Woodward, Christopher (2002) *On Ruins*, London: Vintage.
Woodward, Kathleen (2009) *Statistical Panic: Cultural Politics and Poetics of the Emotions*, Durham, NC: Duke University Press.
Wright, Patrick (1985) *On Living in an Old Country*, London: Verso.
―――― (2009 [1991]) *A Journey through Ruins: The Last Days of London*, New York: Oxford University Press.

Films and Television Programmes

'71, dir. Yann Demange (2014)
Angel Heart, dir. Alan Parker (1987)
Babette's Feast, dir. Gabriel Axel (1987)
Bagdad Café, dir. Percy Adlon (1987)
Distant Voices, Still Lives, dir. Terence Davies (1988)
Fires Were Started, dir. Humphrey Jennings (1943)
Handsworth Songs, dir. John Akomfrah (1986)
High Hopes, dir. Mike Leigh (1988)
House of Games, dir. David Mamet (1987)
Hue and Cry, dir. Charles Crichton (1947)
I've Heard the Mermaids Singing, dir. Patricia Rozema (1987)
Jean de Florette, dir. Claude Berri (1986)
The Lair of the White Worm, dir. Ken Russell (1988)
Listen to Britain, dir. Humphrey Jennings and Stewart McAllister (1942)
London Can Take It! dir. Humphrey Jennings and Harry Watt (1940)
London: The Modern Babylon, dir. Julien Temple (2012)
Manon des Sources, dir. Claude Berri (1986)
The Moderns, dir. Alan Rudolph (1988)
The Nine Muses, dir. John Akomfrah (2010)
Our Friends in the North, dir. Simon Cellan Jones, Pedr James, Stuart Urban (1996)
Patty Hearst, dir. Paul Schrader (1988)
Prick Up Your Ears, dir. Stephen Frears (1987)
Raising Arizona, dir. Joel and Ethan Coen (1987)

Red Sorghum, dir. Zhang Yimou (1987)
Rita, Sue and Bob Too, dir. Alan Clarke (1987)
Roxanne, dir. Fred Schepisi (1987)
Something Wild, dir. Jonathan Demme (1986)
This is England, dir. Shane Meadows (2006)
This is England '86, dir. Tom Harper and Shane Meadows (2010)
This is England '88, dir. Shane Meadows (2011)
This is England '90, dir. Shane Meadows (2015)
The Tin Drum, dir. Volker Schlöndorff (1979)
Torch Song Trilogy, dir. Paul Bogart (1988)
Whatever Happened to the Likely Lads? dir. Dick Clement (1973–1974)
Wings of Desire, dir. Wim Wenders (1987)
Withnail and I, dir. Bruce Robinson (1987)

INDEX

Adams, Mary 60, 61
Addison, Paul and Crang, Jeremy 60, 61, 62
adventure playground movement 83, 84
advertising 58, 100, 101, 134
affect theory 45, 46–51
Ahmed, Sara 53n20
Akomfrah, John, *The Nine Muses* (film) 108–16, 162
Akomfrah, John and Eshun, Kodwo 109, 115
Albertine, Viv 123, 130, 132
Allen of Hurtwood, Lady 83, 84
Altieri, Charles vii
ambivalence 35, 47, 79, 80
anthropology 21, 23, 24, 26, 27–32, 37; 'pattern' analyses 29
architecture: post war Britain 76, 83, 86, 87, 88–91; urban 35, 78fig, 136n10
Ari Up 122, 131
Au Pairs (band) 127, 134
'authoritarian populism' (Hall) 148

BAFC (Black Audio Film Collective) 108, 110
Bakhtin, M.M. 118n19
Barthes, Roland 77
Bateson, Gregory 30–1, 33; *Naven* 29
Beat (band), 'Stand Down Margaret' 135
Beckett, Andy 134, 136n12
Beckett, Samuel 115; *Molloy, Malone Dies, The Unnamable* 114
Befindlichkeit (Heidegger) 39, 40, 43, 44
Benedict, Ruth 29, 30, 31, 32, 33; *Middletown* 32; *Patterns of Culture* 32

Benjamin, Walter 88; 'On the Concept of History' 89
Berger, John and Mohr, Jean 111, 112
Berlant, Lauren: 'crisis ordinariness' 49; *Cruel Optimism* 48, 49; historical sensorium 48–51; 'Post-Fordist affect' US 49
Best, Stephen and Marcus, Sharon 157n2
Bewes, Rodney 90
Birch, Gina 119, 125
Black Audio Film Collective *see* BAFC
Blitz 58, 60, 63–5, 74n8, 82, 92n1; Blitz spirit 55, 71–3
Bloch, Ernst 25
Blurt (band), 'My Mother is a Friend of the Enemy of the People' 130, 131
Bolam, James 90
bombsites 75–91; and the past 90–1; as playgrounds 83–7, 88; in *The World My Wilderness* 80, 81–2
Britain First 158
Brixton riots 130, 131
Burlingham, Dorothy and Freud, Anna 85–6

Calder, Angus, *The Myth of the Blitz* 74n8
Cambridge, University of 25, 27, 28
'Cambridge English' 23, 26, 27, 30
Can (band) 128
capitalism 3, 31, 32, 42, 79, 97, 148
'caring professions' 2
Cartier-Bresson, Henri 152
Certeau, Michel de, *The Practice of Everyday Life* 52n4

Index

Chapman, James 67
children: bombsites as playgrounds 75, 76, 77–90; and propaganda films 69–70; and racism 100–1, 113
Christianity 82, 83
Churchill, Winston 57
cinema *see* films
civil disturbances 57, 72, 107, 109, 130, 131, 134
Clapton, Eric 135n3
Clark, T.J. 124
Clash (band) 130
class: and Cambridge University 25; and furnishings 36; and generational difference 140; Hoggart and Williams on 33, 34; housing and 107; and immigrant disappointment 97, 98, 99; in *The Likely Lads* 90–1; and music 128; in *Our Friends in the North* 142, 149, 155, 156; in *This is England* 149, 151, 152, 156
Clement, Dick and La Frenais, Ian 90
Cochrane, Kelso 107
'cock rock' 123
Cold War 41, 43, 76
colonialism 28, 96–101, 114, 115
commodity culture 9, 125
conative-affective register 27, 40, 48, 50
corruption 18, 83, 142, 143, 144–5, 148, 161
'counter chronotope' 112, 113
counterculture, 1960s 45
Cox, Jo 158, 159
Craig, Daniel 143
Cresswell, Chanel 152
'crisis ordinariness' (Berlant) 49
Crown Film Productions 67
CS gas ('tear gas') grenades, police use of 130
cultural reflexes 26
Curran, Kieran 161
cynicism 49, 79, 161–3

da Silva, Ana 123, 129
The Daily Express 103
The Daily Mail 117n10, 135n2
The Daily Mirror 103, 104, 105, 106, 116
Deadly Headley 131
Debuysere, Stoffel 110
Denmark, adventure playground movement 83, 84
Dowie, Freda 142
dress 33, 34, 36, 105, 107, 108, 123, 135n2
Dreyfus, Hubert 42, 43

Eccleston, Christopher 142
Eliot, T.S. 26, 27
Ellis, Andrew 152

'emotional background' (Benedict) 29–32
Empire Day 96
Empire Windrush (ship) 101, 102fig, 103–4, 106, 116
Enfield, Harry 151
Englishness 70

Falklands War 18, 140, 149
The Fall (band) 128
Favre, Pierre, *Solitudes* (album) 111
feminism 46, 125, 127, 142
Filmer, Paul 22
films: *Fires Were Started* 56, 63; *Handsworth Songs* 108, 109–10; *Hue and Cry* 83; *Listen to Britain* 66, 67–71, 162; *London Can Take It!* 66, 67; *London: The Modern Babylon* 94, 117n8; and mood 4–8; *The Nine Muses* 93, 108–16, 162; propaganda 16, 17, 56, 59, 66, 67, 69–70; *This is England* 18, 140, 148–55, 156; *The Tin Drum* 136n11; *Wings of Desire* 5
Fires Were Started (film, Jennings dir.) 56, 63
Flatley, Jonathan vii, 45, 47, 48
flight attendants 9–10
Forsyth, Brigit 90
Foucault, Michel 73n4
Freud, Sigmund 157n5
Friedrich, Caspar David, *Wanderer above the Sea of Fog* (painting) 114
Frith, Simon 134
Furious Pig (band) 133
furnishings 36

Gang of Four (band) 126, 127
garage rock 128
Gartside, Green 126
gender: Berlant on 50; and generational continuity 142; and music 122–3; Williams and 37
generational difference 139, 142, 155–6
Gerrard, Lisa 112
Getty Images Archive 103
Gill, Andy 126, 127
Gilroy, Beryl 96, 99, 106; *Black Teacher* 100–1
Gilroy, Paul 103, 160; *Black Britain* 117n7
'Girls will be Girls' (TV programme) 122
Glass, Ruth 99, 100
global financial crash 2007/2008 14
Going to Britain? (BBC pamphlet) 99
Gove, Michael 161, 162
Graham, Stephen 153
Grass, Günter, *The Tin Drum* 136n11
Great Depression, US 14

Gregg, Melissa and Seigworth, Gregory J., *The Affect Theory Reader*, eds. 45
Grossberg, Lawrence 37
Guignon, Charles 44, 45
guilt, immigrants 105, 106, 107, 108

habit and mood 37, 38, 50, 54, 63–7
Haddon, A.C. 27, 28
Hall, Stuart; education 96; 'Minimal Selves' essay 95; 'Reconstruction Work: Images of Postwar Black Settlement' 102, 104, 105, 106; on Thatcherism 148
Hall, Stuart and Chen, Kuan-Hsing 96
Handsworth Riots 109
Handsworth Songs (film, Akomfrah dir.) 108, 109–10
Haraway, Donna 142
Hardt, Michael 18n3
Heide, Morten and Grønhaug, Kjell 18n2
Heidegger, Martin 38–45; *Being and Time* 38, 42; conative-affective register 40; on *Stimmung* 16, 21, 38–9, 42–5, 62
Hendrix, Jimi 129
Hersey, John, *Hiroshima* 92n1
HID (Home Intelligence Division) 59, 60–1, 65, 67
historical sensorium (Berlant) 48–51
Hobsbawm, Eric 25
Hochschild, Arlie Russell, *The Managed Heart: Commercialization of Human Feeling* 9
Hodgkinson, Anthony W. and Sheratsky, Rodney E. 67
Hoggart, Richard 33
Hoggart, Richard and Williams, Raymond 33, 34
Home Intelligence Division see HID
Hoskyns, Barney 128
hospitality industry 8
Hoswell, Ros 96
housing 144–8, 150–3; slums 77fig, 84, 86, 144, 145fig, 146, 147fig, 152
Howe, Steve 135n3
Howe, Zoë Street 129, 133
Hue and Cry (film, Crichton dir.) 83
Hulton Archive 103
Huntley, Jessica 98
Hynde, Chrissie 122

Ibsen, Henrik 26
ICA (Institute of Contemporary Arts) 133
image-repertoire (Barthes) 77–80, 83, 86, 88, 103, 122
Imaginary (*L'Imaginaire*) (Barthes) 77
imperialism 93, 96, 97

'Inglan is a Bitch' (poem) 94, 95
innocence, immigrants 104–7, 108
interior design, public buildings 8
Italy 79

James, William 65–6, 67
Jarrow Crusade 1936 142
Jennings, Humphrey 59; *Fires Were Started* 56, 63; *Listen to Britain* 67–71; *London Can Take It!* (with Watt) 66
Johnstone, William 72
Jones, Mick 130
juvenile delinquency 17, 75, 83–7

Khan, Sadiq 158
Khomami, Nadia 159, 160
King, Richard 122
Kozlovsky, Roy 84
'Krautrock' 128
Kwesi Johnson, Linton 94, 95

labour, moods as 2, 8–10
'Labour Isn't Working' campaign 134
Lamming, George 93, 114; *The Pleasure of Exile* 98
Lazzarato, Maurizio 18n3
Leavis, F.R., *New Bearings in English Poetry* 26, 27
Leavis, Q.D. 27
Lefebvre, Henri 52n4
Letts, Don 125, 136n8
Levitas, Ruth 136n7
The Likely Lads (TV series) 90
Listen to Britain (film, Jennings dir.) 66, 67–71, 162; use of sound 68–9
literature 21, 22, 32, 33, 36, 88
'Loadsamoney' (television character) 151
London: bombsites 80, 81–2, 83, 84; cosmopolitanism 158; immigration 94, 95, 97, 99, 106, 107; racism post Brexit referendum 159; riots 130–1, 134; in Second World War 56, 57, 62, 66, 67, 72
London Can Take It! (film, Jennings and Watt dir.) 66, 67
'London is the Place for Me' (song) 94, 95
London: The Modern Babylon (film, Temple dir.) 94, 117n8
London School of Economics 28
Lord Kitchener (Aldwyn Roberts) 94
Lydon, John 120

Macaulay, Rose, *The World My Wilderness* 75, 80, 81–2, 83, 89, 163
Magee, Haywood 105
Malinowski, Bronisław 28

Mance, Henry 162
Marchant, Hilde 105
Marcus, Greil 120, 124, 125, 126, 127, 134, 135
Marwick, Arthur, *The Home Front: The British and the Second World War* 74n9
Marx, Karl 156
Marx, Karl and Engels, Frederick, *Manifesto of the Communist Party* 88, 89
Marxism 27
Mass-Observation 59, 60, 62, 86
Massumi, Brian, 'The Autonomy of Affect' 45
materiality of mood 2, 3, 4–8, 32, 33–8; and immigration 97, 99; and the past 55; and post-war landscape 75, 82; in wartime 64; and Virno 79, 80
Mathison, Trevor 108, 112
McClure, Vicky 153
McKee, Gina 143
McLaine, Ian 59, 62
Meadows, Shane 148, 152; *This is England* (film) 18, 140, 148–55, 156
Mercer, Kobena 109
migration 93–116; archives 108–16; Berlant on 49; Cox on 159; mother country 96–101; reconstruction 101, 102–8
Milner, Andrew 37
Milton, Ted 130, 131
miners' strike 18, 140
modernism 90, 124
'Momentbilder sub specie aeternitas' 113
MOI (Ministry of Information) 60
mood: and attunement 37, 38–45; and habit 37, 38, 54, 63–6, 67; and historicity 3, 10, 11–13, 16, 33, 43–4, 47, 48–51, 54–5, 76, 95, 139, 140–1; as labour 2, 8–10; mood work 2, 3, 6, 8, 12, 13, 16, 17, 67
'mood norms' 41
morale, Second World War 54–73; Blitz spirit 71–3; measurement of 59, 60–2, 63; as mood habit 63–6; propaganda 66, 67–71; 'snapping out' of moods 56–9
Mosley, Oswald 163n1
Mouilpied, Helen de 67
'Mr Newcastle' (T. Dan Smith) 145
Munch, Edvard 129
Muñoz, José Esteban 128

National Front 134, 150fig, 154, 156, 162
national referendum, Brexit 158–63
National Socialism 89, 162

National Union of Mineworkers (NUM) 142, 144
nature 35, 82, 86, 89
neoliberalism 35, 80, 148
New Guinea 30
New Left Review (magazine) 21, 138, 139
New West (magazine) 134
Newman, Randy, *Baltimore* (song) 4
Ngai, Sianne 36, 37
Nietzsche, Friedrich 29; *Umwerthung aller Werthe* (revaluation of all values) 82
9/11 9, 10
The Nine Muses (film, Akomfrah dir.) 93, 108–16, 162
'non-synchronous simultaneity' (Bloch) 25
nostalgia 55, 149, 160
Notting Hill, London, migration 107, 108
Notting Hill Carnival 131
nuclear dangers, anxieties around 76
NUM *see* National Union of Mineworkers

The Observer 78
'Oi' (type of punk) 134
The Old Grey Whistle Test (TV programme) 129
Orwell, George 56; 'London Letter' 57
Our Friends in the North (television series) 18, 140, 142–8, 149, 151, 155, 156
Oxford, University of 25, 28

Paneth, Marie 90, 163; *Branch Street: A Sociological Study* 84, 85
Park Hill estate, Sheffield 152, 153fig
Pärt, Arvo 112
paternalism 67, 84, 103
'patterns of culture' (Benedict) 31
Patterson, Sheila, *Dark Strangers* 117n12
pedagogy, phenomenal 63, 65, 66, 71
Phillips, Mike and Phillips, Trevor, *Windrush: The Irresistible Rise of Multi-Racial Britain* 96, 97, 99, 103, 116n1, 117n11, 131
photojournalism 78, 103–8, 144
Picture Post (magazine) 58–9, 78, 83, 103, 105
PiL (Public Image Limited) 120, 121
Polish Social and Cultural Association (POSK) 159, 160
Popism 122
post-punk 17, 119, 120, 123–8, 132–5; and television 129, 130
Poulson, John 145
Powell, Enoch 135n3
Power, Nina and Akomfrah, John 109, 111
'practical criticism' (Richards) 27
'practices of negation' (Clark) 124

180 Index

Price, Leontyne 112; 'Sometimes I Feel Like a Motherless Child' 113
'primary affects' 46
Prince Far I 130
'problem-solution, innocence-guilt' pattern 107, 108
propaganda, Second World War 16, 17, 56, 59, 66, 67, 69–70
psychoanalysis 53n22, 81
psychological breakdown 71, 72, 86
Public Image Limited *see* PiL
punk 17, 120, 121–5, 126, 129, 131, 132–4

queer culture 128

'race relations' 99
Rachman, Peter 117n14
racism: and Brexit referendum 158, 159, 160; and Britain First 158; civil disturbance 134; and post-Fordism 59; and immigration 95, 97, 99–101, 103, 104–5, 106, 107, 109, 113, 114, 117n7, 117n8; legislation 99; and National Front 134, 150fig, 154, 156, 162; 'stop and search' laws 130; in *This is England* 149, 153, 154, 155, 156
The Raincoats (band) 123, 124, 125, 133, 163
Rancière, Jacques 24
reggae 94, 109, 123, 125–7, 130, 131, 163
Reynolds, Quentin 66
Reynolds, Simon 125, 126, 128
Richards, I.A. 27, 31, 32
Robeson, Paul 112
Rockism 121, 123–9
Roots Radics Band 130, 131
Rose, Jacqueline 161
Rotten, Johnny 120
royal wedding 130, 150fig
Rückenfigur (back-view figure) 114
rumours 61
Rushdie, Salman 109, 110
Russell, Bertrand 163n1

Saatchi & Saatchi, 'Labour Isn't Working' campaign 134
Samuel, Raphael 52n18
Sansom, William 54, 63, 68; *Westminster at War* 63, 64–5
Savage, Jon 125
Scandura, Jani 14
Schubert, Franz, 'Der Leiermann' (song) 112
science labs 7, 8
Scritti Politti (band) 126
Scrutiny (journal) 26, 27

Second World War: Blitz 58, 60, 63–5, 74n8, 82, 92n1; Blitz spirit 55, 71–3; collectivity 57, 63, 64; 'Home Front Morale' 55, 56–73; post war reconstruction 17, 75, 87, 88, 89; West Indian troops 96, 97
Sedgwick, Eve Kosofsky and Frank, Adam 45
Seigworth, Gregory 51
service-centred economy 8, 49
Sex Pistols 120, 121
sexual abuse 149, 153, 154, 155
Sherwood, Adrian 130
Shim, Andrew 153
Shouse, Eric 2
Simmel, Georg 113
Simone, Nina, *Baltimore* (song and album) 4
Sinfield, Alan 71
'situated knowledge' (Haraway) 142
ska reggae 149
skinheads 134
Slits (band) 120, 123, 130, 131, 132, 133, 163
slum clearances Gorbals, Glasgow 77fig
Smith, Mark E. 128
Smith, Patti, *Horses* (album) 129, 130
Smith, T. Dan *see* 'Mr Newcastle'
Smoking Dogs Films 108
Sobers, Norma and Sobers, Theo 97
Socha, Michael 152
Southall riot 134
specialist hospitals ('Neurosis Centres'), Second World War 58
Spender, Stephen 72, 73
Spinoza, Baruch 45, 46
Stimmung (Heidegger) 16, 21, 38–9, 42–5, 62
Strong, Mark 143
'structure of feeling' (Williams) 16, 21–6, 33, 35, 36, 37, 41, 138–9
The Sunday Times 78
'surface reading' 157n2
Sus laws ('stop and search') 130

Tait, Margaret 5
Taylor, Sir Stephen 59
technology 2, 91, 139
Temple, Julian 94
Thatcher, Margaret 11, 12, 134, 135
Thatcherism 17, 18, 148
The Times 62
This is England (film, Meadows dir.) 18, 140, 148–55, 156
Thompson, Dudley 97, 98
The Tin Drum (film, Schlöndorff dir.) 136n11

Titmuss, Richard 57, 58
Tomkins, Silvan 45; 'primary affects' 46
Toots and the Maytals: '54-46 Was My Number' 149; 'Funky Kingston' 125
Toxteth riots 130
Tubbs, Ralph, *Living in Cities* 86, 87
Tulloch, Carol 95

UKIP (UK Independence Party) 162
Umwerthung aller Werthe (revaluation of all values) (Nietzsche) 82
Union Jack 150fig
urbanism 76, 86

Valmont, Tamia, *Solitudes* (album) 111
Vaughan, Peter 143
vernacular expressions 2, 39
Vidler, Anthony 87
Virno, Paolo 79, 80, 89

Wanderer above the Sea of Fog (painting, Friedrich) 114
Watkins, Peter 129

Weiner, Norbert 89, 92n3
Welfare State 17, 49, 79, 80, 88, 155
Wenders, Wim, *Wings of Desire* (film) 5
Wetherell, Margaret 46, 47
Whatever Happened to the Likely Lads? (TV series) 90–1
Williams, Raymond 20–32; background 25; and Berlant's work 48, 49, 50; *The Country and the City* 35; on democracy 34; *Drama from Ibsen to Eliot* 52n3; *Keywords* 26, 36; 'left Leavisism' 31; *The Long Revolution* 28, 29, 33; *Politics and Letters* 26; 'structures of feeling' 16, 21–6, 33, 35, 36, 37, 41, 47, 138–9; 'You're a Marxist, Aren't You?' 20
Williams, Raymond and Orrom, Michael, *Preface to Film* 23–4, 52n5
Wings of Desire (film, Wenders dir.) 5
'Winter of Discontent' 11, 12, 133, 134
Woods, Lesley 127

Young British Artists 11

Taylor & Francis eBooks

Helping you to choose the right eBooks for your Library

Add Routledge titles to your library's digital collection today. Taylor and Francis ebooks contains over 50,000 titles in the Humanities, Social Sciences, Behavioural Sciences, Built Environment and Law.

Choose from a range of subject packages or create your own!

Benefits for you
- Free MARC records
- COUNTER-compliant usage statistics
- Flexible purchase and pricing options
- All titles DRM-free.

Benefits for your user
- Off-site, anytime access via Athens or referring URL
- Print or copy pages or chapters
- Full content search
- Bookmark, highlight and annotate text
- Access to thousands of pages of quality research at the click of a button.

REQUEST YOUR FREE INSTITUTIONAL TRIAL TODAY

Free Trials Available
We offer free trials to qualifying academic, corporate and government customers.

eCollections – Choose from over 30 subject eCollections, including:

Archaeology	Language Learning
Architecture	Law
Asian Studies	Literature
Business & Management	Media & Communication
Classical Studies	Middle East Studies
Construction	Music
Creative & Media Arts	Philosophy
Criminology & Criminal Justice	Planning
Economics	Politics
Education	Psychology & Mental Health
Energy	Religion
Engineering	Security
English Language & Linguistics	Social Work
Environment & Sustainability	Sociology
Geography	Sport
Health Studies	Theatre & Performance
History	Tourism, Hospitality & Events

For more information, pricing enquiries or to order a free trial, please contact your local sales team:
www.tandfebooks.com/page/sales

Routledge
Taylor & Francis Group

The home of Routledge books

www.tandfebooks.com